FUNNY MUMMY

MERRIE LYNN ROSS

COPYRIGHT © 2013 MERRIE LYNN ROSS

Publisher- MediaMorphUs

All rights reserved. No part of this book can be reproduced by any mechanical, photographic, or electronic process, or in the form of a photographic recording: nor may it be stored in a retrieval system, transmitted, or otherwise be copied for public or private use – other than for "fair use" as brief quotations embodied in articles and reviews –without prior written permission from the publisher.

Ross, Merrie Lynn

Adventures of Funny Mummy

ISBN 978-0-9827366-6-1

Published in United States

PRAISE FOR
Adventures of FUNNY MUMMY

HollywoodMag Review: Totally wacky fun...takes over where paranoia leaves off. Love triangles, lust and deceit, cheating and tweeting, back dropped in a funky teen campus scene. We're all in it... as Jilted Jenny, a discombobulated, out of the nest Mom frolics in mid-life madness."

"Merrie Lynn cracks the Hilarious Code with wit, humor, and outrageous antics. Need an upper, read this book." *Paul Ryan, TV celebrity host, author "Art of Comedy"*

Adventures of Funny Mummy is a romp into pathos and folly. Original, just like Merrie Lynn, a one-of-a-kind, "Funny Wise Woman." *Carol Channing, TV star/Comedienne*

"Who said you can't laugh at a lady that is as neurotic as you are? I laughed. I cried, I tinkled."
Lindsay Bloom, singer, actress, Mom.

ACKNOWLEGEMENTS

To All the funny ladies & gents who bring on the laughter: My friends, cohorts, and mentors, who know the truth...Life IS an Improv'.

Shauna Zurbrugg - My brilliantly talented editor, who nurtures my creative flame with patience and precision.

Eddie Medora, artist – Wonderful Mermaid Painting, 'Crack Up Tail' of CC on cover

To our publisher, MediaMorphUs for their amazing vision to bring Funny Mummy to the global stage.

Gratitude to our Media Team for the upcoming 'Funny Mummy' adventures film.

TABLE OF CONTENTS

PART 1   HEART QUAKE   9

PART 2   MID-LIFE BAITS   133

PART 3   HIGH KICK STAKES   263

PART 4   TWISTED FATES   333

In Memory and Gratitude

To adorable Betty, my mother, who taught me to "Look for the twinkle in everyone's eyes".

Especially to my beloved son Byron... your enlivened spirit shines with your wish for all of us to... "BE Real, Laugh, & Love".

Merrie Lynn Ross

PART 1
♥HEART QUAKE

Jenny tried to ignore the resounding clock chimes permeating the walls of the suburban quasi-mansion. Two bells echoed a piercing reminder. Flinching, her eyeballs rolled upward as the sounds invaded the inner-sanctum of her psyche. It was 2:00 A.M. and Richie, her husband, still wasn't home.

With her laptop positioned conveniently on the bed, she was online with God-knows-who. Insomniac night owls, her virtual-reality alter egos were imaginary friends she counted on, erroneously believing they cared about her. This BLOG obsession, a temporary fix in lieu of Prozac, eased her nervous tension and hopefully annihilated a major anxiety attack.

Typing furiously, she grumbled "Oh my misha-gosh", slewing her trepidation's at the cyber-hawkers. She was writing her BLOG:

Don't even ask! That should have been my mantra from the day I met Richie. Instead, I learned to habitually dote on the imbecile with the same intensity that I showered on our twins. Fate misfired by one tiny Y or is it an X chromosome? Therefore, they're not identical. Brian, my son, was born 2 minutes before Samantha, his sister. His prince-ified presence tortures her mediocrity on every front. He gets straight A's to her struggling C's. He's the most popular jock, to her wilting wallflower status. Brian's confidence meter tips the scales with a self-ordained superiority that even I can't ignore. From the moment they popped out of my Caesarian raw tummy their milk-starved curdling shrieks mimicked Richie far more than my wimpy kvetch-iness.

Richie's Russian bloodline boldly dictates a sleazy black market credential that gives him license to bend, change rules or laws, or to invent circumstances for any opportunistic whim. His Ruskie lineage is filled with suffocating drama. Disarming emotional thunderbolts are strategically choreographed to discharge responsibilities, to lay guilt or to inflict blame. My kudos for enduring the wrath of his tyrannical peasant mother, Rifka, for the entire 19 years of our marriage, should entitle me to a full-fledged annulment.

View this diatribe as subliminal verbiage, because in real life I function as a dysfunctional perfectly happy wife. My drone-ish land-locked existence could drive any sane woman desperately mad. The accoutrements bestowed on the coveted title of Mrs. Forrest include being decked out with jewels, sporting a hot Mercedes SUV, entertaining in a well-appointed house in the Burbs, a VIP country club membership, and a wad full of credit cards, far outweigh the compromise. It's probably evident I'm an emotionally battered wife. A complaining wench never getting satisfaction, even after I've yelled, berated or pleaded with my unscrupulous, unfaithful, liar of a husband.

Yet I have my subtle revengeful ways, as well as the not–so-discriminating ones. Like the bumper sticker on my Mercedes SUV that hopefully humiliates Richie at every turn and stoplight. It reads in bright bold red letters: WHY MARRY THE WHOLE PIG JUST TO GET A SMALL SAUSAGE!

The full moon trailed the lone black Mercedes SUV as it meandered recklessly past uniformed street lamps and immaculately manicured greenery. Stars twinkled knowingly, a pre-tease that they were about to reveal the grimy secrets hidden within this hoity-toity suburban maze.

The SUV's driver, Richie Forrest, sang off-key to a blasting rendition of the Rolling Stones' "Satisfaction." He warbled, "Can't get me no-no-noo, yeah, yeah, yeah, satisfaction!" Happily soused, rocking to the beat, Richie threw up his arms. With the pride of an eight-year-old he squealed, "Look, Mom! No hands." Driver-less, the car hit a speed bump, swerved aimlessly off the road, jumped a curb, fishtailed into the cul-de-sac, spun skid marks across a grassy lawn, and then bashed giant rhododendron bushes. Grinning a full-toothed manic snarl, Richie stomped the brakes to the floor, simultaneously throwing the gear into park. VAROOM! The screeching SUV ground to an abrupt halt, stopping several inches from a humongous four-paneled garage door.

Richie's out-of-control routine of entertaining clients (or whomever), drinking too much, coming home late at night, had escalated into a domestic war zone. His self-inflicted pressure-cooker existence of thriving on the success chain was taking its toll. Embroiled in criminal law, his practice had been reduced to defending shoddy small-time crooks and political charlatans.

Staring through the windshield Richie bolted at the closeness of the garage door that was mere inches from his face. His jovial demeanor shifted to panic and a primal need for self-preservation surfaced. In retaliation, inebriated Richie foisted a defensive battle cry at the steering wheel. "There's nothing wrong with me! Stop complaining! Be grateful."

If he had half a wit he might consider that he was a victim of society's soul and body-snatching phenomenon, substituting the authentic self for a treadmill decadent, driven existence. On the other hand, maybe he made a deal with a she-devil behind closed doors trading his sanity for success? Self-involved and unaware of the dangerous precipice he treaded, teetering on the brink of destiny's folly, he could lose everything and everyone important in his life.

Richie stumbled out of the car and slid onto the grass. Jabbering incoherently, he brushed wet dew stains off his Armani pants. Blurry-eyed, aiming a clicker at the four-car garage door, it opened 'ala Sesame' revealing three similar silver Mercedes SUVs parked side-by-side. Snickering with pride, he flagged a grand gesture to the vehicles. "Daddy's home."

The interior of the Forrest foyer boasted a mish-mash of Middle Eastern antiquities spattered with a *nouveau-riche* pizzazz. Richie sheepishly peered inside, and then staggered across the marble floor, creeping toward a winding wooden staircase.

Standing cross-armed at the top of the stairs was Jenny, his miffed wife. Her menacing glare could bore a hole through a steel wall, but it had no apparent effect on Richie's pathetic flummoxed state. He gripped the banister, attempting to tug up the stairs, muttering, "You can make it Richie, boy. One, two, only three more..."

Feigning control, Jenny mustered a deep breath, holding fast to her 'Super-Mom-Wife' persona. "Three? Wrong, Richie. It's Four! Four o'clock in the morning! I've been up all night worrying. Imagining morgues, squished-maimed bodies. Every sick idea going through my head!"

Stupefied, Richie ogled her. "Oops, Jenny's sick."

"Don't schmooze me, Richie. Where were you?"

"Where? Where was I...mmm...I was working."

Her lower lip jutted out in disbelief. "Working? On what? A gallon of brandy, a quart of Stolichnaya, on top of some bimbo?"

Shamelessly avoiding the accusation, Richie teetered onto the stair landing. Almost toppling backwards, he grabbed her leg. She backed away, grimacing. "Just fall, so I don't kill you."

Wobbling, he lunged forward, tugged, yanked, and clawed fruitlessly at her robe in an effort to steady himself. She grabbed his arm to break the fall, but it was too late. Richie flipped backwards and Jenny tumbled over him. Like two rolling pins they bumped down the stairs letting out loud shrieks and expletives. Crash! They landed with an unmerciful bang at the bottom of the staircase.

Oddly entangled in each other's arms, Richie flashed a queasy look at Jenny. Turning green, his eyes bulged, cheeks puffed, chortling a throated gag. Jenny's mouth gaped; her eyes popped back at him as he purged with a vengeance. It was as if a cataclysmic geyser erupted, cascading an oozing "liquid" all over her. "Puh-lease," she whimpered as goo dripped down her face.

"Snap out of it!" He leered at her. "You look messy."

The foyer chandelier swayed to and fro' from the impact of the fall. An upstairs door flew open. Samantha, their eighteen-year-old repressed, rather oddball daughter, raced out of her room. Petrified, she shouted, "Ohmigod it's an earthquake!!" Hearing moans she shrieked, "A burglar?" Peering over the balcony Samantha gazed down at her parents entwined in a pretzel-like embrace. "Mom...Dad?" Racing to their side she stammered, "Are you all right?"

Groaning, checking body parts for fatal injuries, they touched, pawed, sighed, and groped each other. Regaining her composure Jenny moaned, "He's fine. We're fine. Just fine."

Frustrated, Samantha digested the absurdity of her parent's peculiar travesty. Overcome by the barf stench reeking from her mother's gooey-splattered face, Samantha driveled in disgust. "Is this your idea of some kinky trip?"

Jenny, the perfect wife-in-denial, ping-ponged the embarrassing predicament into a zany masquerade. Not over her dead body would she allow this sham of a marriage to become public knowledge. Expert at concealing it in her real world, her only reprieve remained her cyber existence, a BLOG platform to share the hypocrisies that ruled her life. The flimsy safety net provided a courage factor allowing her to stand tall at this crucial moment and face the challenger.

Jenny mustered a pasted smile, "Now-now, Samantha, this is our private little soiree. You just go to bed and pretend you were dreaming."

Samantha plumbed automatically into the depths of her Jungian unconscious and whispered on deaf ears, "Welcome to my nightmare, Mom."

Caught between life's tragedy and her ludicrous cover-ups, Jenny snickered uncontrollably. The sound rolled into a rumbling guffaw, crescendoing into frenzied laughter. "Hah-Hee-Hah-Hah-Hah!!"

To endure the high pitch Samantha covered her ears, and yelled, "That cackle...grosses me out!"

Oblivious to the family banter Richie had removed his shoes and socks. With childlike abandon he counted his toes. "One little, two little, three little pigmies." In self-amusement he ripped a howl of manic-laughter.

Fed up with the mucked-up intensity Samantha sputtered, "Ugh! You guys totally stink!" Exasperated, she backed away from the lunacy and the abominable stench. Hurrying up the stairs, she collapsed in the temporary shelter of her room.

Morning life seemed vigorously healthy in the Forrest kitchen. In the midst of her domestic milieu (hardly a gourmet cook), Jenny loved serving a mega-pancake breakfast to Samantha and twin brother, Brian. Being a doting mom, concerned for their welfare, anticipating what each of her kids needed to excel, offering them privileged opportunities seemed a reasonable parental responsibility.

As their graduation day approached, the more Jenny pushed her involvement in their lives; and of course, the more they pulled away. Desperate to remain a significant and meaningful part of their world her influence wavered, often backfired. Fear of losing control of the twins taunted, knuckled, and curdled like a human meat grinder. Feeling needed, appreciated, and indispensable was at the core of her control issues.

Jenny asked Samantha, "Pancakes with syrup or honey, eggs on top or on bottom?"

"Whatever you think, Mom?"

"Try the honey with eggs on the bottom," Jenny cheerfully replied.

Samantha usually acquiesced to Jenny's preferences. "Whatever," she said. Painfully shy and socially challenged she rarely expressed an opinion of her own. On the other hand, Brian developed a machismo delivery, daily testing his one-upmanship skills on Samantha. He spouted opinions, queries, and challenges about every subject known to mankind.

Brian interjected, "Eggs on the bottom sucks. Dripping yoke mush's up better." To prove his point he squished egg yoke into the pancakes, and then waved a fork of dripping glob at Samantha, forcing her to take a bite.

She pushed it away. Yellow mush formed strings on her white T-shirt. "Now look what you've done!"

Enjoying the effect he teased, "Eat my grits."

In a tissy-fit she belted the first phrase she ever uttered – the one phrase she had incessantly repeated ever since she was two-years-old. "Tell Brian to leave me alone."

Jenny gritted her teeth, "Brian, for the ka-zillionth time, you heard your sister. Chill!"

Looking for a zinger-rise he razzed, "I pulled an all-nighter prepping for the SAT's."

Samantha wouldn't buy into the ploy. "As if you can cram for it."

Richie, miserably hung-over, tottered by holding an ice pack on his cheek with one hand, juggling a ringing cell phone with the other. He continued out of the room, whispering into the phone, "I'm in agony. Set me up with the chiropractor. Okay! Then we'll talk about Maui."

Eavesdropping, Jenny crept around the corner and faced him dead on. "Maui? Did I hear you say Maui?"

"Nah... nah. Howie. Howie sounds like Maui."

"You're gibbering again, Richie," the sultry French female voice hissed into the phone's receiver.

Defending himself he ranted, "I can't win. She's a paranoid PMS-ing wreck."

Jenny retorted, "Try abandoned by a hung-over hedonist."

"I'm above that fib, baby," he winced a cocksure snarl.

"I'm not your baby, egghead." With a triumphant glare Jenny palmed an egg from the carton and squished it on his head. "Drippy yokes mush up good for your bald spot."

Richie dropped the cell. Massaging the slimy egg-run, he grimaced as it trickled off his forehead. "Not fair egging my bald spot." Admittedly he had his hands full. "Nothing I do makes you feel secure."

Jenny spouted back. "Or contented or loved."

Giving up, he threw his hands in the air. "You win." Frustrated by the endless treadmill bickering and unrelenting miscommunications, he went upstairs. To chill his hot temper he detoxed in an ice-cold shower. The beads of cascading water cleansed his mind. Fresh thoughts brainstormed; an idea struck his fancy. Solution-bound he prepared for round two in the battle of the sexes.

Over a pig-in-the-basket waffle Richie faced off with Jenny with high hopes. "How about a time-out?"

"From what? Big fights and hateful days?"

"That'll work. How about a time-out from the stay-at-home mom routine?"

Like a dagger to the heart she whimpered, "Are you insinuating that after almost twenty years of field- trips, homework, discipline tactics and positive reinforcements, it's possibly taking a toll?"

He offered, "How about a week in the wilderness...like at Dune Haven?"

"Trying to get rid of me? Make me a fugitive. Put me in exile. Why not solitary confinement?"

He gently stroked her cheek, "No honey, I'm trying to help you."

"Help me what?"

His voice cracked, "Ahh...feel appreciated."

Twisting her fork into the waffle she whined, "Sure, by sending me to a wacko safe house for women on the verge of a nervous breakdown or killing their husbands?"

Avoiding the killing husband's bit, Richie changed tactics. "Or dying from fatal boredom?" He snapped his fingers. "That's it, the problem. Boredom! You're unfulfilled, fed-up, frustrated. You need to express yourself, as you. The creative Jenny, not just as a mom."

Jenny wouldn't hear of it. "I'm just fine, Richie. I like my life. You and your naughty shenanigans are my only unsolvable problems. Grow up...perpetual adolescence leads to impotence. Only so many shots in the bottle."

Uneasy, Richie tweaked his back and held in his gut. "Not if it's magnum-sized. Come on honey, we almost grew up together."

She nervously nibbled a sausage from his plate. "Right! Going from my parent's home to marrying you. I was just a kid, immature, romantic. Barely older than the twins."

He stabbed his fork into the remaining sausage, "That's my point. You've been shackled for too long."

Yanking the fork from him she flung the sausage across the table at Richie, "Motherhood and being a wife is my life. That's how you feel, isn't it Richie? Shackled and chained?"

Avoiding an all-out assault Richie was on his feet, "Hold that thought. I'm out of steam right now. And, I'm late for a meeting."

"Meeting, smeating! Always running when the going gets tough."

Richie did the unexpected. Flopping cross-legged, Indian-style, on the floor, he closed his eyes, remaining still, as if meditating.

Jenny went over to him, shaking his shoulder. "What are you doing?"

"What! See...I knew you didn't want a stay-at-home dad, unemployed, an irresponsible dead-beat!" Getting up, he planted the usual peck on her cheek. "Think about it. You'd be crazy to turn down a luxury trip to the desert."

"You're not getting off this easy, Mr. Cash-Cow. I have my rights." She had indeed earned her rights. Fifty-fifty in the state of California! However, up until this juncture she hadn't defined them, or owned-up to them. All she could dwell on was last night's gruesome encounter with Richie. She had a right to rectify it. Revolt. Hit him where it hurts most in the prized little checkbook.

Later that morning Jenny consulted with Mr. Peck, a hard-body hunk carpet cleaner, about removing the stains from the previous night'sfiasco. "Mr. Peck, you've got to get it out. It's a carnal blemish on my marriage."

Thinking she was coming-on to him, he took her hand off the barf stain, gently speaking to her. "My dear Mrs. Forrest, you can call me Ed."

"Yes, Ed."

"I really understand you're...tight-spot. You deserve a radical change. A super-duper surprise."

"I do?" Overcome by the kind attention, she giggled nervously.

"Of course you do."

"Of course I do", she echoed, pulling a wisp of hair across her mouth. "What did you have in mind?"

Ed tossed Jenny a teasing grin, "I'm more interested in what you have in mind."

Only Jenny's desperate plea for domestic nurturing could have turned what could have been a saucy dip in the Jacuzzi with a hot guy into a "Living Room Makeover." Ed jumped at the biz opportunity, fielded numerous calls, showed samples of completely furnished rooms. "What suits your fancy?"

Jenny confessed, "I feel down and grey. Like a piñata with no candy inside." Ripping through the choices she selected, "Greige, I want everything coordinated in tones of grey and beige."

Ed cheerfully ripped out the old carpet, replacing it with a 'top of the line' tuft. As a courtesy gesture toward Jenny's posterity, Ed the carpet-layer, would-be lady-layer, positioned two digital camcorders on tripods to document the extravaganza. Ed's assistant, Jade, a saucy little redhead, arrived with an arsenal of beauty products for Jenny's vanity makeover and on-camera folly. Jade primped and crimped Jenny's golden curly-hair, sculpted her high cheekbones, and outlined her full lips in crimson gloss. Jade grimaced at Jenny's understated "Mom" garb. Clueless that Jade was Ed's live-in girlfriend, Jenny mused, and "This must be what Katie Couric feels like getting ready for a big show."

Scrutinizing Jenny's less than feminine tennis shoes, loose fitting pants and jean jacket, Jade commented, "Way more like Ellen."

Put off by the comparison, "Ellen? I thought she never wore make-up and went to a barber."

The camcorder's finally rolled, taping Jenny overseeing the extravagant living room redo. She commandeered a ten-man crew with gusto as they removed sofas and chairs, hoisting in a plethora of new furniture. At the end of the arduous yet fulfilling venture, Jenny proudly viewed her masterpiece. "Ta-Dah!" A monochromatic perfect match."

They toasted with champagne; Dom Perignon, no less. Ed, all charm, gallantly handed her six-dozen yellow roses...her favorite flowers and color! She imagined she was on Venus or was it heaven? He was on Mars or was it lust? Fixing deep into each other's eyes, Jenny envisioned her long-awaited Knight rescuing her from marriage's sinking doldrums. Any other day she knew there was no Knight! No horse! No six-foot tall, dark, handsome miracle woman-pleaser who could read her thoughts and gladly satisfy them.

Ed couldn't help himself. He was unarmored by the flood of emotions and banging twinges inside of him. These strong sensations were being evoked by Jade's presence. Glaring at him from across the room, packing her gear, she mouthed, "Get out _now_."

Covering up his entrapment, not wanting to reveal the duplicity, he flirted with Jenny. "What cat-like emerald green eyes you have." He gazed even deeper. Overwhelmed by what he saw, he flashed a gleaming white-veneered smile. Jenny's pupils were BLINGING neon greenback dollar signs. Seemingly congratulating his lucky score for the day, he murmured under his breath, "Ka-ching!"

Jade broke the trance. "Come on Ed honey, let's go home." He jumped up like the wuss he was.

Jenny's back stiffened into a regal pose. Without missing a beat she dismissed them. "Good day to you both. Good life." Not a twinge of disappointment, she smiled to herself. She knew all along "that lummox was no prince."

The East-Mall parking lot was jammed with shoppers. Cars were circling, blasting horns. All scoured impatiently for a coveted parking space. Jenny headed toward the perfect spot. Going the wrong way, another car fought for position, nicking her side-view mirror.

The driver bounded out of his car waving his shoulder-to-elbow paisley-patterned tattooed arms. "It's your fault, lady!"

"No it isn't. It can't be," Jenny lamented. Too rattled to think of a lie she blathered. "Between Brian's umpteen violations and Richie's DUI's we're maxed-out on auto insurance. Near cancellation." She got out of the car muttering, "I'm in a pickle."

At any cost she couldn't show her driver's license. God forbid this Mohawk-sporting thug would find out where she lived. What if he and his riff-raff friends broke into her home in the middle of the night? What if they dismantled the alarm, or disconnected the bedroom security camera? What if they pillaged and trashed the place? What if...

He interrupted her racing fears with, "Lady, come on, I'm late for work."

"Work?" She hoped her underlying tonal judgment wasn't obvious. "What work could this potential hatchet killer possibly do?" she thought. Luckily, when she examined his fifteen-year-old

Volkswagen Bug, it was difficult to decipher a new ding. The passenger side door was tied on with rope, the muffler hung loose. Handing him a fifty-dollar bill she condescended, "This ought to cover it, sir."

Delighted, he nodded and said, "Most certainly." then rushed into the jalopy before she changed her mind, sputtering and clanking into traffic, the muffler dragging behind.

"Close call" she mumbled, wheeling into the spot. She waited in the SUV. Her attention was preset on a tiny carousel. Youngsters on wooden painted ponies squealed, dipping up-and-down. Parent's spun with them, green with nausea, holding on for dear life. The joy of fluff cotton candy and the aroma of caramel corn surrounded the designated meeting place for a rendezvous with Samantha's ticket to college.

Jenny's Internet prowess had helped her to locate a young woman to take the SAT for Samantha. Never willing to let Samantha fail or hit the reality of her limitations, Jenny kept her floating on artificial life rafts. Rationalizing no distinction between "Learning at your own speed", or "Keeping up with the Jones' " brats, Jenny's heart ached. High school dropouts hit a whopping rate of 48%, a statistic her academically challenged daughter would never become. The cruel reality! Poor Samantha couldn't meet standard test expectations. Years of tutoring hadn't remedied her confidence or the 'how to' do it on her own. Jenny hoped that her daughter's talents were cleverly buried somewhere in a world of fantasies yet to be revealed.

Caught up with the lively organ music and spinning carousal, Jenny's heart skipped a beat. The young woman, Grace, using the code name Smarty-tart, stood before her. An uncanny resemblance to Samantha, Jenny sized her up. "No doubt you're 'Smarty-tart'. You are truly a definite look-a-like to my daughter. The similarity could even fool your mother."

"Or yours," the girl confidently responded.

Matching Samantha's photo ID to Smarty-tart's face, Jenny remarked, "Intriguing." Looking directly into her eyes, Jenny deftly qualified her, "So, you're a certified Mensa – a genius, no doubt! What is your IQ again?"

Without hesitation, Grace answered matter-of-factly, "One-hundred-and eighty-eight on a bad day."

"Well then, let's have a very bad day."

"How bad?"

Jenny was emphatic. "High stakes here. We don't want anyone to question Samantha's wonderful SAT performance, now do we? So, cut the IQ by forty."

The young woman squinted, weighing the unusual proposition. "Forty?"

Jenny continued with conviction. "Better make that fifty."

Grace's eyes rapidly moved side-to-side, computing a negotiable edge. That requires amputated concentration."

Jenny quickly challenged, "Concentration! Isn't that your specialty?"

Sure-cocked Grace replied, "One of many."

Jenny casually slipped an envelope into her hands. "This little bundle should encourage your Einsteinium brain-power...and to conveniently forget we ever met."

Grace, at the top of her "Smarty-tart" game peeked in the envelope, then smirked conspiratorially, "Do I know you?" as she slid the envelope into her backpack.

Solidifying the brilliant choice, Jenny handed Samantha's ID to her. "No margin for error, got it?"

Amused, Grace saw through Jenny's child-like need for dominance. With an air of authority and feigned seriousness, mocking her, she said, "Mistakes are what average humans dwell upon. Recouping and no recognizable error is my specialty."

Jenny gasped, as "Smarty-tart" curved her bottom lip into a Samantha-esque half-smile. With certainty the girl turned away, unobtrusively joining a crowd of pedestrians, disappearing from sight.

Uncanny and untimely, a police patrol car sped by, sirens wailing, blue lights spinning. A twinge of fear grabbed Jenny's stomach. A reminder of the risk, she thought, "What if she gets caught?" A sad pit rumbled in her solar plexus. What compassion could an overachiever Mensa look-a-like have for her precious Samantha who struggled just to be average? Jenny pontificated in her mind, as if on a soapbox screaming, "Dumbed-down, dumb and dumber dummies, WAKE-UP!"

She winced at the irony of the "cheat-to-beat" – an archaic educational system's quota. Hadn't its ineptness failed Samantha? Relegating her to a low percentile shared by the at-risk disadvantaged? More relevant in Samantha's case was the private school syndrome where many of her advantaged peers were also suffering a dismal academic fate.

"Pandemic!" Jenny seethed to herself. It was an outright crime. Wasn't it every mother's duty and unalienable right to fight back and balance the scales of inequity for her offspring?

One-pointed Jenny stayed the Samantha advocacy course. In her home office, a cozy bay off the master suite, Jenny gazed at her laptop. A miracle! Overcoming life's red tape was often plunking a mere keystroke on a data entry system. Jenny had mastered writing query letters, filling out documents and tweaking them to her advantage, no matter what the risk. Massaging a Stanford entrance essay for Samantha would have been a no-brainer, if Samantha gave-up bitching and sabotaging her efforts.

Bleary-eyed, crouched with her knees to her chin, Samantha moaned, "Mom, I feel like I'm tied to this chair. It's like I'm being held against my will."

Not about to rile her, Jenny chose the congeniality approach. "We want to go to Stanford, now don't we?"

"Not WE. ME! I'll write my own essay."

Jenny quibbled, "You can't. I have to help you."

"I can't, Mom...because you always do it for me."

"Okay. You dictate. I'll write."

Defiant, Samantha remained silent. Jenny composed out loud. "I have always been different than my peers."

"Don't say that," Samantha snapped. "Nobody wants a dweeb. I have to get along. Fit in."

Jenny registered her sensitivity. "Good point." She continued writing. "My life is not just about me. I'm a twin. The other half of me is a boy. My ever-so-smart, ever-so-good-natured, popular..."

"Gag me. Why is everything always about Brian?" Samantha whined.

"It's not, sweetie, this is about you."

"Right! I'm not going to Stanford. You go, Mom. You are the real student, not me!" Tied in emotional knots, Samantha scampered out of the room in a huff. Having no meaningful retort to a teenager's wrath, Jenny continued writing the essay. "Being a twin is a special calling in life.

Richie let out a wolf-whistle to get her attention. "How's it going? Samantha grimaced, then slashed her finger across her throat. Richie sailed through the front door, as Samantha made a beeline down the steps, muttering out loud. "I hate her! She doesn't give a hoot about me…it's all about her." Richie glowered, "That bad, sweetie?"

Samantha paused, "Just pretend you didn't see me and then you can pretend you like the living room." She slammed the back door. He remained fixed, momentarily concerned. "How can she be freaked about the living room?" No further explanation was necessary. . Richie glared in disbelief at the transformed living room. Jolted by the unfamiliar surroundings he became apoplectic. "What the hell happened? I don't recognize my own living room."

Touching a silk pillow his testosterone flared. His "King of the castle" persona castigated, "Whose ugly pillow is this?" He ripped at it, flung it overhead. Goose down feathers filled the air, trickling down like bubbles sticking on the new furniture and carpet. "Where is my chair! " He shouted to the rafters, "My comfy chair. Where the hell is it? Jennifer!"

Jenny beamed from her perch on the landing. Delighted, she watched Richie's ballistic response to her handiwork, gloating with a sense of elation, "That's your mad voice, calling me <u>Jennifer.</u>" She descended the steps, approaching Richie.

Every marriage has a demarcation moment, a point where the insults and affronts may have gone too far. Jenny had an inkling this event held that possibility for her and Richie. She knew that being rational about irrationality would bare no weight. It left little space for their minds to meet halfway. Wanting resolution she implored, "Can't we reach that ever-important healing agreement? Can't we agree to disagree?"

Coming out of his frenzy Richie scoured through the pile of invoices strategically left for his disapproval. He choked up. "You're squeezing me like a lemon, dripping the last bit of juice out of me. Why, Jenny?"

Aiming for calm, she clutched at her control valve. "Remember the stain, Richie?"

"The stain? You spent half of our retirement money on a new living room. Because of one little stain?"

"A carnal stain, Richie. It could make you famous."

"Famous?"

"Maybe infamous is more like it?" She slipped the pre-recorded DVD into the player. "Showtime."

On the TV screen Jenny pleaded with Ed, her 'Knight In Shining Armor' carpet man. "You've got to get it out. It's a carnal blemish on my marriage."

"My dear Mrs. Forrest, you can call me Ed. I really understand...your tight spot."

Squirming at the innuendo Richie turned his eyes away from the screen. "Where is he going with this nonsense, Jenny? Have you lost it?"

"No, I made it."

Richie was aghast. "With him? That ape-face? In our house!"

"It was the best afternoon of my life. I was fully ME!"

"In a skin-flick? Like a porno-star?"

Jenny dodged his bullet. "Get real. I made...I did a..."

"You did a <u>what</u>?"

"Ah...a room makeover."

"In one day? You mean this? This bland, no color, tasteless...."

Offended, Jenny snipped, "Tasteless? How dare you insult my studied greige-blend, my monochromatic perfection!"

The TV screen illumined quick cuts of Jenny orchestrating the room makeover. Richie grimaced, grumbled, and groaned as she ecstatically toasted champagne with Ed. Abruptly, the screen faded to a fuzzy snowy haze. He gasped, "What the hell happened next?"

Gloating over his irritation at another man coveting her, Jenny flashed an innocent smile. "Nothing happened."

"Tell me <u>now</u>! What happened?"

Jenny placed a finger over her mouth, gently rubbing up-and-down. "Mum's the word."

Crashing in frustration, fixating on the snowy TV, Richie was determined to get an answer. Clumsily fiddling with the DVD player – definitely mechanically challenged – he pulled connector cords from the TV, the VCR, and DVD player. Red, blue, yellow, black cords tangled around him in a jumbled vice. A captive victim of his own doing, Richie wriggled on the floor, wrapped up in the slew of cords. "Get me out of this mess," he snarled in frustration.

At the sight of his Houdini-esque predicament, Jenny wailed with laughter.

"This is not funny, Jennifer!"

She could barely contain her glee. "Not funny, because it's happening to <u>you</u>."

"Nothing is happening to me." He wrestled with the cords. Trying unsuccessfully to free himself, he mustered a meek, "I'm A-OKAY."

Enjoying every second Jenny seized the DVD, taunting him. "What if your clients see this?"

Richie shuddered, "You wouldn't stoop that low?"

She nodded a she-devil grin. "Of course I wouldn't." For once she had commanded his full attention.

Richie blurted, "I'll be ruined!"

"You're already ruined."

"What do mean by 'already'?"

Jenny tossed questionable credit card receipts at him. "Here's the other half of our retirement fund. Your motels, brunches, quickies."

"Business write-off's," he scoffed.

She focused on one receipt. "Motel Four? Cheap. Cheap. Cheap. No real woman would feel special in a roach-infested dump like that."

On the offensive Richie blustered, "You are obsessed. Over the top. You need help."

"I need help? So now your smutty shame is my fault. You need help, Richie."

"You're right!" With that ploy he screeched at the top of his lungs, "Help!"

Jenny suddenly felt paranoid. "Sshh, the neighbors will hear you."

"Neighbors! You sound like my mother. What am I, a ten-year-old?"

"Nah! You're more like two," she snickered.

Incensed by the jab, he belted even louder, "I need HELP!" Launching a verbal assault weapon he lowered his voice and targeted her straight on. "I need help to get away from you!" His stinging words flew at Jenny like a soul-wounding body blow.

"That was Id kill. Hijacking our marriage. Not OKAY!" Fighting back tears, she fled from the room, leaving him to struggle on his own, twisting, wrapping tighter in the mess.

Brian, who had been upstairs in his room, dashed down the stairs, almost bumping into Jenny as she flew by. "What's up, Mom?" Jenny couldn't speak and sailed onward to the sanctuary of her kitchen. Brian entered the living room where Richie gagged expletives trying to loosen a wire twisting around his neck. Discombobulated by the sight of his father strangling to death, Brian fired a rapid succession of questions. "Dad, are you all right? Are you trying to kill yourself? Should I call the police, the paramedics? What should I do?"

Richie choked, gurgling, "Untie me, you idiot."

Lurking over him, stubble-faced with unruly hair, Brian looked like a huge teen werewolf. Sizing up the wires and cords, "You can thank Boy Scouts if this works." His lip snarled, "Too bad you never showed up."

The growling sting of Brian's 'no show' intent exploded a paranoid rant in Richie's mind. Panicking, he began to reel. "Could my own kid take revenge? Could he be thinking of doing me in? One little twist of a cord, then a snap of the neck. That would be it. An accident for all intent and purpose."

"Dad, calm down," Brian urged. "No one's going to hurt you."

Richie screamed, "SNAP!" before he fainted.

"Dad, what's happening?" Brian shook Richie's shoulders, checked his pulse; faint, but beating. Whipping a couple of light smacks across his face, he ordered, "Dad, wake up."

Richie came to. "Please don't hurt me, Brian, I'll make it up to you." He barely lifted a tied-up finger. "Scout's honor."

"Relax. Your just fainted like a chick. Let me do this. I'll get you out in no time." He raised his fingers in the Scout pledge. "I promise."

Brian concentrated while he began the daunting task of unraveling the maze. He bent over backwards, put his head through a cord, twisted another, and held one between his teeth, reciting every knot in his repertoire. "Slip knot over and under, half-knot back into the slot. Pull, twist, in and out."

Richie succumbed to the process, whimpering, "Will you please shut up."

Meanwhile, trapped behind the kitchen counter, Samantha lackadaisically listened to her mother's endless blather, hoping that the lurid emotions would settle.

Jenny gobbled marshmallows out of a bag. "I enjoyed tormenting him for a moment or two."

Samantha snickered, "I can relate to that."

A portion of a marshmallow hung from Jenny's lip. "But I lost the battle."

Samantha sighed. "It's a marriage, not a war."

"Same difference. You're too young to know."

"Right. I don't want to hear any more of your voodoo negatives. It fries my future brain's future." Samantha snatched her car keys, a Tutti-Frutti yogurt bar, three bananas, and an Energy Blast. "See ya'," she said as she breezed through the doorway.

Left alone to lament her dismal fate, Jenny went upstairs to her office and sat down at her desk, typing feverishly, she hemmed and hawed, dumping simmering intimacies onto her BLOG:

I'm pondering in a pool of doubt. Yet there is a force within me that is greater, more powerful than the little me that drivels and snivels life's sweetness away. This supreme energy is prodding, pounding, begging for an answer to a question. I'm so afraid to even think it. Let alone say it out loud. I remember a tarot card reader telling me at a most critical time in my life, 'The quality of the answer lies in the quality of the question.' I was asking her, 'Is Richie the right one for me?' She would say, 'That is a yes or no answer. Let's open up the possibilities. Rephrase the question.'

'Okay. Is someone else better for me?'

'That is a yes or no,' she said again.

It spiraled in a ton of directions. 'Is the person born yet? Did they just die? Will we meet in another life? Should I throw in the towel? Join a nunnery?'

The barrage of unanswered questions went on for fifty-five minutes of my hour reading. Until, finally, she said. 'Have you become the person that the right person for you - could love? If not, what qualities do you need to cultivate?'

Yipes! How clever was that? It was all about me. Then I blurted some bazaar notion, 'Cultivate? What am I, some vacant piece of land covered with locusts and weeds?'

She gazed at me with the wisdom of an old owl and hooted, 'Whipper-snapper, you're too romantically chained to know who you really are. So, act as if.'

'Act as if what, I asked.'

'You already are who and what you want to be.' A buzzer rang. The hour ended. And I married Richie soon after. Are you with me dear readers? The clue is: settling for less than wholeness is a self-fueling curse. Ask your own question. Go for it.

Right now I'm dizzy with thousand's of sugarplums, smidgens of abstract thoughts, dancing in my head. I see huge red bleeding hearts, tunnels, fireworks, and even my old douche bag. Ooh! Here it comes, an image is forming into a logical sequence. My question is, 'What is in my heart of hearts'? Let's breathe deep. No rush. Don't manipulate. Let the answer come on it's own. I hear it rumbling, grumbling, churning tears and fears exploding in my solar plexus. It's erupting...my heart of heart's answer is that I want Richie to adore me like he used to. I want to be his special love. His one and only main squeeze; his best friend forever. His best lover ever. Oooohhhh YES!

Done. I got it out. It wasn't debilitating. It was a hot turn-on, a horny-making answer. Nevertheless, I have to censor my sudden aroused sensations of lust, visions of hot lovemaking, deliciously, deliriously ensconced in throes of HEAT. Or this noble, pure BLOG will become jeopardized. Compromised. X-rated. I'm going to get that love back no matter what it takes...or costs.

I'm winded now, losing the power-drive, like after the coital climax. I'm left with the dismal reality of wondering why can't WE be like it used to be? Seems that question is asked in vain. Life-Crap happens. Like a plodding disintegration, a gradual descent into feeling alone, then an empty love-starved babe lives with a total stranger, her husband.

It boils down to one irrefutable fact: I refuse to rephrase my question! I'll just scream at Richie. 'Why can't WE be like it used to be?'

What happened to my happy life? It became my 'act as if' you are happy in life. That worked for a while. Then it switched to, 'act as if' so no one will know you are not the happy, cherished, sexiest adored wife.

ACTING AS IF was supposed to cure hair-raising trepidation's, turn rancor into delight or a spineless procrastinator into Wonder Woman. In my case 'acting as if' turned out to be a big fat fib. Diving deeper, paddling, drowning in the next deceit to cover up the next lie. It was like a mermaid swimming in a pool of muck that turned into quicksand.

So what to do? Wasn't it Socrates that said, 'Keep asking questions, and more questions, then you will find the answer? And discover the next question.'

I am so befuddled and muddled I can't even remember my next question, let alone listen for an answer.

Jenny continued on into the night harping secrets, marital qualms, blasting the nonsensical purge onto her BLOG readers.

Four Mercedes SUV'S filed out of the Forrest driveway. Richie, Brian, Samantha, and Jenny, each in their respective vehicles, trailed each other through the suburban maze. At an intersection they waved and split off in different directions.

Jenny counted three beats, whipped a quick U-turn, and followed Richie. The goal was to stay far enough behind and out of sight. No such luck! Richie spotted her. The hide-and-seek game was on. He maneuvered the Mercedes in front of a large truck, blocking her view.

"Damn it!" she shouted at the truck driver. "Move it!"

Richie shot into another lane, leaving her stuck in a traffic jam. "Take that!" he spat.

Jenny pushed a button on her cell, a devilish glint in her eyes. "No rest for the wicked," she sneered.

Richie's cell phone rang. Jenny's name showed up on the Caller ID. "Just give it a break," he said to himself, letting the call go to voicemail. The cell phone call took on a new meaning, as it became a power struggle of dueling wills.

"Richie, it's Thursday, you'll be at the club at about one. See you." Jenny beamed, knowing she had the upper hand, whenever he had his schedule.

Peeling down an alley, he waved, "Have fun, Jenny-kins." Proud of his witty moment of escape, Richie smiled. "Hasta luego, baby."

The Mills Country Club celebrates golf, the nouveau riche, and a few quasi-celebrities. Jenny strolled through the pro shop and impulsively purchased designer golf wear, a token to cover-up her day's snooping. Properly attired, she wrangled a golf cart from an overzealous caddie. Slipping him a few dollars was a note of encouragement. "Mr. Forrest should be along any time now," she fibbed with a big smile.

Aimlessly, she steered the cart across the fresh grown turf. Her eyes were peeled with hawk-like precision, searching the course for Richie. Jenny was in rare form. Choosing not to hide herself from a few familiar golfers, she boldly waved at them. Craning her neck, watching a lone golfer down the stretch, she noted that the long drive eliminated Richie. No way was he that good! A tickle of excitement erupted in her stomach. She giggled. It was probably John McEnroe, a fantasy flame since high school, known to play the course more often now that he was no longer a 'Tennis Pro'.

A rising wind blew her ten-minute-old $125 Coach cap off her head. Hurling above her reach, grasping for it, she missed. The cap sailed in flight like a toy airplane into the wind stream, causing her to lose focus on the trail. The cart veered and raced downhill. Shilly-shallied, it picked up speed, plowing into the depths of a soggy sand trap. The cart partially flipped, landing on top of Jenny who was cushioned by the sand, barely feeling the impact.

Face-up, staring into the sky, dizzily gazing at the rolling clouds forming into shapes, she thought she was hallucinating. One cloud fluffed-up into an angel floating figure eight's in the cobalt blue heavens. Another cloud artfully whisked into the shape of a lion. A giant mouth marshmallow-ed, opened wide, patiently lingering. As opportunity would strike, it devoured the frolicking little angel.

"Brute," she sputtered, spitting gritty sand. "My sweet angel, where are you? Don't leave me." She struggled to free her legs from beneath the cart. Covered in sticky sand, brushing off globs, "Yucky" was her last thought before she collapsed.

Jenny didn't remember the two young caddies lifting her into the cart. Nor did she hear the club's copper-skinned manager, Alfie, whisper, "Why is Mrs. Forrest here today?"

The young caddie answered candidly, "Don't have a clue."

Alfie needed a solution to avoid the required accident report. "Did she sign out for the cart?"

"Not exactly. Mr. Forrest reserved one."

"Ah ha! Dilemma is revealed. The problem is solved. Remember, guys, the key to Mill Country Club's success is, no known marital indiscretions ever take place here. They ask. We don't tell. Avoid seemingly innocent probes like, '...did you see so and so? Or, 'who were they with?' Questions of that nature are never acknowledged or answered to wives about husbands or vice versa. Got it?"

The young caddies echoed in unison. "Got it, Mr. Alfie."

"Good. Now discreetly wheel Mrs. Forrest into the spa. Sergio can take over from there." A stroke of luck that Alfie's VIP diplomacy code momentarily protected Jenny from herself, her obsession; and her impending fate.

The dutiful caddies helped Sergio, the raven longhaired, buff masseur; lift Jenny onto the massage table. He covered her with a sheet and expertly removed her golf shirt and skirt. Sergio kneaded her back with a facile intensity. Nonplussed, he ignored her breast that was peeking through the sheet, exposing a hardened pink nipple.

Jenny's eyes opened. She let out a little "Coo" and an "Ooo." Without missing a beat Sergio responded, "How does that feel, Mrs. Forrest?"

Stretched out in total comfort on the massage table, she answered, "Yucky! That's what I was feeling. Now I feel sooo relaxed."

"So it's good for you, Mrs. Forrest?"

Orgasmic whimpers emitted from behind an adjoining curtain. Escalating passion shimmied through the quiet space. A woman's throaty voice throbbed, "Oh yes. Deeper. More."

Disturbed by the sexual sobs of pleasure, Jenny felt a primal eruption heating her longing loins. "Can't we have some privacy?" she whimpered. Excitation pierced like sticky thorns into her aching crotch. Flaunting, reminding her of the lack of sexual arousal; a deprivation she endured. With each sensuous breath of the woman behind the curtain, Jenny squirmed, a throbbing desire mounting inside of her. Growing increasingly uncomfortable, she became indignant, chastising; "I can't stand it. How rude...and disturbing."

With erotic tension mounting, Jenny became a wild wanton woman. Instead of flinging herself on the available Sergio, she crawled off the table and flung open the thin curtain that separated her from the moaning wailer.

Lying on a massage table, relishing a deep tissue massage was a diminutive eighty-year-old woman gasping in a euphoric state. Jenny stared at the long silver hair covering her gravity-drooping breasts. To ease the embarrassing moment, she spouted a fast quip. "Oh, so sorry. I'm looking for my husband."

The masseuse, a stout English woman affronted by Jenny's intrusively absurd entrance, retreated to a far corner in the room. "Don't do anything rash...I promise you," she pointed to the old lady, "that she's not him. Your husband...I mean."

The old lady bolted up from her prone position, eyes blazing. "Looking for a grimy-lout, eh? That's exactly what I should have done. Henry would still be here today. I let him fool around and he dropped dead. Had a heart attack in his secretary's bed. Go find him girly, before it's too late."

Jenny shook her head in disbelief. Her brain rattled at the thought, "Richie's in-my-face French secretary?" At that instant the sun blared through the window and the light dawned on Jenny. Her suspicions might bare credence, an unfathomable reality. She pleaded to no one in particular, "Oh please, not her! Any other secretary, but not Bambe."

On that note the old lady rested her head back on the massage table. "My hour's not over. Come on and finish that rub down," she demanded. Feeling somewhat relieved and safe, the masseuse edged out of the corner and continued the massage.

Viewing the encounter as a profound premonition, Jenny was overwhelmed with an adrenaline rush. A fire born of the ancient Goddess of Love, Aphrodite, engulfed her. Contacting womanhood's competitive survival rites that were known to the rare few, most likely Cleopatra, Liz Taylor, and the Mata Hari, she bristled inside. How fortunate, she pondered, that her obsession had been sanctioned. "I am entitled to find Richie. I am compelled to win him back."

She quickly grabbed her clothes, gave Sergio a kiss-kiss and a generous tip. "Thank you for holding one more secret discretion. Sergio, you are the best."

"My pleasure is yours, Mrs. Forrest." He looked at her adoringly as he removed the sheet from the massage table and folded it with care, as if still caressing her body. Jenny marched out of the room and into another netherworld of the spa.

Getting dolled-up was a vital part of her game plan. Jenny luxuriated in a steamy Jacuzzi. The Goddess-like ritual also included a manicure, pedicure, makeup, and hairdo – the works. She opted for French nails on both hands and feet. Short, squared, natural with white tips: clean looking. The statement: "Dust-free high maintenance. Don't do laundry, dishes, scrub floors, or mow lawns."

The tricky part was the requisite bikini wax. A sadist's dream-come-true, it became a state of the art profession for the waxaholics. Carla, a trendette, spaghetti-curled clinician, spouted racy choices that sent shivers up Jenny's woozie.

"The Brazilian wax is primo, sweetie. All brilly-hair gone, baldly clean like a baby. Or, we can do the Peek-a-boo, leave just a little fuzz, showing your pinky-pearl. Skip the Boom-Boom Snatch Blast, the under- twenties favorite, bleached to white, then tie-dyed your favorite colors – crimson to aqua with an arrow of fuzz jutting to the hot spot, the pinky pearl. Or there's the old Buzz Saw stand by, the regular – guaranteed bikini proof."

Jenny had gone too far to back out. She opted for the Buzz Saw (scary thought) regular, no fancy frills, at the bargain price of $100. She was handed a mouth-guard. "Just bite down when you want to scream." Swapping on hot wax, Carla comforted, "It's weeding your garden and showing off the beautiful flower so it can open and blossom in the fresh air."

"What bull!" Jenny thought. The hair-to-skin rips and tears *Ssshhizzz's* are louder than any human scream. Pain? Forget it. The worst, like an onion being peeled raw. Some clients spit the mouth-guard out, including Jenny, blending wailing human roars with the *Ssshhizzz*.

At least there was a strategic spa plan for putting the nervous system back on keel. Next, Carla rigorously rubbed on the spa's miracle gel, exfoliating Jenny's mid-age skin. Proudly displaying a gritty-celled sponge, Carla announced, "Black grime is years of life's problems being washed away."

"Ooh, suck it!" Jenny snarled. She could barely imagine. "Then what's left?"

"Only the soft good times, a supple skin." After hose-spraying a body wash, towel-drying her like a newborn colt, Carla topped it off with a head to toe spritz. "This is 'Angelica', a seductive fragrance known worldwide by the rich and famous. Two-thousand dollars per ounce!"

Jenny reveled, "What is that luscious smell?"

"A mix of chocolate and gardenias. Its secret ingredient is pheromone, which is an extract of a fertile woman's juice."

"You're not really serious," Jenny gasped in an almost prudish tone.

"Oh yes. The mating scent is guaranteed to attract and to disarm all men. Anywhere. Anytime."

Exuding a total womanly vibe, Jenny uttered with a sultry humorous air, "Now what more could a PMS-peri-menopausal gal want?"

Feeling like a new woman from head-to-toe, Jenny strolled through the Mills Country Club grounds like a poodle in heat. She checked the dining area. The maitre d' greeted her with a flirtatious air, "You look extremely lovely today, Mrs. Forrest. Is there anything I can do for you?"

The extra glamour effort, a $500 spa overhaul, paid off. Her confirmation was when the maitre d' winked at her, then nonchalantly turned his head, quite aware that she would steal a peek at the reservation list. Unfortunately for Jenny, the list was a disappointment because Richie's name wasn't on it. Convinced he wouldn't change his appointment with an out of town client, she bet he was on the premises.

Rethinking her plan of attack, a familiar voice called out, "Jenny!" She turned in the direction of the caller, and there stood Rachel, the queen of the "Spoil-Us Club". The lunching charity-minded women were the Burb's hilarious social climbing dames, married to mostly elderly or impossible to like power brokers.

Rachel stood a striking six-foot tall, barefoot. Wearing size 12, four-inch stilettos, she towered over Jenny like a looming high rise. The over-bleached, overdone glitzy with heavily padded shoulders, resembled a linebacker in full drag. Yet she was friendly on occasion. Usually wanting something if she bothered to chitchat. Jenny transfixed on Rachel's extreme overbite that would give a battling shark the shivers.

"Jenny, honey, how are you...the kids...Richie?"

The mention of Richie's name sent Jenny's newfound confidence spiraling into the toilet. "Fine, fine, fine," she answered in a pitch one octave higher than her normal tone.

Rachel wagged her index finger. It appeared like a dagger with its extended five-inch curved fingernail, painted in Pucci-like colorful swirls aimed directly at her. "Me too! Good. Good. Fine. Fine." was Rachel's vacuous reply.

The superficial communication style let Jenny off the hook. She breathed a sigh of relief. If Rachel had prodded deeper Jenny would have burst into a fit of incomprehensible tears. It's true she joked about peri-menopause, but in the midst of it all, it never occurred to her that maybe the results of this day's events were the product of raging hormones: The ups, the downs, the unimaginable fears and inexplicable disappointments that were driving her from confusion to chaos.

"Smile, will you?" Rachel's shrill voice brought Jenny into back into the present moment. Rachel cajoled, "What could be so bad? In case you didn't notice, I could be Cinderfella's pumpkin." She laughed loudly at her own joke as she made fun of herself. She was dressed in orange from head-to-toe.

Jenny found it refreshing. She needed to lighten up. But, how? Everyone counted on her; the kids, her mom, Richie. Life seemed so seriously relevant compared to a dilettante's frivolity.

"Come join us, it's the 'Orange Party'."

Jenny hesitated, "Oh that's sweet, but..."

"But, but, but what? No but's allowed in this millennium." Rachel wouldn't take no for an answer. She scrutinized Jenny's blue outfit. Removing her own saffron-colored, beaded jeweled scarf, she draped it fashionably around Jenny's hip line. Rachel nodded approvingly. "Now aren't you a peach, Mrs. Jenny Forrest. Being married is a main criteria to be a member of the "Spoil-Us Club", you know." She held Jenny's arm and guided her into the dining area. "Only a blind person could miss our 'Orange Party'." Giant orange balloons, matching tablecloths and a prism of melon flowers, glowed in the center of the room.

Jenny commented, "How...*orange* it is."

Eight women decked-out in varying shades of apricot, with plumed hats, peachy silks, and tangerine leathers, gossiped among themselves. Jenny smiled. "Boasting a pumpkin patch?"

After a few shallow "Hellos", "Fines" and "Nice", most of the women were so engrossed in their repartee that they didn't take a breath to acknowledge her. Not taking it personally, Jenny chalked it up to typical faire, in the 'all about me' bubble-like cloister.

A waiter rushed to set up a place for her. Three photographers emerged, flashing photos of Jenny and Rachel. Sticking a muscular arm around Jenny's waist, Rachel nudged, "Smile a big one, honeycakes."

Jenny grimaced at the word "honeycakes" that Richie so often abused. Her scowl caught the camera lens, resembling a Pit Bull ready to attack.

Everyone's undivided attention darted to the twosome. One by one they each made the scene as a poser clamoring to get in on a photo. Some of the smiles were frozen. The nip and tuck, Botox and Restalyne gals masked into plaster-faced grins. Chiding each other, "Mara, get in the shot." "Come on, Deanna." In all their glory the ageless socialites freeze-framed in a jovial clump, smiling and exuding a happy time.

Jenny sipped an orange daiquiri – was it her second or third? She found herself an observer in a 'show and tell' of repressed ladies on the loose. Voices rang out, "I'm so grateful to get out and wear my glitters." "Mine are mostly mildew." "If wasn't for Rachel planning my social life, I'd be stuck at home forever."

As the drinks refilled, the stories became more real. Cancer scares, bypass surgery, grandkids on drugs and parents with Alzheimer's. From a hot little newlywed to a granny on a walker, the women celebrated their togetherness. Yet Jenny remained closed-lipped. She couldn't open up. Not here, anyway. Not one of them talked or balked about a rotten marriage. The acceptable dialogue was bashing or bragging rights about their ex-husbands.

Everyone hoisted a chock-packed 'goody bag' filled with delicious chocolate treats, makeup samples, and a Pilate's video. There wasn't an extra for Jenny, but Queen Rachel wouldn't let her leave without one. She gave hers to Jenny. "I spent all night packing the goodies. You enjoy."

"Too sweet and kind," Jenny cooed, feeling honored by the generous gesture. Moved by how close she suddenly felt to Rachel (or maybe buzzed from too much booze) she gave her a warm hug. When Jenny let go of her, Rachel's size 12-inch stiletto heel lodged in the carpet. Rachel grimaced, "Oh, that damn heel's stuck again." Trying to pull it out, Rachel tumbled flat on her back. The force of her weight barreled both heels through a wall. Riveted like a statue with heels jutting out into the dining area, Rachel barely struggled, careful not to twist her ankle, moaning, "Somebody help!"

Jenny and the maitre d' pulled her feet as hard as they could on one side. "You pull, I'll push," Jenny suggested.

Creating quite a spectacle in the dining area, a waiter on the other side of the wall used a hammer to tap the obtruding heels back through the thin wall. Astonished women watched and chattered, "What is that racket?" "Can't they do repairs after lunch?"

One last tug and Rachel was freed. With a big smile, not visibly hurt, she exclaimed, "Once a klutz, always a klutz."

The maitre d' offered, "To save face, we'll just say you hit the treadmill in stilettos." They all roared in laughter. Jenny had always judged the tall drink of a gal by the outside image, a tendency of 'approval by appearances' that someday she might inadvertently change.

After Jenny said her good-byes and made the usual air-kisses, she clutched her 'goody bag' and headed for the great outdoors, happy to see a blue sky and green grass following the flood of orange. Her walk was lighter as she crossed the club's parking lot. Praise the power of play, a daiquiri, and a few gal-friends. Maybe the angel she had seen earlier hadn't left her after all, and was taking care, at least of Rachel, who had survived the fall without a scratch? Jenny had momentarily forgotten about the need to find Richie and she had to admit that it felt good.

Her cell phone rang. Attempting to read Caller ID she held it up, blocking the sun's bright glare. Her eyes fixed. She might as well have been struck by a Mack truck: Leering out of a second story window as if a snitch had alerted him that she'd be standing there, Richie, seeming bigger than life, peered down at her. Shocked and awed, Jenny stammered, "So there's the tawdry scoundrel." The distance was too far for eye combat, but no doubt he had recognized her. Richie quickly closed the drape. A familiar rush of wanton-woman adrenaline pumped through her veins. She was back on the hunt. Nothing could stop her now. Without a diagram of the building it would be almost impossible to pick the right room from inside.

Still feeling a bit tipsy from the daiquiris it was doubtful that she could climb the fire escape, she needed to pull on something to lift up. No matter, she would figure it out. Jenny removed her shoes and placed them neatly in the 'goody bag'.

Thanks to a "Mommy and Me" gymnastic class she had suffered through, she recited a routine on how to lift up on a pole, in this case, the fire escape. "Feet firm. Knees bent. Right foot back." Confused, she stopped the movement. "No, left foot back. Right? Then push. Lift off." Falling forward, clinging to a bush, she pumped herself, "Okay. Second try." Unsuccessfully repeating the drill three times, she stubbed her toe. Holding one foot with her hand she hopped up-and-down, wailing, "Darn! Crap! Shoot!"

On another try she ripped her skirt, skinned her knee. Dabbling tiny beads of blood off her knee onto her sleeve, she then wiped the sweat from her brow. She was unaware that she had smeared a red line of blood across her forehead like war paint.

Remembering the kids in the "Mommy and Me" class squealing, "Yeah, Mrs. Forrest, GO!" fueled her confidence to keep at it. On the next try she propelled into the air, managed a basic somersault and hand-flipped onto the ladder. Struggling with a one-arm chin lift she moved up higher, slowly ascending the free-floating steps one baby step at a time. Unsteady, swaying on the rickety ladder, her heart beat faster than a locomotive engine. The anticipation of who was on the other side of the balcony door had her shakier than the height itself.

Wobbling, she crept onto a ledge, mumbling a pep talk. "You can do it. Only five more feet!" Flat on her tummy she scooted along, moving closer to the window. Teetering a bit, she reached it. To her amazement, the window was open.

A woman's sultry voice could be heard from inside. Richie's French secretary, Bambe, a dimpled beauty with ginger-colored hair and natural 34 D breasts, served hors d'oeuvre's to a client. "Zee croquet's are strictly low-carb," she purred. "Very leetle oil in the preparation. Ahh, and the oyster's gently snail-sauced, with de' escargot."

Straining to see inside, Jenny squeezed closer to the window. Leaning forward, she lost her balance, falling through the drapes. SMACK! She landed on the lap of Richie's client, billionaire heir M. Barrett. Thinking it was a prank he played along and kissed Jenny passionately on the lips.

Breathless, she tried to recover her composure. "Ta Dah! Guess I arrived...just in time." She lifted her arms in the air with a triumphant wave.

M. Barrett applauded. "You sure did."

Richie, caught between a rock and losing a client, clenched his fist. Barely controlling his impulse to sock Barrett in the jaw, he held down his rising arm. Instead, he forced a bland smile. "Cat Woman couldn't have made a more impressive entrance." With the intent of escorting Jenny out of the room, he reached for her arm.

Bambe interrupted the gesture by nonchalantly offering Jenny a plate of hor d'oevres. "How about a lettle taste, Mrs. Forrest?"

Jenny puckered her lips at Bambe like a blowfish imitating her French accent. "For My aphrodisiac lettle snack I will have a whore-d'oevre." Her voice dropped to guttural-throaty "HURRR. Emphasizing 'whore'.

Baffled by the discovery Barrett slid Jenny off of his lap. Jenny lunged forward, her skirt hiked up revealing a black lace thong. Her rounded shapely buttocks faced him dead on.

Befuddled by the sight he declared, "Mrs. Forrest! You're Richie's wife?

Jenny curled her knees to her chest on the floor at Barrett's feet and seductively sucked on an escargot, nodding, "That I am. And whom might you be?"

Barrett, now flushed and beginning to sweat, accused with bravado, "It wouldn't be the first time some gold-digging freaks tried to set me up in some kinky blackmail scheme."

Richie stood between them, defending himself. "That is a preposterous accusation, Mr. Barrett!"

With squinted eyes, Barrett sized-up Richie, and the two women. He focused on Jenny in tattered clothing and the bloody war paint stripe across her forehead. Exuding suspicions and doubt he questioned Richie. "What deal, exactly, were you going to propose?"

Richie was turning pasty-white with anxiety. "Now, this is all an accident. It wasn't planned. It's...it's just a...weird coincidence! Tell him Jenny," he implored with bulging eyes. Had he seen a ghost his expression would have been the same.

Innocently caught in a moment of succulent ecstasy, Jenny gently rolled her tongue over the slippery snail in her mouth, swallowing it with a clucking, "Gulp". All eyes were on her sensual display.

Richie was beyond patience. "Enough already. Jenny, tell him you are here by mistake."

Jenny fluttered her eyelashes. Her eyes twinkled. "Mister whatever your name is? I am sure it is no mistake that you are quite the kisser."

Richie blew up. "This nightmarish moment can't be happening!"

Barrett flashed back, "But it is."

Richie pleaded, "Look, our team has worked over a year building trust. Arranging this meeting with you has been very important to us."

Barrett smiled with contempt. "Looks like you blew it."

Richie paced. He could brilliantly deliver the pitch he rehearsed for months, the masterpiece that he had rewritten a hundred times. This was it, his opportunity for a deal of a lifetime. He couldn't allow anyone, especially Jenny, to blow it for him.

"Jenny, <u>tell</u> him the truth!" Richie demanded. "We can't let this deal fly out the window."

Barrett was on his feet, holding Richie's proposal portfolio in front of him. "Now that's a brilliant idea." Moving toward the window he opened the drapes. Looking down at the distance to the ground he said, "Mrs. Forrest, you are quite the stunt lady and an undoubtedly good kisser."

Richie was mortified. "Barrett, let me explain. It's the deal of a lifetime. One that you would be proud to be part of."

"So, Richie Forrest, the thought running through your head is 'Deal or No Deal?' " Barrett ,taunted.

Appealing to logic Richie replied, "Yes, but you haven't even heard the proposal."

With a sardonic smirk, Barrett added, "I think I got the drift, calculated the odds."

Richie kneeled on his knees like a praying mantis. The room was dead silent as everyone waited for Barrett's reply.

"The decision is, NO DEAL!" For all to witness, Barrett tossed the million-dollar proposal out of the second story window. "Geronimo!" Barrett shouted. It didn't fall like a Newtonian projectile or directly down like a rock would have. It floated, opened up, launching and scattering Richie's gold mine for the world to see. The papers flew, whirling and twirling like glider planes, landing like checkerboards covering the golf course below.

Richie's heart sank as he watched his fortune virtually flying out of his bank account. Solemn, he muttered, "No deal. Bad deal."

That night Richie slept in the guest bedroom, down the hall from the master suite. Stuck in a state of shock and revenge, he felt claustrophobic lying under a frilly little canopy that was draped on top of the poster bed. He stood up on the mattress, did a couple of aerobic bounces, ripped down the silky fabric with entitlement and glee, and said aloud, "Ahh. So much better."

Spotting a magazine on the nightstand, he picked it up. "Penthouse? Why, that sneaky little Brian. What am I thinking? He's eighteen, after all. And I'm forty, sleeping in a tot's bed reading Penthouse." He opened to a centerfold buxom Amazon. A designer, 'slip and slide', lubricated prophylactic fell out between the folds. It was still in the wrapper. "At least I'm raising a son close my heart." Richie gazed at the airbrushed beauty. "Your loss, Jennifer. A hard man is good to find."

Jenny spent the night in the master suite. As she sobered-up, the impact of her actions seemed to take on an amorphous form. Curling up on the orthopedic dual adjustable mattress, she felt so small and alone. She pushed the super-duper button on the remote control to lower the mattress level to air-compress and soften the surface like a feather. Instead of softening, as if Richie was torturing her in absentia, it locked on rock-level hard – his number-one choice. Being inventive and miserably uncomfortable, she propped king-sized pillows under her, and sunk into the soft down. "Ah hah! You couldn't get me, could you, Richie?" she said to herself with complete satisfaction.

Jenny reached for the book hidden safely under her side of the bed, "HOW TO NIX OR FIX A BROKEN MARRIAGE." The hammer and axe on the cover seemed intriguing when she purchased it at Costco's two months earlier. She arbitrarily opened to a page. There was a checklist. Questions in the list included, "Could a stay-at-home mom secretly desire what she was projecting on her husband? Does he have all the status? Is he the boss or the slave? Are you in control of the checkbook? Is he in control of the clicker? Does he care about your feelings? Does he even know you have them? Who would the kids trust if they were busted? Who has the most organisms?" The list went on for fifteen pages.

Jenny's eyes blurred, struggling to answer the rate chart. Was it "Always" or "Sometimes" or "Never"? The ordeal seemed exhausting, so she skimmed to the last page of the test, realizing she needed a calculator to total the score. Desperate for answers she called her mother, Mrs. Rita Gibbons, who was tucked in bed, moisturizer piled on her face an inch thick, and a fluffy nightcap squiggled on her head. As Jenny incessantly rambled on, Mrs. Gibbons put the phone on her pillow and dozed off.

Reading from the book, Jenny recited, "Is your marriage like a backed-up toilet, a dirt-bag, the devil's bidding, a match made in the bedroom?" Tossing the book on the floor, toning like a myna bird, she complained, "Richie is the insensitive dirt-bag, the spoiled brat status-climbing drunk. He needs to change his ways. Not me. I'm okay the way I am. Enablers aren't the dirt-bags, right Mom?"

Mrs. Gibbons grunted an "Eeeh" in her sleep.

"I guess that means I'm right. I'm glad you agree with me. It gives me a sense of peace and tranquility." Within minutes Jenny's exhaustion overwhelmed her and she also dozed off, phone in hand.

Richie had popped earplugs to drown out jenny's harboring incessant chatter that echoed through the walls. He too, was in zzz-land.

The Forrest dining room was bustling with intense conversation. Obviously, this wasn't the best time for a family get-together. Nevertheless, both mothers-in-law were in town and the evening had been planned for months. Mrs. Gibbons, looking perfectly coifed, was an eye-catching contrast to Richie's mother, Mrs. Svartznegger, annoyingly proud to flagrantly flaunt her Russian peasantry.

Samantha had headphones on, intentionally tuned-out from the ego-ballooning fuss being made over Brian who seemed embarrassed as wine glasses were raised, toasting his impending football scholarship. "To Brian, a great athlete," Jenny declared. "A Stanford scholarship boy," she continued. "A true Gibbons," Rita proudly pronounced. "A true Forrest," Richie's mother countered. Mrs. Svartznegger belly-whipped in her usual cantankerous way. "Not Forrest. We're Svartznegger's."

Brian reminded her, "Dad changed it for business, remember, Grandma?" "You remember. Svartznegger means black. Not 'Forrest.' We're black."

Detached from the conversation, Richie mumbled into his cell phone. "No problem. I'm on my way." Snapping the top of his cell into a tiny pancake, he announced to the family, "Got to field an emergency." Without looking at anyone, he stood straight up, giving his mother a pat on the shoulder.

Mrs. Svartznegger attacked, speaking to him in Russian gibberish, "Vas ein fraus-tching dict?"

English translation: "Where are you going? To see a woman?"

Richie replied, "Nein, havblowjob. Ict hasuser slaughten."

English translation: "Don't be ridiculous. I have a big meeting."

Mrs. Svartznegger accused him. "Extermination. Auwx Papa Grimaces. Hookerfleem. Smeetin' smelt."

English translation: "You have the same look your Papa had with the hookers."

Appalled by their incomprehensible repartee, Mrs. Gibbons whispered to Jenny. "Rude. It's so insultingly rude when they talk about us like that."

Dutifully, Richie waved good-bye to Mrs. Gibbons. "Got to go." He patted Jenny's shoulder as if consoling a wounded pup. "Later, honeycakes."

Jenny could barely hide her scowl. "Honeycakes? Honeycakes makes me nauseous, tongue-tied and miserable."

"Okay, how about 'Later Jennifer.' "Without further ado he waltzed out of the room. Jenny followed him into the foyer.

"Emergency? Richie, what emergency? The whole family's here. How can you just leave?"

Mrs. Svartznegger squeezed between them. With a strong maternal embrace, she crooned, "Good-night, son."

"Night-Night. Sweet dreams," he breezed. For show, he planted a skimpy peck on Jenny's cheek, slamming the front door behind him as he darted to his SUV in the driveway.

Seething, Jenny started after him." Richie, if you leave, we're finished."

Mrs. Svartznegger blocked her. She put a tight arm around Jenny and guided her back into the dining room. Full of conviction, Mrs. Svartznegger declared, "A wife needs to get a life."

Unable to hold back her frustration, Jenny fumed a primal-release. She dumped Richie's barely eaten meal on the floor. Ego-crashing with the gourmet mess, Jenny stammered, "A life. I had a life. I want it back. The happy little family! With a husband, who doesn't bamboozle and trick or..." She broke down in tears, "I'm a betrayed woman. They write 'Dear what's-her-name' about women like me. Mama, I'm a failure."

Mrs. Gibbons wouldn't hear of it. "Like hell you are. That jack-ass is mincemeat."

Mrs. Svartznegger felt obliged to defend her son. "Where's the proof he's schtupping somebody?"

"You want proof, 'Cheater Eater's' will get you proof." Mrs. Gibbons dialed a number on her cell phone. "We'll find out about your illegitimate son," she waved the cell at Jenny, "...and your imbecilic reptilian husband, once and for all."

The rest of the evening was a blur. Jenny's mother rattled on about detectives, restraining orders and women's rights. Mrs. Svartznegger surprised them both as she rattled, "So, I had a broken home, a broken fuh-kokting marriage and a broken heart to boot." By the end of the evening the women were in a clutch, holding each other and bearing through their personal pains and tears.

Brian had left hours earlier with a friend. Samantha huddled in her room with headphones on, drowning out the women's cries, deciding if she ever wanted to join the ranks of womanhood.

It was a toss-and-turn sleepless night. Jenny stretched her arm over to Richie's side of the bed, patting it to make sure he wasn't there. Wrenching pangs inside her gut wanted him to cuddle with her. She repeated her night survival routine: hugging the super-sized pillow, stretching it the length of her body, snuggling with the fluffy down. Part of her couldn't fathom what was happening. Part of her felt toasty and warm.

The phone rang several times before she pulled herself out of a dream stupor. She answered, "If it's the morgue...he's not here."

A deep baritone voice replied, "This is 'Cheater-Eaters', for Mrs. Forrest."

She bolted straight up, startled. "Yeah, it's her...the Mrs."

"Mrs. Forrest?"

Hyperventilating, she wheezed, "I mean it is me. I am she."

'We have the goods", the deep voice announced. "We're red-hot on the cheater's tail. Are you ready?"

Unable to utter anything, she breathed "Ahh" heavily into the phone.

"I'll take that as a yes, unless I hear a definitive no."

Jenny gasped a "Guuah" gurgling sound.

"Sounds like a definitive yes. Be ready."

As the eruption of betrayal loomed, her heart filled with apprehensive dread. What had her mother done? Didn't she know that her daughter, the little Jenny, wasn't a grown-up yet? The tender, overly fragile little child part couldn't bare the sting of reality. Hard core resilience was for other people. "Strong people with strong guts who could run butt-naked through life without giving a damn," Jenny mused.

Solving little daily problems was doable. Making little miracles happen for the kids was usually a cinch. However, life-changing possibilities posed terrifying rattraps, sinkholes, and mind-quakes. Caught in a gloomy revelation of Richie's now-confirmed infidelity, she begged the messenger, "Can't someone send in the angels?" Deep within she knew it was a cop-out. Her mother had pushed her off the avoidance fence. It was too late to turn back.

She put on sweats and sneakers and waited at the front door for Cheater-Eater. The white van pulled up to the curb and Jenny got in. "Mrs. Forrest, I'm Cheater-Eater. Just relax. "You're in good hands." His greasy-black hair was slicked back and his pockmarked face with a reddened scar across his cheek, signaled the years of hard-living and scuffling on the streets.

Jenny folded her arms and let out a sigh of resignation. "I hope so." As the high-tech electronically equipped van screeched through the streets Jenny felt the sordid escapade was ego crippling, like being in the middle of some contemptible, inane, self-degrading TV reality show.

Cheater-Eater broke her thought as he spoke into a headset. "We're at the location, ready and waiting."

The moment was surreal and a bizarre terror overwhelmed Jenny as she helplessly sat in a Motel Four's freezing parking lot at 2:00 A.M. waiting for the marriage shoe to fall. To make matters worse, she was hiding in the shadows with a shoddy lowbrow Cheater-Eater. His clothes were smelly and wrinkled. No doubt he slept in them. His vile pungent odor made her queasy down to her toes. Alternatively, was the creepy groveling and churning in her tummy, unadulterated fear?

Cheater-Eater held a camcorder close to her face. "This will tell a piece of the story."

Jenny viewed the murky footage. It appeared to show Richie kissing Bambe in a hotel room. A closer view was more incriminating. A naked bum pumped up-and-down. The left bum-cheek revealed a distinguishable reddish birthmark.

"Oh no!" Jenny cringed. "The raspberry! It is Richie!" She grew a bit faint and put her head on Cheater-Eater's shoulder, sobbing.

He adjusted his headset, speaking into the microphone. "Definite ID!"

Jenny slumped over him. "Is this a crime scene?"

Cheater-Eater lifted her body upright. "They're on their way out of the motel. Are you ready for the confrontation?"

"It's true," Jenny wailed, tears streaming down her face. "He's really boffing her. Why did it have to be true?"

Unknowingly, Richie and Bambe were heading directly toward the Cheater-Eater's camera. Bambe nudged close to Richie. "It's cold. My nipples are getting soooo hard," she smiled lustily.

"Here they come." Cheater-Eater quickly espoused a perfunctory legal statement to Jenny that was necessary to cover him, and then finished with a warning. "You don't have to do this."

Fired-up, Jenny quipped, "And who's going to stop me?" Clearly on a rampage, she leapt out of the van and headed for the twosome.

Cheater-Eater was right behind her. "Remember, we're with you all the way."

Holding her ground like a Terminator Mama, Jenny stepped in front of Richie and Bambe. At the sight of her, Richie froze. It didn't occur to him to run like hell.

Jenny ranted, "The pumping raspberry. How could you? You piece of livered-belly slime."

Cheater-Eater played the DVD footage for Richie. "Take a gander at this, bud."

Richie balked. "That could be anyone's butt." Glaring at Cheater-Eater, he snarled, "Look, you extortionist leper, I am a lawyer. How dare you present this pornographic drivel to my wife?"

Bambe gawked at the butt." eah, zhat ees Richie's strawberry."

Jenny scorned her. "Raspberry! Bimbo."

"My name ees Bambe!" Fuming at Richie, she shouted, "Are you going to let troll-mama call me a bimbo?"

"So, I'm the troll?" Jenny's eyes shot daggers at Bambe's flashy lace dress. "Get her out of here!" Jenny growled as she started to attack Bambe. Cheater-Eater held her back and confronted Richie.

"You were caught with your red cherry down, Richie boy. Haven't you caused enough pain with your cheating and lies? It's time to be a man and choose. Your troll! Sorry! I mean, your wife...or the bimbo?"

Caught between Bambe's buxom bosom and Jenny, who at the moment resembled a disheveled rag doll, he wallowed in a quandary. How could he tell Jenny she was too high maintenance, too demanding, not fun, supportive, or easy to talk to. This wasn't all about sex – the little they had anymore. It was about survival of his manhood. In desperation, he revealed, "I need to rule the roost."

The Cheater-Eater DVD replayed Richie's bum pumping as it flashed before him. He ogled Bambe. She didn't judge, served without question, and believed he was brilliant, funny, and kind. This wasn't all about sex or the passion they shared. This was about his dominance, self-actualizing, and control.

Richie blurted with confidence. "I *do* rule the roost!"

Cheater-Eater relentlessly pursued an answer. "Which one will it be?"

Richie's eyes rolled between the two women. His heart quickened. A survival-based courage surged within. He shuffled his feet, cleared his throat, and stuttered, "I'm sorry Jenny. We just don't fit anymore."

Showing no compassion for Jenny, Cheater-Eater responded like a rabid rat chewing and grinding its prey. "He has made his choice."

Triumphant at winning her man, Bambe took Richie by the arm. Too ashamed to meet Jenny's teary eyes, Richie shielded his face like a cowardly wimp and vanished into the night with Bambe.

Cheater-Eater tag-lined into the camera. "Undeniably, another jilted babe joins the timeless plague of scorned winches." Jenny crumpled in his arms, murmuring under her breath, "He always said we were a perfect fit."

A brutally tough morning followed Jenny's solitary return to her suburban homestead. Within, a bleak reality-check for the Forrest family was on the horizon. In the wee hours, Richie had slipped into the house to gather a few clothes, hoping that he could avoid another unpleasant confrontation with Jenny, then tiptoe out the door before she heard him. However, Brian was up before dawn for a five-mile run with the football team. Richie gave him a heads-up. "Just think that I'm taking a break from husbandry, not fatherhood."

"Do what you have to do, Dad," Brian casually responded as he tied the laces on his running shoes.

"You're not upset?" Richie asked, trying to hide a mild sensation of disappointment.

"Me? Hey, I never counted on you for the little stuff! You weren't there. How many games did you show up for? Bet you don't even know my kick-ass grades."

"So you're still pissed-off and faking it."

"Dad, you're cool. Mom doesn't pay for cars, insurance, and vacations."

Flinching, Richie responded, "Okay, you just shot the elephant in the room and stuffed the carcass."

"Right. And you don't eat people alive? Sorry, that was jacked-up." Brian cracked his knuckles, controlling his frustration.

"I care, Brian. You're my only son. You can come to me for anything, anytime. Got it?"

"I know that, Dad."

"Come on, you're a 'chip off the old block'. You can read a book in two hours, fill a jock strap, and you're a lady-charmer." Smiling with pride, Richie winked. "I saw the condoms and Penthouse on the guest room dresser."

"I don't go in that baby room."

"Yah! Well, who the hell does?"

"Sam, that's always been her play room."

Richie freaked, "My baby daughter, reading girly magazines? What the hell does that mean?"

"It's a *happening*. Don't sweat it." Brian stood up. "Got to split." They gave each other a quick hug, and Brian dashed out the door.

Nevertheless, Richie did sweat it. He belabored Samantha's attention-getting maneuvers. Was it too late to throw a teen daughter over his knee? Why didn't he when she was a bratty three-year-old? Why was it "cool" for Brian to have a condom and a "sin" for Sam? "Whew, I'm in over my head." He elbowed himself, "I'm being narrow-minded, typically chauvinistically piggish, sexist predictable... everything I detest." Yet a paternal voice raked from inside, "I'll kill any sucker that lays hands, or even lustful-lurky eyes, on my daughter."

8.00 A.M.: Plopped on the floor in Richie's room-sized closet, Samantha rubbed teary eyes as she watched him pack. Overwhelmed by consuming warm-fuzzies, she trembled, "It's way sad...I'm going to miss you." In hopes of changing his mind, she clung to him like a pacifier, pouring her heart out. "Dad, you don't judge me. I need you for a buffer. Like when Mom gets too demanding or hyper. Who's going to stand up for me? Who's going to say, 'It's no biggie. It's only a phase. She'll grow out it'?"

"Honey, Dad's only going be five minutes away. I didn't die."

"The truth is...you're my safety valve. You don't know how isolated I am, spending time alone in my room berating, hating and putting myself down." She nervously bit her fingernail, chewing it to the quick.

Richie felt relieved that she brought up the bedroom bit. His personal pact was no peeping, snooping, or prying. That was Jenny's territory. Let her be the invasive baddie while he remained neutral, the open communication channel for teen trust. "Right," he declared. "We'll put an end to alone time in bedrooms," he bit his tongue as he said it, "with condoms and Penthouse."

"Come on, Dad. Look at my skinny-minny body. I'm checked-out on cheesecake." She pushed up size A+ breasts. "See, no meaningful boobs. I'm not physically, definitely not mentally, built for posing."

"Then who the hell goes in there?"

"In where?"

"Scratch that," Richie quickly retracted, not really wanting to know or pry. "We're going to have more quality father and daughter time to work this all out." His voice sounded amplified with lies, she grimaced, "Why don't I believe you? Like I never came first."

"Love is not about first, second, or third. Love just is...and I love you, Samantha."

Hearing she was loved assuaged the natty fear of losing him. "How sweet," she gurgled. "Like a tingling massage on my teensy-weensy quaking heart."

Rolling suitcases into the bedroom's sitting area, Richie and Samantha gawked with raised brows. Jenny was perched on the couch, watching TV with a vacant stare. "Mom's numbed-out again," Samantha droned.

Stupefied, avoiding confrontation, Jenny had retreated from the bedroom when she heard Richie's voice earlier in the morning. Glued to Martha's TV "Shake and Bake" routine, Jenny seemed to listen intently as Martha informed the audience in her patented classic attempt not to sound condescending, "Even a kindergartner knows flour and water make glue. But, what happens when we add the eggs and sugar?" Smiling insipidly, she proudly announced, "We make cake!"

Drowning-out Martha's rap Richie spoke loudly, "I'll be at the Four Season's...if you need me." Not responding, Jenny eyes were misty, slightly crossed.

Samantha pleaded, "Stop him, Mom!! Tell him you'll stop harping. You'll change that irritating perfect wifey-poo routine."

Attempting to reason, to set things straight, Richie explained, "She's a 'Super-Mom', sweetie. We just don't fit the way we used to."

Without warning Jenny bolted from her perch. "How dare you talk crude vulgarities in front of our daughter! Why don't you be truthful for once? We just don't smell the same roses or see eye-to-eye."

Placating her, Richie stammered, "That's all true. Sorry."

Shooting him a menacing glance that spelled a witch's curse, Jenny spat, "Or do we share the same check book."

The sadistic overtone sent shivers down his spine, landing in his groin. Bracing for the worst, Richie retorted, "Those are ball-buster threatening words."

"Not a hollow threat, Richie Forrest. You are in for one big headache. A back-breaker, and most likely a bleeding terminal ulcer." Seething with the wrath of a dragon, she raised the TV's volume and turned her back on him.

After Richie left the house and Samantha fled to hide in her room, Jenny blatantly flaunted her misery in an all-day bed-fest. She was bogged-down in self-torture by skimming a book titled, "The ABC's of Eliminating Infidelity". Reading through bloodshot eyes, she recited out loud, "A is for ABSTINENCE. B is for BE FAITHFUL. C is for CONDOMS (if necessary). D is for DON'T BRING HOME AN INFECTIOUS DISEASE. "She threw the book down." Damn, I never thought about gonorrhea, itchy creepers, terminal diseases that the louse might have given me."

In less than ten minutes she was dressed and on her way. As though she were competing in a trial run for Le Mans, she zipped 85 miles-an-hour down the highway, rushing to an emergency visit to the GYN.

After blazing into the office and demanding immediate attention, Jenny experienced the same demeaning routine: Pee in a jar, dry it off, present it with a pasted helpless grin to Lainie, Dr. Harris' nurse. Then, the humiliating worst part, legs spread-eagle in stirrups with only a tiny sheet between her sanity and Dr. Harris' assault. Jenny fidgeted. "Use the virgin thing, no plastic," she ordered. "The old metal type slides in easier."

Patiently, Dr. Harris replied, "Relax Jennifer, you aren't exactly a virgin. Although on rare occasion the hymen has been known to grow back. We have a new procedure you can try. It's only five-thousand-dollars and you can elect to redo the damage. You'll get the cherry back. It's a great birthday or anniversary gift for the hubby – to rekindle the old flame."

With the sales pitch finished, Dr. Harris, a veteran doctor of thirty years, dipped his glove into more jelly. She let out an "Ouch! That hurts!" before he even touched her. A minor prodding followed and Jenny squealed like a pig in a slaughterhouse.

"Jennifer, we can quell your anxiety."

She clenched her teeth waiting for the next assault, "I'm not anxious. I'm being tortured."

Launching into his customary drug promo, Dr. Harris encouraged "At least try Xanax, or a low dose of Prozac. You'll be stabilized instead of banging your head against walls, being flattened by impossible situations, or stomped-on by difficult people. Trauma will just fade into a circle of breath gently, going in and out. No more blind fury or hair-splitting when you don't get your way. You'll just dance, boogie right through it all."

Using all her mind power to prove the jerk wrong, Jenny imagined swinging on top a Ferris wheel. Visualizing the car moving downward, she sensed a rocking sensation. It jolted her tummy into her throat, releasing a repressed wail, which was perfectly timed as Dr. Harris scraped cells from her vaginal wall. "Scrape! Got it. All done." Watching him take the specimen to a countertop, she relaxed.

Striving to keep a steady tone, hoping to elicit a conscionable awareness in Dr. Harris' stone heart, Jenny said sarcastically, "Your Mother must be proud she spawned a pill-pushing drug dealer. What dose are you on, Doc?" Ignoring the insult, he marked the specimen and jotted notes.

Peering over his shoulder, she defended proof of well-being. "As far back as my great-great-great-grandmother we've been self-medicated mainliners, inveterate chocoholics. Filling up on mass doses of serotonin and endorphins, running '10 K's', screwing our hearts out, and blasting super-duper fun into our brains. So shove those meds down your throat, Doc. Enjoy the greed-mongering pharmaceutical's pathetic synthetic solution to life's sweet sorrow." After blowing her wad of frustration, she reached into her bag and pulled out Listerine mouth spray, taking a couple sprits.

Calmly, without engaging in her fury, Dr. Harris observed with detached arrogance, "I can see you're irritated and experiencing a hollow verbal victory."

"At least I can feel. Even if I am wallowing in the shittery of life." Without missing a beat she changed her tone, "Enough medical chitchat. So, will you have the test results in a couple of days?"

"Yes, Jennifer. Take care of yourself. You're capable of giving me high blood pressure. I can't imagine what you're doing to yourself and the unfortunate souls around you."

"Thanks for the usual upbeat pep talk, Doc. I feel so much better." She left her sarcasm and wit in the office, taking only doubts and lingering pangs of hurt with her.

Dr. Harris locked his office door, fetched a bottle of Schnapps, and downed a shot, questioning how long he could continue his unforgiving work. Hadn't he delivered the Forrest twins, helped Jenny through post partum, and circumcised Brian, put Sam on birth control?

It's true. He struggled morally with what damage the psychotropic drugs he pandered might cause. Downing another shot, he swore that his profession defeated him. All he had to offer was a guess-job, a dart-shoot that meds weren't destroying brain cells and creating neurological defects. True, they could alter mental symptoms, elevate or debilitate moods, alleviate erratic behavior, emotional suffering. Or they could exacerbate the very symptoms that were being treated. There were miserable side effects such as dullness, groggy-brain, weight-gain escalating to liver disease, diabetes, or even death. Always weighing side effects against the plus side. Looking for the right dose, the perfect cocktail.

Nodding at his family's photo next to a slew of hard-earned medical certificates mounted on the wall, he recommitted, "Just do my best and wait for cures." Until then he was forced to mask the underlying causes by writing prescriptions for psych drugs, or was he?

Debating in his mind he pondered, "Why not nutritional supplements, holistic alternatives? Were they too risky to entertain when someone was on the brink of suicide or homicide? Hadn't a dose of Geodon whacked-out a patient into a psych ward, ending-up in worse shape than before his drug-taking months were weaned away? What about a combo natural remedy with a low-med dosage? How to get insurance companies onboard?

The intercom buzzed, shaking him back to his schedule. "Janet Murphy's here with the newborn," his receptionist announced. Dr. Harris smiled at the thought of the pink chubby baby. In spite of his inadequacies, babies were still being born, and the human race was not extinct. He put the Schnapps bottle away, revived –ready to go. "I'll be right in," he replied.

By nighttime Jenny was overly restless. Her period had started, most likely induced by the metal invasion. The curse of cramps sent her reeling to the medicine cabinet, downing a couple of Midol's. After an hour they weren't working. Checking the bottle's label. "Oh God, they expired last year."

Wracked by a 'charley-horse' in her left foot, her big toe folded upward, causing it to arch and tighten like a vice. She rubbed the cramp, trying to pry her toe back in place. Standing up, she lobbed her foot on the carpet in an attempt to ease the pain.

It finally made sense to Jenny why women during menses, often crazed, listless, and temperamental, were barred from the sweat lodge, or in other traditions banished from temples, or even sent away from their homes. The saving grace was being spared a few slaving workdays from hog-tying, scalping traitors, or being a nurturer to a tribe or harem.

After what seemed like hours of torture, Jenny fell asleep. Catapulted into a nightmarish-surreal dream, hazy images flashed of Bambe fondling Richie, fixing his tie, nuzzling on his ear. They sat on a dais, on stage with other honorees. An MC rattled off kudos. "The energy behind the man of the hour, our sensational Richie Forrest, is his most current, his most beautiful wife of them all. Mrs. Forrest, will you please stand up?"

Decked-out in a shimmering Stella McCartney gown, Bambe exuded prize-winning "Hot" and "Luscious." Facing the star-studded crowd, including Dr. Phil who was gaping at her striking movie star charisma, applauding, Bambe glowed in the spotlight. Suddenly, a flash of Richard Gere on a speeding motorcycle with a come-on smile entered the room, blowing a kiss to Bambe who waved back, exposing an intimate view of her body.

Jenny appeared in the room, overhearing the MC's rave, salivating at Richard Gere. Swaggering, Gere nudged her, flinging the 'bird'. Having jogged from Brian's football practice, she was wearing sweats and was sweating. Humiliation engulfed her.

In bed, wriggling like a drowning worm, Jenny moaned, "Faker! I am the real Mrs. Forrest."

Still in the nightmare Jenny raced on stage to claim her rightful place. Two security guards, Brian and Samantha, apprehended her just as her hand grabbed Richie's shoulder. Ripping, holding on for dear life, tearing the sleeve off his tuxedo, she was kicking and screaming as the twins carried her away.

The sweating was real. She awoke drenched with her pillowcase ripped to shreds. "You're destroying me!" she cried from a mangy, confused, hyperbolic state. The blaring TV caught her attention, bringing her back to present time. A cleaning product, "WipeyWipes", was featured in an infomercial. The product demonstrator cheerfully polished a metal cabinet, declaring, "WipeyWipes" is the cleaner's-cleaner, cleaning clean. Don't miss out on this one. You can be the cleanest cleaner. Only eight-dozen left. Seven. Six. Five..."

Needing consolation and nurturing that only power-shopping could fix, Jenny emotionally plugged into the hype. She dialed the number on the screen.

An operator answered, "WipeyWipes, your name please."

"This is the real Mrs. Forrest. Please send me a dozen, make that two-dozen, WipeyWipes."

"Your address please?"

Jenny went blank for a moment. "Yes, this is my still my home. Even though he's not technically here. I am. I'm alive here."

The operator interrupted in mid-sentence. "Bling. Sorry, you're a second too late. We're sold out. How about next month's delivery?"

"Next month? That's not fair," Jenny huffed. "You don't understand! I need to be the cleanest cleaner. Right now!"

A dial tone rang in Jenny's ear. "How dare you hang up on me," she yelled into the phone. The receiver slipped from her hand, dangling off the bed's edge. The grating dial tone signaled an ominous warning. "My life is suspended in chaos. On hold." Unable to bare it, she ripped the phone cord out of the socket, and then covered her head with a pillow. Childlike whimpers turned into a hum, repeating a familiar Elton John song lyric, "...never knowing who to turn to when the rain comes in."

The Forrest laundry room resembled a QVC warehouse. House products were piled from floor-to-ceiling. Jenny hunched over the sink like a washerwoman, vigorously scrubbing at her vibrant sign of fertility. A crimson red menstrual stain had ruined a 650 thread-count, pure Pratesi cotton sheet.

Lifting the sheet from the double dryer, Jenny examined its pristine whiteness with pride. She positioned her portable TV/VCR combo close to the ironing board. In great anticipation she removed the shrink-wrap from a Martha video titled, "How to Train a Fledgling Housekeeper." She would finally learn to iron sheets! Jenny copied Martha's gentle ironing strokes. Martha elaborated, "The secret to the perfect roll is not only distilled water, but mainly temperature, temperature, temperature!"

Jenny became so enamored with the host's delivery that she stopped the rolling motion and just watched. The iron sat still for a few seconds. A scorching smell brought her back to the sheet. Quickly prying the stuck-to-the-sheet iron it was too late! A big brownish iron imprint had seared through the material, branding her fertility-cleanse, which was now completely defunct.

Still captivated by the instructions on the video, Jenny had no time to fret. It was folding time. She watched with full concentration, following Martha's lead. "Take the bottom edge - bring it up even with the right corner. This is where it gets tricky. You slip your thumb into the left side and fold it under."

"Thumb is the word," Jenny said to herself, amused at her own wit. "I am all thumbs!" Wrapping the bottom edge over the top, she leaned down and slipped into the center of the sheet. Moving to the left, then to the right, becoming more entangled in yards of white fabric, she crashed on the floor. Thump! Arms and feet bound tight.

Trapped like a mummy she rolled, wriggled, and squiggled. There was no way to freedom without help. She knew what she had to do. Letting out a blood-curdling scream at the top of her lungs, Jenny begged, "Samantha! HELP!!" Right behind the screech came the thought, "What will the neighbors think?" Her next thought was, "Who the hell cares?" So she let out another big one. "HELLPP!"

Samantha didn't intentionally ignore the pitiful outburst. Her earphones and the reverberation of the hip-hop blare were the culprits that shut Jenny out.

Thanks to a new hearing aid, her next-door neighbor, Mr. Grosse, a retired bandleader, did respond. He put on a pair of slippers, scuffling out on a rescue mission. He rang the Forrest buzzer, pounded on the front door. "Open up." No one answered. Huffing and puffing, jogging to the rear entrance, he kicked the door open. Heading in the direction of the cries, he called-out, "I'm coming." Finally standing over Jenny, he gazed down at her mummified body. "What in the world...? Aren't you a sight, Jenny Forrest"? He rolled, twisted, and jostled her out of yards of cotton, releasing her from bondage.

She squirmed, totally embarrassed. "Geez, Mr. Grosse, how awful for anyone to see me in such a ridiculous predicament."

Pleased to be of service to someone, he smiled. "I promise you, that's what neighbors are for."

At the kitchen table they chatted over cups of Chai tea and munched on toasted bagels. "Neighbors aren't supposed to be strangers," Mr. Grosse remarked. "Where I grew up we bartered – we traded. You have the potatoes. I have the bacon. We shared everything. It was a loving little community that lived and basically died together."

Jenny giggled, assuring him, " Well, we're not dead yet."

"Not until you stop laughing," he said.

A warm smile exuded from her as she replied, "Sounds good to me."

On the way out, Mr. Grosse spotted the Grinnell ebony baby grand taking full stage in the living room. He motioned, "Mind if I pound out a tune?"

"Please, you're just full of surprises." She smiled motioning him to the piano.

At the keyboard he crooned a medley from honky-tonk to New Orleans-inspired jazz. "When you're smiling, life smiles back at you. When you're laughing, your heart's happy, not blue."

She joined him, swaying, "When you're crying, you dump all the pain. Keep that smile on, you'll be happy and sane." They giggled. They sang. It had turned out to be a perfectly wonderful neighborly rescue not only of the body, but also of the spirit, the mind, and heart. When Mr. Grosse went home she almost felt sad.

Dashing to the computer Jenny could hardly wait to share the experience with her loyal BLOG readers. She wrote with fervor and enthusiasm, yet something profoundly foreboding and mysteriously dark clicked into her keystroke:

I felt so comforted by Mr. Grosse's reminiscing about simpler times. But the light switch went off, amplifying the darkening madness of these unpredictable times. Isn't life spiraling out-of-control, quaking and shaking? Not just for you or me personally, but for the whole world? Calamities bombard like a swarm of bees, stinging our sensibilities. From bad air quality to endangered species, wars, terrorism, famine! You guys can continue the Armageddon list. I'm exhausted. I'm taking a bathroom break. Please go to the message board and share your doomsday or happy thoughts. Maybe some visionary out there has a solution?

Jenny took a cold shower to ease the hot flashes and her hot temper that seemed to flare up over anything, at anyone, at any capricious time. She returned to the BLOG and read the one lone entry from screen name "DeathSport" on the message board:

Hey, DeathSport here. Anyone else notice the visual terrors whizzing all around us? The horror show culminates with the greedy obliterating the needy. I see hundreds maybe millions of hands with bony fingers all grappling for the same big slice of pizza. Smithereens of stringy cheese drips away, even a tidbit of pepperoni is out of reach. A 'no win' for the little guy. Too much competition! Too many bodies traipsing across the earth. Pounding its surface, consuming and exhuming.

Jenny gasped at such depth of truth. Wallowing in dread of the unfathomable possibility, she began to write. Automatically and with compulsion, she dumped her guts on the lone writer:

I know I'm not a deep thinker. Thinking scares me. If I started dwelling full time on the suffering, I might have to do something about it. And what would that be? To blow myself up in front of a TV camera screaming, STOP THE INSANITY! Right now I can't deal with it or come up with solutions or options. How about you, DeathSport? You see it all. What to do? Being obsessive, I must remain apathetic and take my place as an ordinary stay-at-home mom, but I can't do even do that. My reliable rank is about to change.

So, why rush the kids off to college because I'm supposed to, or because Dr. Spock says so? What if he's right? They stay here and I control their every move. They end up dependent on me for life. That's a death wish, right, DeathSport? That terrifies me. What if they don't find their true calling and end up on the street begging for that slice of pizza? And when I die (hopefully I'll be laughing), and hopefully they will have graduated from college, living a full and productive life on their own terms (laughing).

Jenny stopped writing. "Ah Hah! I see 'DeathSport' has checked back in on the message board."

What's up, everyone? It's DeathSport here with a one-line Armageddon blaster. Forget Spock. It's Anarchy-Time, people. Use your VOTE POWER and get the greedy evil-doing bastards out of town!

Jenny responded. ***Thank you, DeathSport, for that food-for-thought.*** She glanced at her diamond-studded Rolex. "Oh my God, it's 3:00. I'm late for Brian's practice". Winding-up her online time, she wrote: ***Until next time...keep smiling, my dear readers.*** Jenny didn't continue the thoughts when she logged-off the Internet, but that didn't mean they weren't inside her mind, lurking and waiting to overtake her – someday.

The week had been hell-bent for Samantha, especially when Jenny basically had to kidnap her on SAT test day. Samantha's fragile self-esteem had been doubly blistered when Jenny was forced to reveal that a Mensa look-a-like was taking the test for her.

Samantha's teeny voice faltered, "A cretin is pretending to be me? Everyone will know."

In fact, as it turned out, the students were so nervous no one even noticed if Samantha was there or not. Days later, even her so-called best friend Lisa asked, "How'd you do? Could you believe the math?"

Samantha felt crushed like a lowly worm. How more invisible could she be if her best friend assumed she was there? Gathering a full-blown windstorm inside, she mustered a slingshot retort aimed at her fair-weather friend, "So, how did you do? Wasn't it all a breeze?" In Samantha's shy and passive world she had delivered a major comeback to a perceived major put-down.

Over the following weeks Jenny kept her daughter in the dark. The reality of the test results weren't in and Jenny needed to find a backup plan to secure Samantha's place at Stanford.

"I still can't believe it," Samantha admitted to Jenny. "Being invisible, like some freaky ghost, was a major reject, a double major diss."

"You didn't take the diss lying down, honey. You stood up for yourself. The mark of a true winner! Who better for you, than <u>you</u>?"

"<u>You!</u>"

"Think again." She tickled Samantha's tummy like she did when she was a baby. "You deserve a treat. How about a triple-fudge sundae?"

Through ticklish giggles Samantha croaked, "How about a trip to Paris?" Laughing, they sauntered off arm-in-arm to Bloomies Ice Cream Parlor. Sharing the biggest dessert on the planet, they ate pounds of fudge, caramel, strawberries, bananas, cashews, and whipped cream. Two spoons battled, clanked and dipped as they melted in the decadence. Such a posh regal excuse for real mom-daughter bonding.

"Ahhh. Oooh. Such comfort food," Jenny slurped as she savored every morsel like it was the last drop of nourishment on earth. Her cell phone rang. Jenny picked-up. Lainie from Dr. Harris' office rattled off the SDS results. Jenny repeated, "Just a little yeast infection. That's really nothing, right? Okay, the 'one night' blue box at any drug store. Fine! Thanks, Lainie." She clicked off.

Samantha stared at her, hot fudge dripping from her virgin lips. "Are you fooling around, Mom? Did I really have to hear about your disease-catching indiscretions?"

In an authoritative tone Jenny clarified, "Samantha, let's get this straight. Neither one of us is fast and loose. Sharing a bathroom is enough to spread germs and all kinds of creepy-crawlies."

Samantha crinkled her nose. "Gross! Brian's been in my bathroom, too. Hurry, let's go to the drugstore and get that blue fajingy-box."

"Good idea," Jenny agreed. And off they went, sharing another intimate mother and daughter unforgettable moment.

Jenny dropped Samantha off at home and then headed to Brian's football practice. Today's visit held special relevance in support of Jenny's master plan to get the kids off to college. Coach Watkins had grown too pork-paunchy for a jock. Over the last couple of years he rapidly declined from a dominant personality to a kiss-ass. It was public knowledge that he was floundering, needing an immediate boost of recognition to enhance his upcoming retirement package. Jenny's trump card was that he relied on his champions, young talent like Brian, to promote himself.

From the sidelines Jenny and Coach Watkins watched Brian toss an impressive long pass to a teammate. "Bravo!" she cheered. "He's got the arm, doesn't he?"

With candor Watkins replied, "He's my star player."

Satisfied with his response, Jenny seized the opportune opening for driving home her agenda. "By the way," she said delicately, "if Stanford wants Brian, they'll have to take Samantha."

Scuffling dirt under his foot he replied emphatically," That's way out of my hands."

"Fine. Then Brian won't be your kudos-kid salary booster."

He shrugged off the insult. "We're talking Stanford."

"He doesn't need Stanford." Lying through her teeth, Jenny proclaimed, "He's been contacted by USC scouts, to name one...of many interested parties."

"Oh, really." His tone had a challenging edge, so he smiled in an attempt to cover it.

She quirked one eyebrow, "Samantha did quite well on her SAT's."

"Is she out of Special-Ed?"

She gave him an audacious grin and declared, "What moron told you that?"

"Brian."

Gingerly smoothing over the moment Jenny prodded, "It wouldn't take much for you to step up. Put in a good word to one of the good old boys."

He shuffled his feet, uncomfortable with idea. "Well...I don't know."

He shuffled his feet, uncomfortable with the idea. "Well...I don't know."

Taking a more personal ploy, she softened her tone. "They've never been separated. Nor will they ever be. Please let them know that." Her passion, short of begging, struck a chord of human kindness.

His eyes softened, "Well, when you put it that way. Maybe I could put in a word."

Nodding with appreciation, Jenny's eyes sparkled. "You won't regret it." She offered him an envelope. "Two tickets to the Super Bowl, hotel and airfare. VIP all the way!"

"Did I hear Super Bowl?" Ecstatic, his athletically trained reflexes were on overdrive. Coach Watkins knelt down. Stood up. Knelt down again. In perfect form bracing his body in a runner's start position. Focusing, breathing, anticipating like a wiry greyhound at the start of a race, his eyes twinkled. "I've been waiting for that starter-gun to sizzle in me again. And it just loaded big time. I haven't looked forward to something in so long. Are we talking *Super Bowl*? Hot damn!"

"Not talk. You're going."

He whipped an about-face. His body became rigid, stiffening harder than a cardboard box. His brow furrowed, "No. No. No."

Jenny grinned ruefully, reassuring him, "I hope you don't consider this offer to be a bribe. It's gratitude. Your well-earned ticket to fame."

Reluctantly reaching for the treasured envelope, Watkins muttered, "I couldn't. I shouldn't!"

"Who are you kidding?" Jenny pulled it away from him. He pulled it back. She pulled. Both were tugging, creating a mini tug of war. "You shouldn't, but you will." She let go. He had the prize. They burst into laughter.

Coach Watkins peeked inside. Elated by the sight of the tickets he squealed like a young kid, "A dream trip comes true!"

"That seals the deal," Jenny smiled in satisfaction. "Stanford will love them." Her attention shifted to Brian running with the ball. Motioning to a lunch pail, she called out, "Brian! Lunch!"

Caught off guard, he glanced at Jenny for a nanosecond. Two players ferociously tackled him from behind. Brian scrambled to his feet limping off the field. "Oh shit!"

She shouted, "Brian, Brian, are you all right?"

Calibrating high up on the pissed-off scale, he scowled, "How could you mess up my concentration?"

Teammates bullied, "Is 'Mama' messing with your concentration?" "Assuming you can concentrate."

Brian usually held his cool. He had been seasoned since first grade to take the heat and jive from guys who were ribbing him. His stomach didn't churn into unstoppable hiccups anymore. Over the years, his skin thickened like a blubbery whale. Insults and putdowns ricocheted off him like shallow darts. But today his composure began to crumble as another teammate taunted, "Brian, there's your mommy again."

His patience had dwarfed to zero. Didn't she know the pressure he was under? Winning was mostly on his back. Quarterback's can't make excuses. Quarterbacks can't have their mom lurking around, especially at the last practice before a play-off game. Holding the lunch pail high over his head, he yelled at Jenny, "Dunk it!" Taking aim he lobbed it into the intended trashcan over fifteen feet away. BANG! Bulls-eye.

"The audacity of the punk, "Jenny steamed. She'd like to shoot him with a peashooter. All morning she had been sweating over a hot oven to prepare the lasagna fricassee, her special Italian-French combo. What did she get for it? No thanks! No respect! Didn't he realize he might have just tossed out the fifty-thousandth meal she had prepared for him? Add it up: Three-to-five meals a day, counting snacks, protein drinks and fudgie treats for eighteen long, monotonous years (including holidays, Christmas and Thanksgiving), had to count for at least ten meals each.

Every last detail counted. Shopping, preparing, serving, cleaning up...all took planning. Minutes, days, years of her life had passed; gone, never to return. Sadly, much of it had been wasted on the often-burnt charcoal-like uneatable meals. Even take-out, home delivery or going out to eat counted equally in her book. Hadn't *she* orchestrated and handled it? All done in vain for what? Her ungrateful poop of an offspring!

Bursting to chastise his cocky ungrateful attitude, raw instinct took over. Jenny talked herself down. "No power plays. No ego busting! Not the time to draw the battle line."

Tipping his helmet at her, Brian cantered like a stallion down the field. She muttered to herself, "Don't take it personally. It's his impending manhood reacting."

The football field was his turf, not hers. That truth stung. What part of his life was hers? Quickly losing her place and influence, she had to measure how far to push her will, to carefully choose her battles. Power struggles had taken their toll, creating lack of trust, emotional freeze-outs, and high anxiety. Talking to Brian had become worse than walking on a tightrope. More like a blind person trying not to stomp on Big Bird's eggshells.

Practice was over. Brian walked fast, distancing himself from her. She always felt bad when he ice-cubed her with silence. Jenny's guilt meter was flying kite high. This incident was her fault: a result of poor judgment, bad timing. Longing for a bear hug squeeze and his Tom Cruise sheepish grin, on impulse she chased after him. "Brian, wait up!" She jogged with all her might, huffing and puffing.

Fearing she might collapse, he slowed down, letting her catch him. "Take it easy, Mom."

Breathless, she waved concert tickets at him. "Limp Biscuit live. It'll be a family outing."

His eyes flicked up defiantly, "No more outings! It's <u>my</u> life remember! I need my space."

"Third row seats, Brian. These cost a bloody fortune." Jenny wheezed.

He cocked his head with determination. "Not my problemo, mama-sita. Try Samantha." Returning a devilish grin he raced off like the Road Runner, leaving her to sulk in a dustbowl of disappointment. Jenny couldn't stand being shut out or left alone. Her obsession with the kids deflected her tendency to dwell on her own personal dilemmas. Keeping busy with endless "To Do" lists staved off the inevitable self-reflection and questioning what to do with her self-inflicted miserable life.

As Brian disappeared from view, Jenny's forlorn look quickly vanished. As if he could hear her, she shouted, "No little wimp's wrecking my day!" Without hesitation, she pushed a speed-button on her cell phone. Samantha's voicemail announcement shrieked over a mind-twisting metal guitar. "You got me."

Impatiently, Jenny responded, "Samantha, we pay sixty dollars a month to keep tabs on you. And, you deliberately turn off your cell. Please! Turn the thing on." She ended the call, and then text-messaged an SOS – three Sad-Happy Smiley's.

Samantha was in rare form. Feeling popular for a change, she was hanging out with a group of friends watching a raunchy episode of "South Park." Her cell phone vibrated in her lap. Glancing at the Caller ID she saw that it was Jenny. No way would she embarrass herself and speak to her mother in front of Jack, the "rad" guy that she was leaning on.

Still needy and ruffled, Jenny pressed redial. "Samantha Forrest, this is important," she insisted. "You need to answer me <u>right now!</u>" She continued pressing buttons, text-messaging. The second text message caught Samantha's attention. "Oops, three sad faces." Mom meant it. Samantha's thoughts overpowered her. Maybe something tragic had happened. Mom was so jumpy and uptight since Dad left. Maybe she killed him or he committed suicide. Anything was possible. Samantha's breathe quickened.

She recalled the late night news. An upscale wife went bonkers and ran over her husband with a car. Another woman stabbed her husband with a kitchen knife and claimed she was hugging him. Samantha hoped Jenny hadn't gone completely wacko and had done the unspeakable. Maybe she did. Wound up like a spin-toy in a frenzy of doubt, she sneaked into the privacy of the bathroom, locked the door, and returned the call.

Jenny answered with great surprise. "Forget the first and the second message."

Relieved her mother wasn't a murderer, Samantha still felt invaded. "Give me my space, Mom."

"But, honey I have tickets for Limp Biscuit."

"Limp who?"

"Don't play games, Sam. Third row seats. You must want to go?"

Samantha ignored the question and hurried back into the room with her friends. She casually set the cell on her lap. Grating "South Park" character's voices blasted in Jenny's ear. She yelled back, "Bad connection...can't hear you."

Gloating with satisfaction Samantha turned off the cell. She viewed the victory on a par with blowing in a pup's face and riling it to chase its tale.

Oddly, Samantha's impression that her mother was "losing it" proved fairly accurate, albeit without the 'Murder-Queen' take. Even the neat stack of envelopes filled with extraordinary tickets, excursions all strategically organized, indicated a desperate need for Jenny to belong and to buy the love of her children.

Alone in what was once her seemingly safe bedroom sanctuary, Jenny lost sleep. Insomnia prevailed as her new worst enemy. Like a sneaky little rat taking refuge in the house, it crept into her mind, dwelling in dark spaces, surfacing unexpectedly, munching and crunching her perceptions. No sense whacking at it with a broom, trying to sweep out racing thoughts. It would cleverly outsmart her and scurry into tiny crevices, staring her down with beady eyes.

As the days flew by and sleeplessness grew, she felt hypo-maniacally wired with mounds of energy 24/7. "This is what it must feel like to be on Meth," she thought with a sense of irony because she had never taken drugs of any kind. The kitchen's clock with its bold black letters and seemingly fast-spinning hands served as a wakeful barometer.

It was 7:00 P M: Jenny was in the kitchen enjoying her favorite "Chef Harry" DVD - renowned for his down-home healthy cooking, he rolled dough on a large wooden table. Jenny mimicked the procedure as Chef Harry shared a piece of history.

"Apple Betty pie is a true slice of Americana. Even today it ranks as a favorite in the Deep South. In fact, Apple Betty is said to have healing powers. When feuding families got together over piping hot Apple Betty they usually forgot what they were mad about."

Chef Harry broke out in a song:

"Folks say Apple Betty is why people learn to love. And her spicy flavor causes babies to be born. When our countrymen were battling the North against the South. No doubt the bloody war ended when Apple Betty helped them out."

Jenny wanted an Apple Betty miracle in her life: it had been a family tradition since she discovered Chef Harry. With great expectations she put the mixture in the oven and waited for it to bake. Suddenly she grew very sleepy and curled up on the couch.

Life's not fair when insomnia takes a hike and goes into hiding. Somewhere between an all-done Apple Betty and a hardened charcoal burned version, the oven alarm buzzed, waking her from a pleasant sleep.

Jenny stirred, smelling the familiar burning stench. Quickly rising off the couch, she scrambled into the smoky kitchen. Scraping the black gunk into the trash she made a decision. "Why let a little inopportune nap disturb my miracle?"

Rewinding the Chef Harry tape, she started a new pie. By midnight the Apple Betty was perfectly done. She sat alone with only her mind demons to squabble with. Was this an opportunity to make amends and friends with the nagging culprits? Even adopt a new positive point of view? The thought of emotional change produced hunger pangs.

With an insatiable appetite she nibbled at tidbits, then cut a larger piece, then another. She binged, devoured, gobbled up the entire pie. Overtaken by nausea and heartburn, she stumbled to the toilet and threw up. With her head hanging over the commode, bulimic and worn she gagged, coughing up the last of the Apple Betty. With remorse she whimpered, "My Apple Betty miracle just slipped away." Bulimia wasn't new to her. Since a teen she found comfort in emotionally-charged bingeing.

Hearing the gagging, her mother would pound the bathroom door, "What are you doing in there, throwing-up your guts?"

"Cleaning the toilet bowl," was the usual answer. She became a bowl-cleaning expert, leaving no visible trace of her mess. Not admitting or realizing she had a problem, Jenny didn't know that Bulimia existed until she heard a woman on TV revealing her secret malady. "I'm trying to beat Bulimia, which is a life-threatening disease."

Swirling in apprehension Jenny couldn't believe it. "How could eating too much, occasionally throwing up, be fatal?"

The show had been on for only ten minutes. Jenny had wolfed down a bag of baked chips, two packages of M&M's, and gulped a frothing hot chocolate. She squirmed uncomfortably as a doctor described the side effects. "Bulimia, binge-eating, is a disease that can cause a stroke, heart attack or rotting teeth."

Pulsing in her skin, Jenny lowered the sound. Staring at the woman's mouth opening and closing, Jenny's jaw dropped, her lip quivered. Tears flowed from the woman on TV as well as from Jenny. Unable to watch one more unbearable second, all she remembered before shutting off the TV was irrationality shouting, "Eat and enjoy, dummy. What's your problem?"

After her Apple Betty purge, getting through the night was a challenge. The big black spindles of the Forrest clock stopped on 1:00 A.M.

Jenny wasn't a typical coach potato. Her viewing habits included interactive activities such as exercising to Suzan's ten-minute workout tape that guaranteed moving a sloth-coucher off their duff. With Suzan, dynamo personal trainer accessible 24/7, pounding and stretching sagging bellies, cellulite thighs, limp muscle tone into shape, Jenny wasn't more than ten pounds overweight. The bouncing dimples on her backside and thighs had to go, along with the signs of cheesecloth fat hanging and swaying under her arm.

Suzan, the famed workout maven, boasted a beautiful pint-sized hard body, fully endowed with silky blonde hair tipping the top of her rounded derrière. With a charismatic cheerleader delivery she whipped the struggling Jenny into line. "Be a 'ten' to a better you. Let's firm up that tummy. Crunch. One. Two. Up. Hold. Hold. Breathe."

Stretching full out on the mat, hands behind her neck, Jenny lifted her back a couple of inches above the floor. A little crack popped in her mid-spine. Suspended off the floor, a vice-like cramped muscle held her in position, "Geez, I'll split in two," she groaned, not daring to budge a fraction of an inch. Her purview was the freshly painted greige-colored ceiling. Agonizing over her predicament she mumbled, "I'll be stuck here forever."

Unable to see the TV screen she listened intently as Suzan commanded with gentle authority, "Just a teeny higher. You can do it."

Jenny strained. Every muscle in her body clenched rigid, stiff and fixed. She tried hard to move, release her position, or just lift a tad higher, lower. "Anything but this agony."

"Don't hurt yourself." Suzan warned.

Jenny grunted, "What happened to the 'No pain, no gain' bit?"

It was as if Suzan's hand tenderly reached out from the TV, massaging her aching back. POP. The tension released, Jenny let go, banging her head on the workout mat. She lay there in awe, envying lithe Suzan, body-sculpting her tight little body tighter, dancing, smiling, enjoying every aerobic second. Jenny rubbed the crook of her back. Crackling noises made her leery of looming osteoporosis. "Isn't working out supposed to stop the old-lady hunchback? Too bad," she thought. "Better give up midnight workouts. They're too taxing and energizing, especially for an insomniac."

By 2:00 A.M. Jenny performed like a raving kamikaze madwoman. Japanese style, with a giant cleaver in hand, she hacked, whacked, sliced and diced an array of veggies from carrots to cucumbers. She reached for more veggies. The bin was empty.

Wearily gazing at the clock, the dials spun to 3:00 A.M. Jenny sat cross-legged on the kitchen floor staring straight ahead. In a semi-stupor she fixated on a mutant spider crawling up the wall. After a few seconds she gyrated with leg-spasms. Then she clunked-out cold on the kitchen floor.

It was 8:00 A.M. on a Thursday: Jenny had been up since the crack of dawn, another night barely snoozing three hours. Coming into the kitchen, still panting from a jog, she opened the fridge. "No OJ? How could they drink two gallons?" Settling for prune juice, she recoiled at her only option. "Yuck, prune's like castor oil." She poured a glass, downing it like medicine. The jog had failed her. It hadn't quieted the rising hypo-state: another result of fatigue.

Milling in the food panty, Jenny was further nonplussed. "Where's the rice cakes? Rats are probably nibbling crumbs on Brian's floor." The weekend food stash seemed low, erroneously signaling an impending crisis. "What if there's no bread and they want a sandwich, or butter? We're almost out." An impulsive need overwhelmed her to immediately replenish the food supply. With time fleeting there was no chance to shower, brush her hair or bother with bright red lipstick. Instead, she threw on Brian's baseball cap, slipped on dark Christian Dior sunglasses, and hurried to the supermarket.

No apparent changes had taken place at the market, except her heightened senses. From Jenny's perspective the lights were brighter, including the colors of the fruit. Red apples glowed. Shimmering bananas seemed to have a life of their own. Each piece of fruit she touched had a vibration, a unique and distinct feeling. The bruised ones seemed to say, "Be gentle with me." A healthy-looking peach beckoned, "Please eat me." She put the succulent peach to her lips, taking a giant juicy bite.

The newly appointed produce manager detested fruit snitchers. He uttered a haughty warning to Jenny, "Sampling?" He pointed to the sign that read in bright bold red letters, "NO SAMPLING! EAT AND PAY".

As a regular shopper her accustomed status was VIP treatment. Succulent fruity-samples were always offered. Usually she turned them down. The 'keep-your-hand-out-of-the-cookie-jar' childhood syndrome prevailed. It was still more fun sneaking a taste and getting by with it.

The manager's protruding chin gave him a snooty look. She shrank to an eight-year's-old as a déjà vu reminder crept over her: Bravely waiting at her local market until no one was looking, she had snatched a ten-cent lollipop, then ran for her life. All the way home she licked the raspberry coating, anticipating the chocolate caramel inside.

At the sight of her mother nagging guilties hammered within her head, "Spill the beans, you rotten thief." Sparing no clemency for the wicked, it was too late to retrieve the digesting lollipop. Like a broken dam overflowing, the petty crime confession driveled out. "I stole a lolly."

Mother didn't admonish her, as was expected and deserved. She simply said, "A ten-cent lolly?"

Wanting off the hook Jenny cried, "Punish me, please, before the police come to get me!"

Looking at Jenny curiously her mother left the room. Saddled with the newfound delinquency, Jenny made the first moral decision of her life: she broke into the piggy bank she'd been stuffing with spare change and hoarding for two years. She held it up one last time and gave it a tender kiss on the snout. "Bye-bye, little piggy." She closed her eyes, smashing it on the kitchen floor. Pig ears, a tail, and the snout, scattered in a holy mess. Jenny gathered a handful of coins.

Without hesitation she ran full-throttle back to the store. Counting out ten pennies she handed them to the storekeeper. "This is for..."

He interrupted her in mid-sentence. "For the lollipop you took." Amazed that he knew, every muscle in her body tensed. The hair on her neck stood up as she waited for the deserved scolding. The ordeal was eternally unbearable as he stared beyond all of her defenses and fears, penetrating deep into her soul.

"I knew you'd come back."

Feeling even more remorse, she panicked. "How did you know that?"

"You had to come back to get another lollipop, now didn't you?" Smiling, he handed her a big red one, her favorite. "That's for doing the right thing."

In that moment she understood the difference between right and wrong. Between justice and injustice, being considered a fugitive or a good kid.

However, this current situation was different. This little peon produce manager wasn't about to intimidate her. With a crooked smile, she handed him the half-eaten peach. "So yummy. Life's a peach. Try it. <u>You</u> pay."

Shocked, he stood there as peach juice soaked into his nicely starched white apron. He struggled with store policy: "The customer is always right." Skeptically, he let her walk away.

Jenny strolled through the food aisles checking labels, examining ingredients for safe health. Scrutinizing a can of red beans she read aloud, "450 mg's of sodium?! Bloatsville!" Scouring the ingredients on another can, "350 mg's potassium. Healthy." Viewing another she winced, "Lactamium! That's a death warrant." With abandon she tossed the tins on the floor.

Strolling down the same aisle, Dee and Mara, gals from the "Spoil-Us Club" Orange Party couldn't believe the mess Jenny was creating. Her loud food rant attracted onlookers. One woman ducked a flying can whizzing past her nose. "She's trying to kill me," the woman shouted.

Jenny threatened, "Eat this poison and you are a dead woman."

Opting to avoid a possible assault, Mara turned her back away from Jenny. "Let's get out of here," she whispered to Dee. Mara led and Dee followed as they hastily wheeled their shopping carts into the bakery area. Unaware of their presence, Jenny stopped her cart nearby. Salivating over a double-layered ice cream cake brought her within earshot of the gossiping twosome.

Dee, a youthful 'Soccer Mom', dissected Jenny. "Poor woman's getting a double whammy! An empty nest and an empty bed."

Mara, the catty socialite, spit crucifying barbs. "She was the last to know. Even her kids knew. And then that awful love-at-first-orgasm motel fiasco..."

Repulsively, Dee sniggered, "Ugg. Who can relate to a loser like her?"

"Vile, isn't it?" Mara confirmed. "Just consider her an *ex* "Super-Mom'."

Reality smacked Jenny in the face faster than a runaway train wreck. Becoming the neighborhood's laughingstock knocked-out her last bit of dignity. Feeling unjustifiably ostracized and cruelly putdown, she lashed back, "Witchified-hunters." With lightning rod retaliation, she jerked the shopping cart around, aiming it at the gossiping vipers. Giving it a heave-ho strong push it bounced, wheels grinding, rumbling directly at them. Dee jumped out of the way, crying, "Holy mother of..." CRASH! The cart toppled over. Rows of stacked cookies, pies, and cakes launched like rockets across the aisle. Banana cream pie-faced, Dee yelled, "What a mess!"

Mara screeched, "Call Security!"

Emotionally spent, feeling like a pyramid of cards caving in when it's poked, Jenny didn't dare glance back at the wreck of cans and pastries strewn everywhere. Empty-handed and in tears she raced from the store, ending an hour-long grocery jaunt into hell.

Whenever the racing thoughts started Jenny could rush to the computer and let the creative juicy demons flow into her BLOG. But this time she was trapped, shaking and seething, too frazzled to drive.

Sitting like a clump of mud in her SUV, smack in the middle of the grocery store parking lot, silly nonsensical chaotic images danced before her. An arousal of up-and-down sensations rattled every body cell, engulfing her like an unpredictable ocean storm. Angry waves unmercifully pulled her into an undertow, reeling into unknown scary depths. A toothy shark pulled her even deeper, lashing into a dark cave, drowning her in the fear of total annihilation.

When calmer waves emerged, she effortlessly floated to the top, relaxed and safe. Revitalized, she miraculously swam to shore, buoyantly able to accomplish her daily tasks. The panic attack had passed. How amazing! She actually felt better: More like herself. Was this euphoric feeling what emotionally balanced, or "normal" (whatever "normal" was), is supposed to be?

"Normal?" she said aloud. "Not my goal." A neurotic childhood taught her that. Memories flooded through her mind of being an Army brat living abroad, changing schools thirteen times (hard to believe, but true). Many nights were spent trying to cope in a new place, desiring to make friends. She fantasized a future of eventually settling in the Burbs, attempting to live a normal life. She remembered wishing on a falling star, "I want to live in suburbia and have a big kitchen of my own."

Conflicted by daily discipline routines executed by her commando father, a high-ranking officer, imbedded different notions in Jenny of how to handle life. His job was to control the ranks below him. He trained soldiers to think, "Safety first!" and to respond and behave in the best interest of their fellow men and country. That was noble and true. Deeply ingrained in her core she adopted the M.O. of being in charge, in control as her survival norm. Deviation from this norm, along with any kind of chaos, brought out her fragility and the need to either attack or run away.

One thought led to another in a series of epiphanies. Suddenly, she became a newborn witness to her erratic behavior. A yellow light seemed to flash caution, time to get back on track. To take charge of her life! Unfortunately, that included taking charge of everyone else around her.

A supermarket security officer shined a yellow-bulb flashlight into Jenny's face. Then he tapped on the window to gain her attention. "Everything all right?" he asked. The question and his presence jarred her back to the incident. Unwilling to speed off like a criminal, she murmured in a tiny voice, "I'm okay, now."

He prodded further, "Still feel like nerve gas on the loose?"

"No, more like a deflated tire...needing air." Head hanging out from the window, she inhaled a deep breath. "Oh, that's better."

"Being a little paranoid doesn't make us crazy," he remarked. Pointing to Dee and Mara who were standing outside the front of the store he added, "Just stay away from those crackpots." Smiling with a peculiar understanding as if he'd been there – on burnout toll road and back – he walked away.

Jenny detested Dee and Mara's snooty-snobby reactions to her overreactions. Not reacting was inhuman, reserved for the stoned-faced, someone like Brian's karate instructor Master KuKu, a Korean black belt who attacked and ravaged his opponents without a blink or wink of an eye.

Jenny intentionally drove by the two self-appointed snob-keepers who were seemingly guarding the shopping outpost, and tossed a flappable wave at them. Intimidated by Jenny's direct awareness of them, they pretended not to see her. Cool as a cucumber, Jenny shook her head and laughed out loud, taunting them. "You think you clones are normal? No danger of me becoming normal. " Normalcy was as improbable a task for Jenny as asking the tide to stop coming in. And more foolishly, expecting it to listen.

Several days of spring rains had taken its toll. Minor flooding and a few leaks in the Forrest house were finally repaired. Every weed known to mankind had surfaced, choking the luscious cornucopia garden.

José, the gardener, whistled while he worked. His son, brother, and cousins all pulled, wrapped, and stacked weeds. They heaved refuge foliage into an old beaten-up truck. Mariachi music inspired festivity. They joked and worked in perfect timing to the beat.

A cloud of dark smoke spun up the street as a Harley motorcycle grinded to a halt. A bald-headed Hulk Hogan-ish man in shiny black leathers dismounted a few houses down the street from the Forrest's. With a dozen long-stemmed yellow roses tucked under his arm he approached José. "Say man, got a surprise delivery for the little lady of the house." José eyed the character and kept working and whistling.

"Hey, all I'm asking is to hang out in the bush until she gets here. She'll love these." He pointed to the roses.

A bit territorial José tightly clenched a rake. Hulk Man slipped a couple of dollars to him. Holding a blackened fingernail over Jose's mouth, he lowered his voice and said, "That means keep your mouth shut." José registered stone-faced, he nodded, and continued his work. It wasn't clear if he was fearful or if his loyalty stopped with a buck.

A few minutes later, Jenny drove down the street. A red Corvette and José's old truck blocked the driveway. She parked out front. Unseen, Hulk Man lurked in a nearby bush. Admiring José's handiwork Jenny proclaimed, "Good job, José. What a relief to see my beautiful rhododendron and sweet peas again."

José smiled. "Glad you're happy today, Mrs. Forrest." He emphasized 'happy'. Even the gardener was aware of her erratic moods of late.

Jenny inhaled the fragrance of a full-bloomed hydrangea. "Stop and smell the hydrangeas. Heavenly."

Hulk Man, actually a deceitful court server, lunged out from his hiding place. "Mrs. Forrest, is that you?"

Still enraptured from the hydrangea scent Jenny unsuspectingly replied, "Of course it's me."

Menacingly, with sadistic pleasure, he thrust a large manila envelope at her, along with the roses. "You are legally served, Mrs. Forrest."

"Served what? Roses?" Jenny asked. She looked inside the envelope. Quickly skimming the pages her eyes landed on the killer words, 'Irreconcilable differences.' "What is this?" she shrieked.

"Divorce papers!" Like daggers she whirled the roses and the envelope back at Hulk Man. Seething, she spat, "Richie...that lowbrow, seedy underbelly. He's divorcing me before I had a chance? Divorce...the rotten scum-bum!"

Ignoring her wrath, Hulk Man ran up the street like a rebel-rouser bandit, hopped on the Harley, slammed his snakeskin boot down on the pedal and kick-started the engine. The bike lifted into an airborne wheelie, speeding-off.

Exasperated, Jenny picked up the divorce papers and chased Hulk Man down the middle of the street, shouting, "'Irreconcilable differences'? A friggin' lie. Try shylock...betrayal!"

Neighbors peered out of windows, gawked from porches, admonished in protest, "There she goes, disturbing the peace again." "The community board should file a petition." "Shut up or move!"

Oblivious, Jenny walked past the jeers. No way would she concede to the legality of being served. She snarled with the biting rage of a caged lion, tossing the documents in José's battered truck. Only one thought dominated. "Dumb move, Richie. You just ignited the 'War of the Forrest's.'"

In a mega-hypertonic state she bumped her 'funny bone' on the Corvette's side mirror. "Ouch! Damn kids! Brian knows that friends park on the street." Rubbing the elbow sting, she headed inside the house, ready for war with the first person in view.

Brian had forgotten to meet his buddy Steve, and wasn't at home. What auspicious timing for Samantha! Touted as the second most popular guy in school, after Brian, of course, Steve was hunky-gorgeous. Samantha in all of her nerdy-fluster, was left alone to entertain the serendipitous gentleman caller. One little giggle had led to another. Hands touched. Next, a tentative embrace! A first intimate moment blossomed when Steve whispered, "You are the most beautiful girl I've ever touched." That declaration led to her first tongue-waggling kiss. Writhing in her tight jeans on the den couch, they were clenched in a steamy embrace.

Samantha giggled, "You are so cool."

With a perfunctory response, he pressed his body against her, "So are you."

In the kitchen, dithering over the divorce ordeal, Jenny wiped her face with a sopping wet dishrag and meandered into the den. As if a vacuum hose had sucked the breath out of her, she grabbed the sofa's edge, steadying herself. Not sure whose wriggling body was on top of whose, she moved in for a closer view. Gaping at her supposedly innocent wallflower daughter making-out and enjoying it, Jenny was thrown back in time, reminded of the premature results of her own messing-around days. She had been just a few months older than Samantha when she missed her period. Diagnosis? Pregnant!

"No, no, no!" Jenny panicked, "I have to stop them." Then she lost it. "Samantha! Stop that before you get pregnant!"

Samantha bolted up. "Mother! Holy shit! Go away!" She screeched in total embarrassment.

The young man rolled off her, rising to his feet. "Sorry, Mrs. Forrest. We never did the deed. Sam has protection, anyway. She told me that she's on the pill."

Jenny and Samantha locked eyes. "The pill? When did you go on the pill?"

Feeling humiliated beyond repair Samantha furrowed her eyebrows, "Go away, will you?"

Steve pointed to his zipped-zipper. "The pecker didn't peek," he grinned, pleased with his humorous play on words.

Raising a fist to strike him Jenny thought better of it. Instead, she threatened, "Jailbait! Assault. Prison."

He backed away. "Geez, I didn't mean to offend you."

Samantha added, "See? Our clothes are still on."

Jenny's voice rattled. "Enough. I have heard enough, John."

Both he and Samantha blurted in unison, "Steve."

"He's <u>Steve</u>," Samantha corrected in frustration.

"I'm Steve." Extending a hand to shake Jenny's, she recoiled. He found himself pumping air instead of her hand. "Pleased to meet you," he continued.

Jenny refused to acknowledge him. "Good-bye, John," she commanded in an icy tone.

As he headed out the front door the young man mouthed the words, "I'll call you, Sam."

Samantha threw herself on the floor. In a childish fit of exasperation she wildly kicked arms and legs, pounding her fists on the carpet, sobbing big wails. "Thanks for ruining my life! I finally found someone who could get past my knobby knees and braces."

"He just wanted to get into your pants. My mother warned me and I wouldn't listen."

"Then why should I? Can't I just be normal for once? Be like the other kids?"

Jenny stammered, "Heaven forbid. They're being brainwashed into shopping mall addicts. Manipulated by sexy ads, big red lips, cleavage, pierced bellies."

"Give me a break. That's you!" Near tears, she put her head between her knees.

"Samantha, please listen to me. You're a good kid. You don't have to become a media-hyped drone!"

Samantha rapidly shook her head back and forth, "I hate your stupid time-warped ideas. You are soooo out of it."

"And you aren't?" Jenny fired back, tensing her jaw.

Jenny heard her voice snapping at Samantha with the same judging tone as her own mother's. Remembering a stinging blow during one of their battles, her mother had warned, "Mark my words, young lady. Someday you'll have a kid as awful to raise as you." Those words had stuck in her head all of these years. Now the time had obviously arrived. Now it was Jenny's turn to reason the unreasonable with Samantha.

"I'm only trying to help you. I don't want you to make a mistake that could ruin your life."

Samantha shot back, "You mean like taking the birth control pills Dr. Harris gave me to help my acne?"

"Oh, no. I forgot." Jenny's heart sank with Samantha's broken spirit. "Forgive me," she quietly pleaded.

"I'll never forgive you...how could I? You ruined my first kiss," Samantha accused, then jumped-up from the floor and fled to her room where she would pout for hours.

???

Jenny had put off the inevitable long enough. Scheduling a consultation with Mick Hartford, a notable divorce lawyer to the rich and famous, left her wondering how much he'd charge for services rendered. She reminded herself to beware of oak-paneled offices. The price of service went up exponentially in high-ticket conference rooms. She felt comforted that cheapo Richie could represent himself, draining less of their savings.

Rather than wearing St. John she dressed down in a dreadful geek-chic suit, a ten-year-old birthday gift from her mother-in-law. Calculating every move that morning, she was hoping to ignite a tad of sympathy in Mick Hartford's jaded heart.

Mick entered the room with a movie star air, flanked by two assistants who were attentive to his every move. Most certainly a flick of his eyelash would have some meaning in Mick's high-powered world. After the perfunctory salutations, he got right down to business. "Mrs. Forrest, you know the drill. You've lived with an expert on the matter of divorce for years. There are two important questions. Number one: Who will be the first to file?"

She diverted her glance for a second and then looked him directly in the eye. "I wanted to be first."

Sensing the hesitation he stated, "Let's be straight forward. You 'wanted' to be. But were you? Did Richie file first?"

Not willing to shoot herself in the foot she admitted, "The dork...excuse the crude slander..." she covered the faux pas with a cough, "...filed first."

"Good break for you. Saves tons of hard-earned cash. Mitigates missed payments, late notices, and even foreclosures. He pays the cost of drawing-up the papers. We answer. Makes it simple. Now, for the second question: Do you want to rake him over the coals or let him disappear into the sunset? Either way, you'll get the same settlement." He cocked his head back. His styled salt-and-pepper hair and tan face gave him an irresistible boyish charm. He smiled confidently, waiting for her response.

"How hot are the coals?" Her lips compressed into a calculating grin.

"I thought you might be savvy. There's no way Richie could have married a pushover." Before she could answer he held out his hand, "Looks like you made the right decision, shall we proceed?"

Her lips quivered, his warm brown eyes offered comfort. She was tempted to pour her heart out, tell him everything, which would prove utterly disastrous, she was certain. Controlling the impulse she answered with a bright cheery tone, "Go get him, nothing would make me happier." They shook hands. She noticed how soft his skin was, all brains no brawn.

As Jenny left Mick's office she understood why he was the best. He knew that money and revenge were both relevant in a divorce settlement.

No sooner had the door closed in the office, Mick placed a phone call. "Richie, my man. I'll guarantee your net worth on your

Funny Mummy

tombstone. Play ball. For a slam-dunk, you draw up the terms. We'll sign."

???

Jenny was having a "Monday Blues" day as she handled little nitpicking chores such as cleaning hairbrushes and replenishing electric toothbrushes. As a diversion Jenny sorted through the mail. She jostled Samantha, who was curled up on the couch. Jenny held up two identical envelopes. "They're here. The acceptance letters from Stanford."

Samantha shivered, tugging her sweater over her mouth. "Or the rejection!"

Jenny opened one of the envelopes. "We got in!"

Samantha bounced on Jenny's lap. " 'We'. Which 'we'? Me or Brian?"

"Brian."

Samantha ripped at the second envelope. She closed her eyes, handing the letter to Jenny. "I can't. You tell me."

Jenny cried out, "We're in!"

Simultaneously, a female voice gasped a loud moan, then cries of passionate delight from upstairs. "You're in, Brian. You're in."

Startled by the cries Jenny cringed, "Who the hell was that?"

They both let out a shriek of concern and headed upstairs. Barging into Brian's bedroom, Jenny and Samantha glared at Brian's naked bum pumping up-and-down over another naked body. His left rear cheek boasted the familiar Forrest raspberry birthmark.

Clutching onto each other as if they'd just seen a ghost, Jenny and Samantha wailed expletives. Staggering out of the room, holding on to each other, Jenny mumbled, "Breathe. In and out..."

Samantha chimed, "In and out." Breathing perfectly in sync they ambled down the hallway. Retreating into Jenny's bedroom Samantha comforted her mother. "Good job. Just keep breathing."

Orgasmic echoes rippled through the second floor. Samantha and Jenny pounded their fists on the bed.

"He got laid before me," Samantha wailed.

Jenny cried, "Get that little harlot and raspberry junior out of my house!"

"It's not a harlot. It's Lisa," Samantha explained, as she put her head between her knees.

"Little Lisa from third grade?" Jenny's mind reeled. "Not little Lisa!"

Rocking back and forth, filled with envy, Samantha countered, "Think like the most downloaded web Lisa, the freakin' Prom Queen who's soon to be nineteen-years-old and madly hooked on your chick-magnet son."

"You mean your brother. How can he fornicate when we're at home?"

"Your rules, Mom. Always preaching to us. 'Do whatever you have to do at home, drink, smoke pot. Do it at home, where you're safe.'

Jenny rubbed her temples. "That's not what I meant". Weary from the commotion Jenny pleaded, "Give me a break before I break."

"Mom, I'm the one who's in bad shape." Samantha's nostril's quivered, searching for the right words. "Being a virgin is like...being a freak ejected in a time capsule. So everyone forever and ever will know...I'm a reject."

"You're not a reject. You got into Stanford. I'm so proud of you. Your whole life is about to change forever. You have a grand opportunity to better yourself. Look what happened to me. You have a chance to become somebody great and make a difference in this bloody world."

"Ya' think?" Samantha clutched herself as if holding onto a ray of hope.

Sensing the upbeat shift in her daughter, she slipped on her sneakers, "Come on, let's celebrate your good fortune!"

Samantha perked up. "You mean like a brain-drained trip to the mall?"

Laughing at the pun, "Just what the doctor ordered. Come on," Jenny beckoned. Grabbing her bag, her eyes gleamed with pride. "Mind if I call you 'Dr. Sam'?"

Following her into the garage, Samantha giggled, "A doctor? No way!"

In all their glory, the Forrest gals unwound on a die-hard shopping spree. Carousing trendy boutiques

Samantha tried on tall studded boots, a push-up bustier, dangling fake magenta curls, and electric blue false eyelashes.

Jenny scrutinized the punk look. "Are you going for Osbourne worst-dressed?"

"Eye candy would be better. I don't know a 'what to' from a 'what not to'." She sniveled like a kitten up a tree.

Jenny rattled on as she caroused the racks, gathering an outfit. "No horizontal stripes from the waist down. Lighter colors on top. No white shoes after Labor Day. Two inches below the knee is dowdy...two inches above the knee requires lean and leggy." Jenny handed her a hip straw cowgirl hat, lace-trim shirt and cords. "This is more you."

Samantha nodded, "You would know since I don't know what's me or not me."

Jenny felt empowered as she taught her daughter how to become a fashion-maven. "Style is feeling good in it, flowing, moving, stiff or soft. You'll know when it works."

Samantha wandered into the jewelry store where they sold designer copies for a fraction of the cost. A

commission-only, no-salary salesgirl salivated at the sweet fish that were entering her net. Without pause, tantalizing with a navel heart-cubic Zirconium stud, she pitched. "Now if you like hearts, this is the bomb."

"Earrings? Only one?" Samantha asked, disappointed.

The salesgirl looked at Samantha as if she had two heads. Where had this girl been living? On another planet? Regaining her friendly demeanor to make the sale, she explained, "This is a 'Belly' ring, a notorious fashion statement. Try it. The jazzy part is that it's removable, interchangeable with the blue, green and yellow stones." Sensing the upcoming sale, her eyes glittered brighter than the stones as she placed a green one into Samantha's hand.

Jenny watched Samantha slip the gem into her bellybutton. "What do you think, Mom? It's removable."

Jenny's eyes lit up. "I say we take two."

The salesgirl was delighted, "Excellent choice."

Jenny popped the little gem into her navel. "Thank you, Richie. Too bad you'll never see it." In a dream-like moment Jenny rubbed her tummy counterclockwise. "My lucky Buddha belly. Rub the belly, make the wish." Jenny closed her eyes. "I wish I was twenty years younger and fancy-free." Gesturing to Samantha, she encouraged, "Come on Sam, give a try."

"Too weird, Mom."

The squared-faced, blue-eyed salesgirl jumped at the chance. "Could I try?"

Jenny nodded. "Touch the belly. Make that wish."

How bazaar! There they were in Bloomies, enchanting a salesgirl most likely with only fifteen dollars left in the bank, on the verge of being evicted for late payment, and was silly enough to rub Jenny's tummy in search of a miracle.

Hopeful and bright-eyed she said, "I wish I could meet a gazillionaire and fly off to Tahiti."

Stuffing purchases into new Coach luggage, they loaded the SUV. Samantha suggested, "How about a hip chick flick? There's a cool fantasy film, 'Big Girls Don't Cry', where these girls gang up to help this dork guy be cool. They dress him, stud-train him, and then auction him off on eBay for mucho bucks like he's a hunk."

Jenny nodded. "Classic Pavlov. Train a man like a pet. Punish. Reward. He'll jump through fire-hoops to please."

"Racy, huh?" Samantha giggled. "I don't know the ending, but I bet one of the trainer's buy him."

"I'll bet it's someone else, but that sounds about right." Jenny lived and breathed for Samantha's rare bursts of enthusiasm. "A matinèe sounds great. Let's go!"

At the concession stand, they jostled super-duper-sized popcorn, red licorice, and vanilla-berry Frosty's into tiny cardboard boxes, maneuvering through the lobby on their way into the theater. They settled into deep-tufted rocker-chairs, awkwardly balancing the treats on their laps. Munching and slurping, mom and daughter shared the darkened theater's womb-like ritual, sprinkled with a sinful sugar rush.

Samantha tingled on the seat's edge, anticipating the movie's ending. On screen an assimilated eBay auction was in progress. Dollar amounts were rising fast. Bidders were feuding. It was now down to three seconds. Suddenly, a new name appeared – "Hot-stuff69" – a daring last-minute bidder. The auction ended.

Coming from out of the blue, "Hot-stuff69" was the winner. Samantha was disappointed. "I was right, it was one of the snappy-snippy bitches." In the final scene of the movie a limousine picked-up the winner. In a surprise twist, she was the dork's old nerdy girlfriend who he had supposedly dumped. The dork and the nerd tricked the catty, and sometimes mean-spirited, "cool chicks." The couple gleefully shared the eBay winnings.

"How cool, what a great ending!" Samantha jumped up, applauding. "Mom, you won, right? Oh, thank you!" she gave Jenny a hug, "There's hope for me, Mom. There's definitely hope."

"Remember that and I will too" Jenny sighed. "So what's the lesson? Big girl's don't cry...over spilt milk or losing?"

Funny Mummy

Brian had a lot on his mind. Getting into Stanford meant playing major football, juggling parties and keeping up the grades. It was almost midnight when he climbed the steps to his room. Something was blocking the bedroom door. Thrusting his body weight against it, forcing entry, he exclaimed, "Holy crap!" Shopping bags and a slew of boxes were piled ceiling high. The bed was loaded with new sheets: the works. All of this was a surprise to him, "What the hell?" He pushed the intercom button. "Ma, what is all this junk?"

Lying in bed with an ice pack plunked on her forehead, freezing out a migraine, Jenny pushed the intercom button. "You'll be sending me yellow roses when you go to school. You need every single hand-picked item, whether you know it or not." She flicked off the speaker and turned off the light.

Minutes later, Brian's cell phone toned a raucous rap-beat. He answered, "Brian on the horn."

Richie greeted him from his SUV. "How's it going, son? Want to get a bite?"

"Dad, you are so tuned-in. Ma is so tuned-out. Way gone. Out of control. I can barely get into my room. Call it living in a storage bin. All this junk she buys for the dorm." He waved a heart-shaped cookie cutter. Juggled a sewing kit. "A sewing kit, Dad! I don't know where the hell she thinks I'm going."

Richie chuckled. "I'm sure she thinks I am definitely going to hell."

Brian appealed to him. "Dad, you've got to help me. This is not working. Get her off my case."

"Done. Handled. You can count on me. So, you want to get a burger?"

"I'm zonked-out. Maybe another time, okay, Dad?"

"You got it, son." Concealing his disappointment, Richie bit his tongue, not mentioning that he was only four houses away. The street lamp glowed brightly on the SUV as it slowly passed the house. Stopping for a moment, he stared at Jenny's darkened window. His heart leaped. Thumping his chest with remorse, he said aloud, "I miss the family life, the kids, the squabbles, the love." Being nearby gave him a feeling of comfort, calm, and peace. He was surprised by how "right" it felt.

The night wore on. Jenny's headache subsided. On her way to the kitchen to put the ice pack away she heard loud, pained groans. At first she thought it was coming from Samantha's room, then from Brian's. She peaked in on Samantha.

Holding her jaw in agony Samantha cried, "Mom! My jaw, my teeth..."

"Here we go again." Jenny had been there before on double-trouble dental duty. Dreading another round she panicked. "From dueling tooth fairies, knocked-out front teeth, root canals, braces, extractions, caps. Dentist bills up the kazoo."

"Mom, stop. I'm dying."

She hovered over Samantha. "Open up...let me see."

"No, I can't," Samantha groaned.

"You won't? Open or I leave."

"All right. Just a quick peek." Samantha opened her mouth wide. Jenny peered inside. A giant red blob throbbed in the back bottom of Samantha's mouth.

Jenny took a deep breath. "Wisdom tooth time."

"No one's touching my tooth," Samantha recoiled.

Jenny handed her the ice pack. "Put this on for now, it'll help with the swelling."

With great curiosity Samantha asked, "An ice pack...how did you know?"

Another moan reeled from down the hallway. Jenny stampeded into Brian's room. He was holding his jaw, rocking back and forth in a fetal position on his bed.

"Brian, what's hurting?"

"My jaw, Mom. My teeth. I'm going to die."

Jenny shook her head, sighing. "Twins are so connected. It's so strange. So predictable."

"Mom, stop it," Brian demanded. "Look in my mouth."

"I don't have to. I already know what's going on."

"You don't know. You haven't looked."

Jenny acquiesced. "All right, let me see. Open up."

He opened wide, glaring at her, praying for relief. She gazed inside the darkness. There were two red throbbing blobs in the back and top of his mouth. "Wisdom tooth time," she announced with certainty.

Up-and-down from her bed and down the hallway all night, Jenny hopped from one bedroom to another applying ice packs, coaxing Tylenol down their throats like worm-feeding squawking baby chicks. Finally, dawn arrived and all was quiet on the Forrest front. As the twins slept Jenny watched the clock hands spin.

At one minute to 8:00 she speed-dialed, aiming to be the dental office's first caller. To her astonishment, she was. "This is Mrs. Forrest with an emergency."

The assistant replied, "Isn't it always?" and proceeded to set up the usual dental appointment from hell.

At the dental office with two moaning teens in tow, Jenny felt that she had touched upon a stroke of genius! She had brought a distraction with her to avoid the typical complaints from the twins as they waited. Reaching into her purse, she retrieved their baby book and a string of teeth. She had strung every tooth they lost into a prized necklace. She pointed to various teeth. "Here's your first baby tooth, Sam. Here's Brian's."

"How in the world can you tell that one's mine?" Samantha asked.

"Brian's were white, yours have a kink of yellow."

"Not now. I can't take it," Samantha pouted.

Brian whinnied like a baby colt, "Why pull all four wisdom teeth at once?"

Jenny replied matter-of-factly. "So we don't have to do it again."

Twin dentists, Dr. A. Nathan and Dr. B. Nathan shared a large dental room, housed with two identical dental chairs fully equipped for each respective doctor. Jenny scampered in the room before the twins. She handed each doctor a plastic baggie.

"This is Samantha's, that one's Brian's. Please put all four teeth in a baggie. Don't mix them up."

Dr. A. swished and gushed, "I just love your tooth necklace concept. We should patent it."

Dr. B. disagreed. "You can't patent someone else's teeth, jerko!"

Jenny corrected, "Pearls, darlings. Think Pearls. These 200 millimeter molars you're extracting are the crowning bangles for my precious necklace."

Dr. A. announced, "I'll take care of Brian. His teeth are the whitest, most translucent and glowing."

"No fair," Dr. B. complained. "Last time I got wimp yellow tooth."

"Cut it, boys," Jenny admonished. "We don't have all day." She left as two nurses escorted, rather dragged, the twins into the room.

Brian pleaded. "Laughing gas, OK, bro'?"

"Me too," Samantha echoed.

Dr. A. insisted, "Not until you get the needle."

Dr. B. added, "Then you get the happy treat. Now pick a chair!"

Dr. A agreed, "That's fair. Let them choose their poison."

Samantha yelled, "Poison! I'm out of here." She bolted out of the door, but the nurses grabbed her by each arm and trotted her back to the room.

Brian implored Dr. A. "You promise the gas?"

Dr. A. nodded. "But promises are made to be broken."

Brian sized-up the drolly twins. "I'll take Dr. A." Brian jumped in his chair.

Samantha punched his shoulder. "You always get Doctor A. and I get Doctor yellow fang."

"Oh, really." Dr. B. fanged his big yellowish teeth like a Sumu wrestler, lifting her into his chair. Foisting large red straps he waved them at her with the wrath of a monster, snapping them hard in the air. CRACK. The sound was terrifying. "You can sit here peacefully without the strap-in or you can keep up the bull."

Eyes wide, Samantha responded, "No straps. I'll sit."

Dr. B. hooked a water-drain hose in her mouth and swabbed a numbing antiseptic across her gums. With sardonic pleasure he raised the anticipated long needle. Moving closer to her open mouth it seemed to stretch in length, dagger-ish. Dr. B.'s pupils glared a wild red hue, his teeth jagged nearer to her face as if to devour her. Samantha's mouth gaped in a frozen position, waiting for the battering.

For up-close vision Dr. A. wore gigantic black goggles with coke-bottle-thick lenses. Brian thought Dr. A. looked like a bug-eyed alien from Crypton! The overhead blinding beam-light resembled a spaceship operating room. Brian was sure he was a human specimen being tested and dissected. He squirmed, wondering if he'd ever get back home alive.

As if on cue, Dr. A. glanced at Dr. B. as they plunged the needles into the twin's jaws, digging deeper and deeper, gashing past flesh and bone, possibly touching their brains. Otherworldly screams reached the waiting room. Jenny continued filing her nails to avoid feeling the contact pain.

Shortly thereafter inside the dental room, displayed as treasures on side matching tables, were the two baggies, each containing four gigantic pearl-ish teeth.

Partying like frat boys, Dr. A. and Dr. B. shared a round of laughing gas with their twin counterparts. They chuckled and roared themselves into a silly fit laughter. In high-pitched Donald Duck helium-squeaks, they congratulated their fine work. "Job well done." "We are the tooth fairies."

Hearing the laughter, Jenny relaxed. "Hallelujah, the gas kicked in."

The days were slipping by as the countdown to Stanford life for the twins had begun. Jenny was in top form commandeering at the computer. Wearing an earpiece, she blabbed a mile a minute. "Enough dormitory red tape. We're paying twelve-thousand a year for that minuscule cubicle. Email the floor plan. Now!"

Highlighted on the computer screen a Stanford dorm room popped up in full color.

"Very good. This I can work with." Jenny expertly mounted, manipulated, and inserted various objects into the virtual room: A lamp, bed, dresser, and clothes hamper, among other items. She rotated objects around the faux room, arranging and rearranging.

Samantha gawked at it. "The truth is, I can't do anything by myself."

"You've watched. You've learned. Now, you'll <u>do</u>," Jenny instructed.

"I don't function alone. Maybe I shouldn't go."

"You won't be alone. Call me morning, noon or night...and I'll always be there."

Samantha tinkered with a portable alarm clock. "Is it winding back for spring and forward for fall?"

"Wind forward for spring. Back for fall. It's all about light. The days are shorter in winter, so we wind back." Gently explaining, hoping she was simple and clear.

Samantha flapped her palm against her forehead, "See, I don't know anything...I can't remember anything."

"You'll learn. You'll know. You'll remember." Jenny continued her mission: Shopping online. She added a straw rug to the purchase cart. The finished product pleased her. "Well, Samantha, how do you like your room?"

"It's nice," With a deadpan glance at her mother, she flicked on the fire engine blasting radio alarm.

Irritated, Jenny flicked it off. "Nice, that's it?

Samantha exaggerated a loud jabbing yawn, "It's your room. Not mine."

Exhausted by the continuous effort to keep Samantha on track, Jenny's eyes sunk to the back of her head. "Here we go. What's not to like?"

"You, Mom. You don't listen or really see me. You don't care what the hell I think. Admit it."

"I'm finished. I've been slaving for hours on your behalf. No thanks. Pick whatever you want."

Samantha couldn't believe that Jenny had acquiesced. "You know I don't know what I want."

"Good you can see that. When you do know, you'll go after it. You'll get it. Nothing will stop you."

Samantha timidly asked,. "Does that apply to guys?"

"Preserving, being available and picking the right one...applies to everything."

"I hope you're right," Samantha mused, "I guess I have to figure out what I really want."

"Good start. Want me to help you?"

"Enough, Mom...I need to do it myself." Feeling pumped and encouraged, Samantha grabbed her cell phone and sneaked into her room where she closed the door and locked it. She took a deep breath for courage and called Steve.

"Hi, it's me, Samantha. I really wanted to get out for a sec. Ah...it's my last night before I go to Stanford. How about it?"

"I'd love to. But...like I'm grounded. Unbelievable, huh? " Trying to win her sympathy and to convince her he was not putting her on, Steve coughed, gagging a bit dramatically.

Hiding her disappointment Samantha remarked, "Too bad."

"I'd invite you over, but no company's allowed," he said in a somber voice.

Giggles could be heard in the background. A girl's voice simmered, "Hang up, Stevie. Talk dirty to me."

"Shhh," he muttered.

Samantha felt the blood rush out of her. Not knowing what to say or do next, she was motionless and silent.

Cutting through the silence, Steve asked, "Hello, are you there?" As his date wriggled the phone from his hand. Samantha could hear the 'plop' onto the bed. She boiled inside with jealousy, singeing from the sucking zeal of their kiss. Masochistically listening, she fantasized that she was the girl in Steve's embrace. She wished she knew the cool thing to say, at the right time. She wished she wasn't always on the outside praying to get in. Why wasn't she popular, smart, and savvy? In desperation she screamed into the phone, "Talk nerdy to me! Friggin' you both too!" She knew that made no sense. Exasperated, she ended the call with "go...friggin' screw yourself.

Sometimes the classic saying, "Out of bad comes good". Samantha had identified what she wanted. "I want a boyfriend." The harder one to admit, the one that hurt was, "I don't want to be a goof-ball lame brain." If knowing what you want and don't want was the first step to getting it, she needed more facts and 'How-To' information.

The rest of the afternoon she browsed a bookstore, hanging out in the "Hot Love" section. Embarrassed at holding a stack of books that taught how to arouse a man, she hid in the kid's area, propped on a tyke seat.

Perusing each book, the main point seemed to be, "Don't nag a guy. Praise him. Tell him the good things: 'Great shirt. Love your bald head.' Refrain from the temptation to say, 'It would make a great bowling ball.' Remember Grandma's stand-by recipe. 'Praise, flattery, honey.' These strategies are so potent that in no time you'll have the wimp eating out of your hand (or wherever else brings you pleasure)."

Samantha felt ecstatic, satisfied that she might have discovered the Holy Grail to a man's heart and loins. This new information gave her a lucky confidence boost, a secret seduction arsenal that would hopefully serve her wishes at Stanford.

Part 11

THE MIDDLE – MIND BAIT

Three Mercedes SUV'S pulled out of the Forrest garage. Jenny, Samantha, and Brian drove their respective vehicles through the cul-de-sac. A moving van followed. The big moment had arrived. They were off to Stanford.

The trip up north was breathtaking. The caravan meandered through the wine country, over hill and dale. Closer to the coast the leaves had tips of orange, yellow, and crimson, reflecting a refreshing change of season. A fall welcoming with its crisp awakening air enlivened the senses and everything seemed to indicate that it was an auspicious time for the Forrest's new beginnings.

Stanford's campus reeked of an eastern Ivy League college. Red brick Tudor-style buildings were interspersed with evergreens, fountains, and benches for meeting and hanging-out with friends. The caravan pulled in front of an all-girl dorm. Samantha was the first stop.

Overly zealous, Jenny leaped out of her car, spouting her first command to the movers, "Okay. Are you guys ready to unload?" She turned to Brian and Samantha, "You need to guard the truck. Make sure they don't break anything. I'll run in, get things ready."

Samantha blocked her. "I need to go in, not you."

"Don't start, please. The movers need to know what to do or they'll mess it up. It'll only take fifteen minutes."

Brian's eyebrows lifted. "Right, Mom...fifteen minutes, sure thing."

"Time me," Jenny challenged.

He looked at his watch. "You're on."

With a gleam in her eye, Jenny smiled. "You buy lunch if I do it in fifteen."

Brian returned the challenge. "You buy if you don't."

Samantha's nerves rattled, her teeth chattered. "Mom, promise if my roommate's there you won't say anything crazy. Not a word! Don't talk. Just don't make me look like a dork."

"Trust me. I would never do anything to make you look...stupid." Nearly biting her tongue, Jenny grimaced. Then attending to the movers she said, "Unload all the white box's marked 'Samantha'." Turning to Samantha she gave her a hug. "Don't worry honey, it's all under control." Then Jenny headed for the dorm.

Samantha literally was praying, "Please, dear God, don't let her mess up."

Inside a darkened hallway, Jenny boldly ignored a sign that read, "DAY LIGHTS OUT" and flicked on a light switch. "What about night-light's out?" she muttered. "Do they want you to just trip and kill yourself?" Clambering the stairs to the third floor, she stopped every ten steps to take a breath. Reaching the landing she searched the corridor for Samantha's room. "Viola! Room 313! Thirteen is our lucky number," she exclaimed. Wiggling the key in the lock, she opened the door. The room was identical to the layout on the computer screen: stark and sparse with two single beds and matching dressers.

Curled-up in one bed, under the debris of clothes and smoking a cigarette was Tanya, a no-study partying sex-pistol. Jenny scrutinized her, "You must be our new roomie?"

Tanya glared back in disbelief. "<u>You</u> are the Forrest chick? They said you were offbeat. But this...is way not right."

Ignoring the familiar teen angst Jenny met her attitude straight on. "Would you mind putting that cigarette out so you don't burn up the place?"

"You're like coming in here and totally taking over. Just like <u>that!</u>" Tanya angrily snapped her fingers.

"You'll get used to it," Jenny remarked in a dismissive tone. "How about getting out of bed so we can rearrange a few things."

"Major rudeness," Tanya huffed. "This is my bed, okay? That one's yours."

Ignoring her, Jenny walked a few paces measuring a corner of the room. "Perfecto. It's all going to work."

The movers arrived, carting a floor-to-ceiling desk-bed contraption. "Right there, near the window, remove the single bed." Jenny instructed. Working fast as little beavers, they installed a shower massage and mounted a shelf in the bathroom where Jenny stacked Samantha's toiletries and towels. Then she quickly hung a flounce sheer curtain over the window. The movers laid a woven rug on Samantha's side of the room. With nothing new on Tanya's side there was now a striking contrast.

Samantha bounced in the door with Brian. Stunned, she gasped, "It's only been fifteen minutes and you're done."

"Told you," Jenny proudly declared. "Brian's treating us to lunch." Jenny held up the computer printout of the finished room. It was identical.

Brian applauded. "Mighty impressive. A perfect match."

Tanya hadn't made a sound. She remained crouched in a fetal position, hiding under the covers, murmuring, "It's the invasion of the Forrest-snatchers. In fifteen lousy minutes my life is trashed, destroyed, decimated."

Noticing a twitch under the covers, Samantha moved toward Tanya's bed. "Hi. Is anyone there? It's Samantha, here. Your new roommate."

Tanya peeked out from her hiding place, one eye focused on Samantha. "Thank you, God. It's like a roomie-type person. Not a taboo frazzled mom-type...like I just escaped." Then she saw Brian. He smiled his sheepish grin. Their eyes locked. It was lust at first sight. Her demeanor immediately shifted to sultry. "Hi. I'm Tanya."

"I'm Brian. Samantha's older brother."

Jenny chimed in, "By two-and-a-half minutes."

Uncomfortable watching the obvious mutual attraction Samantha balked, "Such a big deal...a few minutes."

In disbelief Tanya shuddered, "<u>You</u> can't be <u>his</u> twin!"

Samantha made a cross-sign with her fingers as if warding off evil spirits, "I wish."

"Whoa! I better leave before the fireworks start, guys. I'm off to my pad." Brian flashed another sheepish grin. "Nice meeting you...ah, Ms...ah?"

"Rice...like Chinese rice," Tanya purred.

Still flirting, Brian added, "Tanya Rice. Nice name." He gave Jenny a quick hug. "See ya', Mom." Then planted a kiss on Samantha's forehead. "Hey Sam, have fun," and quickly slid out the door.

Jenny followed him down the hallway. "Brian, wait! The movers have your furniture."

"No need, Mom. I'm off campus. Way off! And off limits to you!"

Confused by the comment, Jenny asked, "How can that be?"

"Dad covered it. Movers are handled."

Jenny's eyes bulged. "That snake went behind my back. He's finished."

"Come on, Mom. This doesn't mean I don't love you."

"Right. You just want me to crawl in a hole and disappear."

Brian sensed her distress, "No one's banishing you, Mom. Drive carefully, looks like a big storm's coming." Comforting her with a long good-bye hug, Brian continued down the hallway while Jenny watched, a mixture of sadness and frustration whirled within her.

It was dusk – grey and dreary. Strong winds and heavy rain pounded the SUV as Jenny made her way south on a small, winding road. Having left the 101 to stop for gas and a snack, she missed the on-ramp, lost in thought. Already feeling sorry for herself, like an orphan returning to an empty home, her movements were automatic and trance-like. Jenny was miles away from the freeway before she realized her mistake.

Straining to see through the blurry windshield, she barely avoided colliding with an oncoming car. The SUV swerved, bounded over a pothole and careened into a muddy ditch. Jenny smacked her head against the dashboard. Disoriented for a couple of seconds, she rubbed the small lump growing larger on her forehead. "This sucks," she moaned. Reaching for her cell, she touched the pre-programmed button for 911. Nothing happened. "Damn, no service. This can't be happening!" she exclaimed. "I'm in a dire emergency...you bum-out on me." She slammed the cell phone into her jacket pocket in disgust.

Checking the GPS map she traced the green line with her finger. Following twists and turns, sadly disappointed, she realized the location was inconsequential. "Cripes, I'm lost." Rifling through a side-pocket on the door, she cheered, "Yay for preparedness." Discovering the rarely used umbrella she slid out the door into a foot of rainwater. Opening the umbrella, she braced for an unknown trek. "Where the heck am I?"

Ferocious winds blew, flogging the umbrella. Struggling to keep it open, it buckled and bowed. "Damn it again," she muttered. Schlepping and waddling she tripped in the sloshing mud. The cell phone flipped from her pocket, rolling into a ditch. Mushing her hand into the brown sludge, scouring about, trying to find it, she couldn't see through the downpour. "Just my luck! I give up!"

Drenched and freaked-out she plunged onward down the road, slipping and sliding. In the distance a rundown farmhouse was barely visible. A lightning bolt struck nearby, illuminating the sky. The house on the hill lit up like a lantern. It looked and felt eerie, horrifying, reminding her of the film, "The House on Elm Street."

Thunder roared, sending shivers piercing through her bones. Not sure if she was trembling out of fear of the unknown, or from the freezing rain, she prayed, "Please, no psychopaths or ghoulish fiends lurking in that house."

With nowhere else to turn Jenny headed for the ominous wooden porch. The rickety steps creaked as she mounted. Mustering might and courage, she tugged on the cowbell hanging from the entryway. After a few beats, no one answered. Pulling faster and faster the bell's deafening clang rumbled into the night. "That should wake the living dead," she said through rattling teeth. However, no one answered. She pummeled her fists on the door. "Somebody, please! Help me!"

Elma and Festus Barton, an elderly couple known by the local's to be pranksters with questionable motives, lived in the farmhouse. Festus, sporting a Santa white beard, peered through the peephole. Barely able to make out the image of the rag-tag-looking woman glaring back at him, he said to Elma, "Wished I had my glasses. Can hardly see who's out there."

Elma, who looked like a cross between Mammy Yoakum and Ma Barker, handed her spectacles to him. "Take a gander through these, Festus. Sure's better than gawking blind."

With granny glasses hanging off his nose he squinted at forlorn Jenny. "Looks like one of them homeless gals hankering for a place to bed."

Elma removed her glasses from Festus' nose, put them on herself, and peered out. "You might be right! Best we spare the poor varmint a meal."

Festus opened the door. "Wasn't expecting company was we, Elma?"

Jenny shivered from head-to-toe. "I'm not really company. I just need to use your phone."

Festus checked her out for some dodgy agenda. "Looking for the kindness of strangers?"

Near crumpling Jenny broke down. "My car ran into a ditch. I traipsed through muck, sloshed through the rain."

Elma believed she was spouting the truth. "This Gucci lady's no gutter-mouth tramp." Recognizing the Gucci bag dangling from Jenny's shoulder cleared up that possibility. Elma reached out, "Poor thing. Come on inside before you catch your death of pneumonia."

Relieved, Jenny whispered, "Oh thank you, ma'am."

In an "Alice in Wonderland" fashion Jenny walked through a portal that, in time, would reveal itself.

The rain continued to batter the windows, rattling the doors. Jenny felt comfy zipped in Elma's couch potato robe as she poured out her woeful heart to Elma who fussed over her, offering soup and a lending ear.

Sitting in a well-worn recliner Festus happily watched an "I Love Lucy" rerun on TV. His laughter interspersed the conversation. Jenny sniffled and sneezed. Elma took a spoon in hand pretending to conduct an orchestra. A chuckle. A sneeze. A guffaw. A sniffle and then a giggle. "What a symphony," Elma laughed.

Jenny desperately needed someone to confide in. She was ready to open up all the way with this old woman. Why? She was clueless.

Elma simply asked, "Feeling better?"

Flooding with emotion Jenny let it fly. "Better than what? Misery? Yesterday? Last week? Or the year before? I carry all my damn feelings in a bagful of shame."

Elma kept a safe distance. "You're ticking like a stink-bomb," she said. "Time you had a tantrum, girl, and got it out."

"I have plenty of those. Dumping on my kids, Richie, my mom."

"Under that bluffing piffle you're toting a potful of pain, dipped in a tar of misery."

Jenny bawled, "I don't like <u>me</u> anymore. Don't like me by myself. I am a 'we' person. Being just an 'I' is like...nobody's home."

"You think you're the only heart-crash! Felt the same way after every one of my divorces. First three were the worst, then I lost count." On TV Lucy dumped water on Ricky's head. Festus laughed out loud. Elma grinned adoringly at him, "That was until Festus here, came along."

Jenny confided, "I'm the dopey romantic, a 'forever girl'. A freaking dumbbell living the 'death until we part' bit."

Showing disdain Elma commented, "Ball and chain girl, eh?"

Jenny was lost in a reverie of funk. "Richie was the first. My only."

With a knowing smile, Elma nodded, "Got hot 'n heavy. You got preggers?"

"How did you know?"

Elma ignored the question. "Too bad you wasted it. No smutty memories to keep you going."

Festus' ears perked up. "First-timer, heh? We can change that right quick. Where's Finster?"

"Mind your business, you old coot," Elma chuckled. Showing her affection for him, she rubbed her red tufted slipper against his leg.

He sighed, contented as a clam, "Umm, feels good sweetums'.

Elma sat in her matching recliner next to Festus. She glanced at Jenny spread out on the couch and offered, "You'll love the little trundle guest bed, never got a complaint yet."

Jenny raised her head, nodding with gratitude, "That's so kind, how can I make it up to you?"

"Help us with the chores that a fair-exchange".

Jenny nodded, not having a clue what she had bargained for. Relaxing together, the threesome spent an uproarious evening watching Lucy reruns one after another. Jenny roared a cackle minus the usual mania. "Hah-hah-hah!" The contagious giggle caught the old couple, who laughed hysterically. Slapping their legs, rocking to and fro'.

Festus yelled, "I just peed my pants!"

"Uh...me too." Jenny candidly admitted as she sashayed past them and into her room.

Elma and Festus were refreshing company for a pent-up anal-queen. It was so freeing to "let go" for a change. Relishing a reprieve from her frenzied bondage, tucked in a trundle bed wrapped in a fluffy womb-like comforter, Jenny slept like a baby.

How could a city gal possibly anticipate the loud, relentless, squawking "Caw!" of Caruso, the rooster, at the break of dawn? Hoping to drown-out the intrusion Jenny pulled the covers over her head. It was a futile attempt, so she trudged out of bed and put on the overalls hanging on a hook. Sunrise meant chores were waiting. Time to work off the kindness of the stranger's and pay her debt for food and lodging. Jenny was up for the challenge and the much needed down-home nurturing.

It was both weird and wonderful for Jenny to get a reprieve from catering to a lazy brood, serving breakfast to them every day with nary a thanks. No doubt she wouldn't mess in Elma's kitchen. Elma fluttered about whipping up hominy and grits, pork belly's, and deep-fried potatoes.

Jenny asked, "What's the pasty white stuff you're cooking everything in?"

Festus gleamed, "Lard, all fat. Good for a big sweet fanny."

"Or a coronary," Jenny added.

Elma poured Jenny a third cup of robust black coffee. "Finish that mud and you'll be climbing walls and working like a banshee."

Jenny downed the sour brew. "It's got a buzz for sure," unaware she'd need more than a caffeine pick-up for the hacking day's workload ahead.

Out in the barn Elma manipulated the teats on Winifred, the cow. "Up-and-down, fast. Squeeze. Squeeze." She repeated the motion for Jenny's benefit.

Jenny took the teat in her hand, "Up-and-down fast. Squeeze." Winifred blew her milk-wad, squirting Jenny in the eyes and face. "Yipes!" she exclaimed. With the palm of her hand she wiped her face. "I didn't even breast-feed."

"Don't blame you. Two twin suckling's pulling, sagging teats to your knees." Elma cupped imaginary breasts in her hands and rolled them from knee to chest.

Jenny laughed at the antic. "Gravity's no friend to even a twenty-year-old. But, now I regret it."

Elma smiled a gold-toothed grin. "Don't believe in regretting. It kills living. Should I regret pulling my teeth and going for the gold? Won't bring 'em back, now will it?"

"No regrets after a twenty-three hour labor-torture screaming, 'epidermal'. Thank God for my Caesarian. Two eight-pound heads jamming-out would have killed me."

"Yep. And you lose your dignity with them doctor's staring up, and poking where the sun doesn't shine."

In the hot midday sun Jenny sweated like the pig she was feeding. It's snout kept kicking mush back at her, as if offering her a bite. She scooped the last bit of corn into the trough and eyed her chore list.

"Insanity" was the first word that crept into her head. Here she was in the middle of nowhere, getting ready for the next insult – shoveling cow manure. "How did I refuse Richie's offer to go to an expensive spa, a luxurious time-out. Was I crazy? He sure thought so." Ready to bolt, she tried to remember where she put her car keys. It couldn't be that far up the road.

As if Elma read her mind she appeared with two shovels. "Gung time, girly."

Jenny rolled her eyes. Reluctantly picking up a shovel she headed to the barn. "Now I'm a castaway in a pauper's den, shoveling shit. A definite time-out from civilized life, could this be a solitary chain gang?"

"Don't get your britches in a pretzel, until you've tried it." Elma was firm, yet lighthearted.

To Jenny's amazement the smell of fresh hay overpowered the manure. She shoveled the hard ones first, tossing them in steel bins. The mushier ones wedged on the shovel, so she kicked at them with Fetus's old workout boots. Sooty gunk-cakes stuck to her clothes, hands, and face.

The more she shoveled, a soothing rhythm, a sense of earthiness, permeated her spirit. In a short time she no longer resisted the task. It was as if the task was doing her. Like she was "One" with the shovel, with her movements, with life. As if time stopped, she was in the zone recalling an earlier time: A blur of changing diapers, the sweet aroma of baby powder, replaced dung odor. In an altered state of being she heard the chirp of birds, pheasants, doves, crows cawing. Aware and vibrantly alive, she was part of the magical force of nature.

The day was filled with continuous surprises. Cast in the hands of fate, Jenny was in the wonderland of self-discovery. Taking the shovel from her Elma offered, "Come and get yourself cooled-off."

Jenny beamed, "That was great shoveling."

"Tag along, got a lot of showing left", Elma said with a knowing twinkle in her eyes. In an instant she took off at a quick paced gait. Jenny barely could keep up with her. They headed across the property to a fast-flowing stream. Uninhibited and free, Elma stripped off her clothes and dove into the water. "Come on in, nothing like skinny-dipping."

A bit more modest Jenny kept her dirty work shirt on until the last second before she peeled it off, dousing herself in the cold water. "Whoa! What an ice cube."

"Freezing buns, eh?" Splashing and turning with the playful spirit of a dolphin, Elma was radiant.

Dog-paddling to stay afloat, Jenny asked, "Is this what you do for fun?"

"Naw. I usually count the rings around my neck, like an old oak." Elma burst into explosive laughter.

"Come on, your skin is flawless, hardly a wrinkle."

"I stitch, starch, and iron it." Elma continued to laugh.

"What's your secret? Dermabrasion, alpha-hydroxy, growth hormones?"

"I'm done growing. Outside, that is. The inside keeps me very busy. Look, it's simple. I don't use fancy creams. Don't give a hoot what people think. Not bothered by their blaming prattle, wagging gossiping tongues, pointing battering fingers, 'icking' at me. Pay no mind at all to their phony praise. I gave up pleasing."

Treading water, Jenny declared, "Wish I could say that."

Elma scanned the water and deftly reached her hands below the surface, snapping her wrists. Within seconds she wrangled a fish, flipping and flapping for its life. "Thank you, carp. You'll make a fine supper." She tossed the fish ashore.

Astonished, Jenny shook her head in disbelief at what she'd just witnessed. "Amazing, Elma."

"What's more amazing, I don't get jealous if my man's eye strays on another woman, or does whatever. Don't pay that any mind."

Jenny pondered. "Oh, so you just ignore losing him? No revenge, nothing, huh?"

"There is something. If you love him, show it." A glint of sunlight bounced her reflection on the water making her appear larger than life. It was like an apparition speaking the words, "Get us another fish."

Stunned by the vision and the request, Jenny stammered, "Me?"

Staring at her with the eyes of a sage, Elma suggested, "Isn't it time you picked one yourself?"

Without hesitation Jenny aimed to catch a fish. She slipped her hands underwater. "Oh, I feel something." She flailed, splashing headfirst into the water. Coming up gurgling, she sputtered, "Where'd it go?"

"You missed one. No worry. Always another one coming along."

"You sure?"

"Of course I'm sure! True about mostly anything. You end up getting what you need, usually not what you want. Now get yourself a fish."

Jenny focused on the water's depth. Elma instructed, "Be patient. Wait. That's another secret for the catch."

Feeling a tickling sensation, Jenny giggled, as school of minnows sailed through her legs. Caught up in their dizzying freedom dance she impulsively chased them, swimming deep into a world of scintillating color. Golden fish with large shimmering tails fluttered by her. Like a mermaid, feet slashing the water like a tail, she joined the school of fish swimming by her side. She transfixed on a small one with big rotund black eyes staring back at her.

As if to say, "Hello, glad to see you," the little fish swam closer, within reach. She grabbed it and quickly surfaced. Holding her prize it flapped between her fingers. "Got one!" she declared with pride.

"That one's too small. Give it back," Elam ordered.

"Oh, you're kidding?" For a moment Jenny's heart sank as she stared into the fish's pleading eyes.

"Little ones aren't for eating, they're for growing." Elma headed for shore. Jenny gently let the fish go. As it swam away she smiled, "Thank you for the fun, little guy. This is your lucky day."

The sun hid under a cloud. The open fire-pit exuded the sweet aroma of sizzling carp. Elma flipped the fish over. Jenny watched the fire, then observed nature's green-tufted fields, the simplicity, and natural beauty of the wilderness, feeling totally at home.

Elma chattered, "Getting fed. No worry. See, I'm not wrinkling at fifty-two."

"Fifty-two? I thought you were...ah?"

"Seventy-seven? Got cha'!" Amused at her own joke, Elma doubled-over, laughing.

"I used to laugh a lot," Jenny said with regret. "Making people crack-up was my daily dream. Sadly, I traded my pranks and giggles for a cackle at about thirteen...when my dad left us."

"For another woman, heh?"

Reflecting on her own setback, Jenny sighed. "Isn't it always?"

"Not for Elma. I've left a few and I buried a few." Hidden under her haughtiness the years of heartbreak fermented.

Jenny glared at the dark clouds hovering over the valley. Elma sniffed the air, "the Thunder beings are coming. We're in for heaven's bath. Its going rain a big one." They packed up the left-over fish and headed back to the farm.

That night a heavy storm blew out the electricity in the middle of a Lucy rerun. Festus moaned, "We're going to miss our Lucy...need my laughs. Can't get me a good night's sleep without her." Turning to Elma, he said, "Get that gal up on the pole and fix it right soon."

It was pitch dark. Elma lit a candle. Puffing on a corncob pipe, something Jenny had never seen in real life, Elma blew smoke rings in Jenny's face.

Putting her hand over her mouth Jenny coughed back in Elma's face. "Have some mercy, second-hand smoke is lethal."

"Stop harping, get on them work boots. We're going up!", Elma announced. Slipping on slickers and boots, they headed outside.

Festus yelled words of encouragement from the porch. "Don't get yourself fried on one of them hotwires."

Jenny was appalled as they headed into the storm. "What kind of man let's women go into harm's way?"

"And what kind of women do it, anyway?" Elma laughed like it was the funniest thing she ever said. "Poor Festus can't do no climbing with that metal in his hip. But, don't tell him I told ya."

Elma led the way up the electrical pole, climbing as fast as a goat. Jenny slowly slogged on each metal rung, blinded by the dizzying rain.

"Come on slowpoke, I need you to flip the switch," Elma screeched from the top, opening the electrical box, holding it steady with both hands. Lightning splintered across the sky, rattling the wooden pole.

Jenny finally reached the top and looked in the box. "Hanging wires are mind-boggling dangerous. Elma, do you know what these are for?"

"Yep, I know not to touch 'em. See this switch? Push hard. Now push." Together they pushed with all their strength, but nothing moved. Elma started to laugh, louder and louder. Jenny could barely hold on. "Elma, please!"

"Imagine no laughing with Lucy ever again, now push." They gave it all they had. The switch ignited. "Get going before we get hit by one of them lightning bolts," Elma shouted above the whirling wind and grumbling thunder.

Jenny went down the pole faster than a goat. Elma followed. At the bottom the unthinkable blasted: A bolt of lightening struck Jenny in her back, knocking her to the ground. She writhed for a second and scooted across the soggy grass like a jet-propelled car. She stopped, sitting erect. Shaking her head she declared, "What a blast!"

Elma was at her side in an instant. As light from another bolt of lightning lit the sky, she gazed deeply into Jenny's eyes. Satisfied that Jenny wasn't hurt, she said, "Well, you're alive and saved, girl." Helping her to her feet, she continued, "Your whole body was just redone in a split second. Dead, gone, renewed. Whatever you didn't need is gone."

Jenny staggered, leaning on Elma's arm as she touched the back of her coat that was singed from the hit. "I feel a little dizzy, but I'm okay," she assured Elma as they headed to the house.

Elma tucked her in bed, gave her warm soup. "They say once you're struck you can feel and see what other's are blind to. Healing and psycho-psychic stuff - new personalities. Oh, no mind, you're just a city-girl ready for a change." Jenny was asleep before Elma finished her prophetic words.

The next day Elma gathered chicken eggs. As Jenny came near a hen squawked loudly, winging its feathers. Elma observed, "Mama-hen's like you. Protects chicks from rain. Difference is, hers aren't grown yet." The baby chicks toddled behind one of the Mama-hen's.

"Mine aren't ready to make it in the world," Jenny winched. "Anyway, I'm not ready to give them up. "They still need me."

"Rubbish. Controlling keeps fun away. Can't make 'em do nothing they don't want to, anyway. So why bother?"

"I tried, created miracles to spare them of life's rotten pain." In quiet desperation, Jenny clenched her fist.

With uncanny understanding, Elma was gentle. "Doing for them what a hurt thirteen-year-old couldn't do for herself."

Jenny's face softened, recognizing the truth of Elma's words.

Elma grabbed at a chicken. It slipped her grasp. In a madcap chase she pursued it across the yard as it flapped its wings, squawking. Chicks ran in circles, crisscrossing the yard. Finally she nabbed her prey, pulled a knife from her boot, and with one WHACK, sliced its head off. Flinging the head to the ground, the body ran headless across the yard. Running out of steam, it fell to the ground, dead. Elma handed the torso to Jenny. "You go inside, feather it, drop it in a pot and we'll have us a good supper."

Jenny's mouth hung open at the grisly sight. "Wasn't that Ellie, or Minnie? How could you?"

Bristling at the mere mention Elma barked back. "Like you never got a store-bought bird. Or never ate an egg...a poor little chickie that was never born. Don't play-act me, girly."

Inside the kitchen Jenny cleaned the bird, sneezing at feathers that were flying up her nose. "Smelly old bird," she sniffed.

"Ah, now you don't like Ellie or is it Minnie?" Elma teased. "That's how short your life is, girl." She took the bird from Jenny and popped it in the boiling pot. Looking over her shoulder Elma said, "Time to move on, bumpkin. Get yourself a new identity. That's what I did every time I got divorced."

"Really?"

Elma was convincing. "Identity theft's catching on. It's all over the news. The latest craze."

Jenny balked. "I wouldn't risk it. Isn't it a felony?"

Truly in her element Elma recited. "In the words of Dickey Pillhouse Nixon: 'You ain't a criminal, until you get caught,' Elma chuckled. " Danger makes you feel alive."

While the bird was boiling, they sneaked down a wooden hatch into a hidden room in the cellar. The two women began to play, giggling like two kids in a candy shop. The room was filled with an array of clothes, wigs, and hats. Elma helped Jenny concoct a would-be identity makeover.

Jenny donned a white-haired wig and granny-spectacles. Looking at herself in a floor-length mirror, she considered what Elma had said about danger. "Me? Live dangerously? I'm your basic cookie-cutter, desperate housewife."

Elma snickered, and whipped her hips into a mean bump and grind. "Variety and adventure is what life's all about."

Not amused Jenny took off the wig. "Not for me. Being an Army brat, traveling like a nomad, changing schools thirteen times…I was sick of making and losing friends. I longed for the 'same old, same old'. Even Ground-hog Day sounded good to me."

Refusing to be stymied by Jenny's stuck-ness, Elma pumped her with enthusiasm. "It's time you popped your head out of the hole. Time to drop the old traveling baggage. You're not that Army gal anymore. Have a ball. Let your hair down…while you still have some."

Filled with mixed emotions, Jenny squinted, "What does Festus think about all this?"

"Festus doesn't know anything. To him I'm clodhopper Elma." Lowering her voice to a raspy twang, "Before that I was 'Rachel', a honky-tonk hairdresser." Elma affected a bawdy-toned voice. "Then there was 'Clara', a mean-ass bootlegger's wife." Plopping an Afro wig on Jenny, she crinkled her face with her hands, scrunching each cheek, forcing Jenny to look in the mirror. Elma cracked herself up. " 'Dem's seen betta days. You look like a dead squirrel."

Jenny tried on a reddish wig. Bobbing her head back and forth, she assessed this new look. "Not bad."

Elma encouraged her. "Now try a sweet little redhead drawl."

Her nose twitched at the thought, Jenny balked. "Oh, I can't."

"Yes you can. With a little practice, bingo – you're another person. You fib a little. Put on the jokesters. Rip it up. Have fun doing whatever it takes. You can play the part."

Jenny considered, fluffed her fingers through the red hair, affecting a slow drawl. "Howdy, Elma. I'm just sooo delighted to make your acquaintance." The identity change was no longer just play. Jenny was excited, almost enrolled. "This could really work," she marveled. "The kids are gone. Richie's gone. A little variety might actually be fun." Adjusting the wig, trying different expressions, she considered, "At least for a week or two."

"There ain't no time limit. Only what you make it."

Jenny fast-paced a series of wardrobe changes: a tailored business suit, an airline hostess, frolicked in chef's garb, created a very nerdy-geek look with clunker shoes. Displaying a 'holier than thou' bit, she posed as a proper school-marm.

Elma imitated a British accent. "Crumpets, please."

Jenny answered with a Cockney flair, "Never touch the lardy buggers, me-self."

A man's voice with a proper English accent interrupted their soiree, "That would be my choice, my lady." Festus, the prankster, peeked his head from behind the door. "Howdy gals." Fixing his eyes on Jenny, "Now isn't Ms. Prissy here looking fine."

Jenny blushed, "I'm trying on a new persona."

"You mean a new ID. Now that includes a driver's license, birth certificate, career opportunity, the whole caboodle."

Pacing back and forth Jenny was deciding, reeling in the possibility of setting herself free, letting go. She burst forth with, "A new ID it is. Farewell to the tied-up, uptight, unappreciated Jenny Forrest."

"Smart move," Elma agreed, then changed her jovial tone. The businesswoman surfaced. "Well, Jenny dear, time to square the score."

Gulping, Jenny asked, "Meaning what?"

Festus added, "Time to negotiate for your new ID change. Is that your messed-up Mercedes out in that ditch?"

Thrown off-guard Jenny muttered, "It must be."

"Well, I was thinking how you could repay the kindness of strangers."

"Yes. I want to do that." Her eyes lit up, becoming overwhelmed to hear more.

Elma held up a photo of a sassy 1956 pink Cadillac convertible. Festus, like a 'pot and pan' salesman, made his pitch. "A prototype classic. Retooled and totally refurbished from the chrome bumpers to the rolled leather seats. It's a beauty."

Elma hammered, going for the close. "Only one-thousand of them made. A priceless retro-trade, wouldn't you think?"

Jenny smiled. "Wow! Didn't Elvis have a classic Cadillac?"

Festus wittingly assured her, "One and the same."

"Sounds like an amazing investment." Jenny paced, twirling her hair, imagining, considering, thinking of the retro car's potential value and prestige of ownership.

Laying it on thick Elma pleaded with Festus. "Come on, Festus, trade it for that wreck of a Mercedes. She deserves it."

He hemmed and hawed, grunted and grumbled. "Well...I guess...if she really wants it?"

"Oh, I do!" Jenny exclaimed. "I'll take perfect care of it, I promise." She searched in her bag and, to her surprise, discovered the previously missing keys. Gratefully, she tossed them to Festus.

A glint of joy crossed Elma's face. "Our pleasure. Probably the first time we gave a sucker an equitable deal."

Festus jounced a little skip. "You got that right."

Elma informed Jenny, "Now, I'll clue you in on the protocol. You're getting the chance to start a new life. Your new ID has no money stealing attached or false credit cards. Our clients do honest day's work. We see to that, help get you started, and get you up on your feet."

Both relieved and excited by the possibilities Jenny uttered, "Great. I need all the help I can get."

Festus answered, "Understood." With one hand on top of each other, they made a three-way handshake.

Outside the barn a spontaneous celebratory hoedown was in progress. Country music blasted from a radio. Rodeo gal Elma spun a lasso, jumped through the loop. Festus stomped his foot to the beat, clapping and hollering. Jenny klutzy-scuffled, grinning, "It's my turn to live an adventure."

Elma and Jenny twirled arm-in-arm. "Round and round they go," Festus joined in. "Swing your partner and dos-à-dos." They romped, kicked-up their heels, and did a little jig.

The next morning Festus and Elma admired Jenny's beguiling transformation. Decked-out in a retro 1950's look, she sported pointed sunglasses, red hair, and pedal pushers. Festus wolf-whistled. "Boy, what a dame. You'll find yourself a new beau, for sure."

"Better stay in touch," Elma said as she handed Jenny a piece of paper. "Follow this. It'll show you your way." The threesome squeezed a hug.

"How can I ever thank you?" Jenny asked, as tears welled up in her eyes.

Festus eyed the Mercedes SUV in the driveway. "You already have."

"Remember, if you're ever in a pinch just repeat old Elma's saying," Elma clapped her hands three times directly in Jenny's eyes, " 'One day at a time! No muss. No fuss. No cuss.' "

Jenny eyes widened, and in a sotto voce hypnotic tone, repeated. "One day at a time! No muss. No fuss. No cuss."

Festus broke the trance-like moment. "Time to be off with you, gal."

Bright-faced and glowing, Jenny climbed into the refurbished '56 pink Caddy convertible. The license plate read LUCY. Settling into the soft leather seat, she smiled at Festus and Elma. "Meeting you two character's on your territory turned out be a hoot and a life-altering uprooting." She started the engine, put her hands on the large pearl steering wheel and drove off the property, backfiring and chugging down the road.

Tooling along the highway with the Caddy's convertible top down, her hair blowing wild in the wind, a quirky, revitalized Jenny captured her new life. Rocking out, she sang a medley of songs that ranged from "Pink Cadillac" to "Bobby McGee." Blissfully immersed she belted, "Freedom's just another word for nothing left to lose..."

The Caddy pulled into a parking space in front of Stanford's Administration Building. Jenny got out of the car and viewed her reflection in the car window and adjusted her wig. Not recognizing this new person staring back at her, doubts began to spin in her head. How did she fall for this crazy scheme? Here she was at Stanford in a disguise getting ready to interview for a bogus job. Her only recommendation was an old lady with a past life that existed in a cellar of costumes.

What was she thinking? The charade of the last two days seemed surreal. Grumbling at herself, she thought out loud, "The whole plan's ridiculous. What am I, nuts?"

Whipped and discouraged, she climbed back into the car. Fiddling with the big round pearled steering wheel, a feeling of hope fluttered in her belly. Then she recalled sitting alone, desperate, staring at the

SUV's steering wheel. "I felt like a dowager racing to PTA meetings, soccer games, client dinners, grocery shopping," she stammered to herself. In frustration she banged her hand on the dashboard, then clutched it with all her strength. "That does it! Never! Ever! I vow right here for the rest of my life, I'll never go into that suburbanite grocery store again."

Maybe Elma was right. An identity change brings 'newness' to life. The thought was invigorating. The moment of doubt had vanished. Armed with a newfound courage she sauntered toward the Administration Building steps.

Once inside, her nerves took hold. Trying to remember her new M.O. she rehearsed the lingo in the stairwell. "Hi. I'm Lucy Ball. No, I'm Lucy Hall...I mean, Hallbally! How the heck did Elma come up with Lucy Hallbally?" Incomprehensible, the ID matched a driver's license, social security number, and the works.

Several moments later she was a job-hunter inside Human Resources. A first interview in twenty years. The only significant employment on her résumé was selling shoes at Baker's right before she got pregnant. She commanded her chattering mind to quiet down. "Shut up. We've got business to take care of."

Other applicants in the waiting room breezed through the obligatory personality career test. Jenny reviewed the application, began to fill it out with a pen, painstakingly pondering over every question. Time passed. She sat alone. All the other applicants were gone.

Jenny read the query list out loud. "If you were the only person left on earth how would you spend your day: 1. Making friends with the animals. 2. Gathering food. 3. Hiding in the forest." She tapped the pen on her cheek. "Can't keep picking 'hiding in the forest'. Maybe I should pick making friends?"

Feeling defeated she lowered her head. "I just can't do it." How could she perform miracles for everyone else? Stuck in a "Can't do" headspace, suddenly Samantha's difficulty performing simple tasks made sense. Stricken with fear, Jenny felt like a failed 'Superwoman-Mom' unable to answer a question geared for pre-schooler's. Dejected, she crumpled the application into a ball and tossed it in the trash. A woman's voice caught her attention. "Ms. Hallbally, you're next."

"Hello! I'm still here." Jenny responded. In a last ditch effort she retrieved the application, smoothed it out. Faking her best pasted-on smile she entered the room. Ms. Missy, the upbeat no-mess-around Human Resources Director stated, "You're here on a favor-owed." Jenny sat across from her, observing the stark desk with only a pad and a gold pen on it. "I'm a friend of Clara's...I mean, actually an acquaintance of Elma and Festus. They told me you could help me find a life...I mean a job," Jenny sputtered.

Ms. Missy quickly scanned the application. She kicked-back in her chair and took a moment to size Jenny up. "Let's cut the formality. Elma sent you – that is all I have to know. Is your new ID actually 'Hallbally'?"

Jenny cleared her throat. "Ahh, that's me. Hallbally. Lucy Hallbally."

"What did Elma charge you for the get-up?"

Indignant, Jenny quipped, "No payment changed hands."

Ms. Missy corrected her. "You mean cash. They scored merchandise."

Jenny rejected the implication. "My Mercedes? However, I got a retro, a one-of-a-kind classic. A perfectly equitable trade."

"You know Elma is eighty-seven, right?"

Jenny laughed, flashing seven fingers twice, "Seventy-seven."

Ms. Missy retorted, "Let's get down to raw business etiquette – the protocol. First rule. Know what we don't know. Elma's one of the toughest, meanest bootleggers ever to cross the Mississippi line. She'd kill for a gold tooth. So, if she sent you, you're gold, girl."

Not wanting to upset her, Jenny feigned naiveté. "I am?"

Ms. Missy tapped the application with her pen. "A felonious personality. Great criminal mind. Sneaky. Lie when you have to. Will compromise your dignity. Demean your self worth for the cause. Let me guess…ex 'Super-Mom'!"

Amazed, Jenny quivered. "It still shows?"

"They'll come after you. They always do."

"Who?" Nervously flinching, Jenny learned back in the chair.

"Family. Did you leave with the money?"

"Of course not. I have credit cards."

Scrutinizing her, Ms. Missy said, "Traceable. Our specially rigged ATM can handle it. Gobbles the records, chews the paper trail. Remember the cardinal rule for laying low is to join the team that's looking for you."

"Very clever, inventive, resourceful." Jenny turned on the charm.

Ms. Missy leaned in closer to Jenny and focused on her with a concentrated gaze. "Natural charmer, eh? The best job we can offer is Campus Security."

"You mean like a cop, or a peace officer?"

"Not exactly. More storm troopers. Like an interceptor. Spying on students, busting shenanigans, enforcing infractions. To be frank, we're short on staff, so it's a perfect fit."

Jenny leaned forward. "You just said 'perfect fit'?"

"Yes, I did."

This was the sign she'd been waiting for. "It is so perfect. Spying on my...on kids...is my life. They need me. Actually, I need them."

Ms. Missy nodded, "I'm sure you do. By the way, dorm housing is included as a perk." Reaching in a desk drawer she pulled out a work contract. "Review this and sign it." Jenny quickly scanned the document, focusing on the moral code. She put her hand over her mouth to keep from laughing out loud, 'No' fraternizing with the students (or faculty)'.

Showing concern Ms. Missy asked, "Have a problem Hallbally?"

"Oh no, I agree with all of it, especially the moral code." Without further ado, she signed "Lucy Hallbally" on the dotted line. They shook hands and Jenny was on her way.

The pink Caddy cruised by the People's Bank. Not wanting to be seen, Jenny scoped the area, then parked down the street. Carrying a satchel tucked close by her side she nonchalantly strolled to the ATM machine. Glancing behind her one more time, secure no one was looking, she entered her PIN number.

The wait seemed to take forever. A cranking 'Grrrr' sound sprang from the machine. It began spitting out a stream of one-hundred dollar bills. Jenny beamed as the cash poured into the open satchel. Hurriedly, she shuffled the last of the bills inside, closed it, and snapped the lock. In the blink of an eye she raced to the Caddy. Making doubly sure no one was watching, she did a 360-degree scan of her surroundings, and then lifted the trunk, hiding the satchel under a pile of clothes.

A smile of relief crossed her face. She pulled out a list she had concocted with Elma. She checked off number two: "Go to bank." Reviewing her achievements she glanced at number one: "Interview at Stanford." Grinning, she mused, "That was a piece of cake." On to number three: "Get a place to live." Since her new job came with housing, she beamed, "Well done." She liked the positively creeping back into her consciousness, along with the lightness of being.

That evening Jenny entered the Stanford dorm. Strange the lights weren't on, it was dark and dank. This time she decided not to flick on the light. The apparently inconsistent rules were to be followed, at least for now. She lugged her heavy suitcase up a flight of stairs. Stopping to catch a breath she realized she was on Samantha's floor. Peeking from the stairwell she glanced toward Samantha's room.

An adrenaline rush jolted her. "My God, I've been assigned to this dorm as a security guard to troll my daughter's turf. What is wrong with this picture? I got a new identity with the intent of getting a life of my own. Here I am spying, doing the same thing I've always done to my kid."

Elma's last words to her rang in her ear. "One day at a time. No muss. No fuss. No cuss!"

"Yes!" Jenny comprehended the meaning. "One baby step at a time. No complaining or blaming, until I get my own life up and running." She raised her confidence level even more. "This is just a way station, not permanent digs. And, this disguise is way too good for Samantha to ever catch on." Or so she hoped.

She trudged up one more flight of steps. There it was – room 413. Turning the key, gratefully muttering, "A divine plan. Right above my darling Samantha," she entered the stark room. The moonlight twinkled into the room from an open window. It illuminated one bunk bed, a couple of chairs, and two chests of drawers. Jenny was perplexed. What floor plan was this? Only one bunk bed? Someone who was occupying the bottom bunk was snoring and grunting.

Jenny quietly slid into Elma's couch potato robe. Attempting to climb the ladder to the top bed, she bumped the sleeping stranger. Without missing a snore an arm whipped out with a karate chop, clobbering Jenny in the eye. She flipped backward, crashing to the floor.

Rubbing her aching back from the fall, she balked, "Ugh! You could have killed me. It was just a little bump. A mistake!"

As if nothing had happened the slugger remained shut-eyed, snorting, clucking guttural "ufff's."

Half-dazed, Jenny unzipped the robe, wiggling out of it. Cautiously climbing the ladder, she arm-pumped onto the bed and crawled under the covers. Hard metal mattress spring bumps kneaded her body like thorns. This was not a fun massage. She moved sideways, flipped on her back, tried rolling onto her stomach. "Oh, what pain," she murmured as sharp springs jabbed her skin, pinching worn bones. Clutching a hand over her mouth, biting a thumb to squelch a scream, she could only utter an "Eeiii!"

From downstairs a familiar metal guitar riff blasted through the floor. The shockwave decibel mixed with the retching bass-level snore of her bunkmate, twanged her sanity. Squeezing hands over deafened ears, her eyes bulged, fixing on the paint-chipped ceiling. Contemplating her predicament, sharing a seven square-foot room (smaller than her closet at home) with a barbarian, Jenny wondered, "Where is all of this leading to? Why am I here? What am I doing? What's the upside? Is it downhill all the way?" Not a single answer came, only questionable doubts. "Why won't the demons let me sleep?" As a last resort she begged under her breath, "Little sheep come to me. One sheep, two sheep, three", she continued counting, at 1,005, Jenny was asleep.

The moon's soft glow peeked through the dorm window. Still on the top bunk, fast asleep Jenny was snoring. Aggie Lane, pug-nosed and freckled, a former female wrestler turned hard-core security-lifer, was up and ready to go. A "No excuses, no mess-around attitude" proceeded her. Aggie busily spit-shined her combat boots, in a rhythm that matched Jenny's snore. When she was finished, she stood up and shouted unmercifully in Jenny's ear. "Rise and shine, Hallbally!"

Jenny thought she was dreaming, hearing her dad commanding a wake-up call, "Get the hell up, Jennikens!" She half-opened a bruised eye, groggily glaring at the large woman's stern expression. Touching her aching face Jenny flinched. "Ouch! Are you talking to me?"

"Don't see anyone else here. You look nasty. Someone's hung over. Cut the gab. Get dressed."

This dame meant business. Jenny tottered off the ladder, quietly slipping into the bathroom. Dousing her reddened, soon to turn black-and-blue face with cold water, she gently patted it with an industrial scratchy white towel. A uniform was laid out for her on a shelf. "That's weird," she thought as she brushed her teeth.

Aggie warned, "No time for primping, Ms. Suburbanite. Security Boot-camp's at 0500. Get your fatigues on, pronto! "

Unsure how to handle her, Jenny peeked out of the bathroom door, saluting, "Heil! Commando, whoever you are."

"Sergeant Aggie to you, Hallbally." Without resistance Jenny dressed silently, repeating her mantra, "One day at a time. No muss. No fuss. No cuss."

A sign read "Campus Security Boot Camp." Reputed as a heavy-duty out-of-bounds training center, some of the participants' attended in lieu of a jail sentence, others as candidates for a permanent security squad position, or to compete as part-time recruits. Jenny appeared diminutive compared to most of the husky muscular ladies in formation. Aggie was flanked by Helga, the head security maven.

Helga drilled the Campus Security Boot Camp code. "Cadets, listen up. Why are we here?"

Reading from a list, the group repeated in unison, "To preserve the bodies and the minds of our teaching staff."

Helga blasted, "Who rules the campus war zone?"

"We rule."

"How do we dominate?"

"We patrol, catch, and penalize the enemy."

Helga spun her student riot-act tactics. "Student punks disrespect, fornicate, litter, and destroy our campus. We will defrock the spoiled-brat vermin that molest our territory with graffiti trash."

She kicked into a goose-step. "We shall prevail."

The cadets marched behind her, bellowing, "We shall prevail."

Helga commanded, "Louder!"

"<u>We shall prevail</u>!"

Workouts at local gyms boast aerobic classes, spinning and sweating on a treadmill to get into shape. Such techniques for a hard and toned body are a total delusion at a serious training camp. Not at all in tip-top combat shape, Jenny's aching bones and muscles proved it as they screamed for mercy while trying to keep pace.

Grunting and puffing, lagging behind the cadet's on the running track, Jenny's feet were as swollen as they'd been when she was pregnant. While jumping rope she tripped, becoming tangled in the synthetic material, nearly strangling to death. Doing push-ups she flopped face down from exhaustion. In the middle of a bungee jump a mild apoplectic shock overtook her. Hanging and swinging in mid-air she wailed, "Get me down!" In a relay, scaling a wall, Jenny inched up three feet and slid down two. Tugging up again, gaining a few feet, she ended up reeling downward at wildcat speed, landing smack on her fanny. Dizzy, visions of little tweety-birds spun overhead. Jenny threw her hands into the air declaring, "Kaput! All done! Time to go to beddie-bye."

Aggie on her watch, demanded. "Shake it out, Hallbally. Get off your ass. Climb!"

Shaking her head, feet, butt, Jenny returned to the wall, glaring at Aggie. "Can't you see I'm climbing more feet than anyone!" Pulling up six feet, she slid down five feet... "Just 'cause I can't reach the top."

"Button the excuse lip. Climb it," Aggie growled.

Mustering all her strength Jenny struggled, slipped, balanced, clenched her teeth, and in hair-splitting, fingernail-scratching finality, reached the top. With arms overhead waving victory, she waited for acknowledgment. "No cheers?" she asked. No one noticed, or cared. "Nope, guess not."

Jenny held strong to the rope as her partner ascended the wall. Very agile, the young girl was scaling upside like a monkey. Jenny faltered, her grip weakened. She pulled harder. "Trust me. I got it," were her last words before letting go. The cadet plummeted, echoing "Moron!" on the tumbling plunge.

Nearing dehydration Jenny slipped away from the crowd to rest on a rock. Pouring cool refreshing water on her face, she chugged from a canteen. "Ohhh, water shortage...then death follows."

Helga watched Jenny for a moment, letting her have one long gulp before grabbing the canteen. Taking a long swig, swishing the water around in her mouth, Helga spit it out. "No sissy-breaks in the field. We persevere through draughts, floods and panty raids."

The next challenge was sloshing about in mud. Jenny and Jan, a twenty-year-old twelve-pack-ab's opponent, slithered together in a mud-wrestling contest. Bumping butts and slinging mud at each other, the cadet flew in the air, charging at, and squishing Jenny facedown in the slush. "Gotcha," Jan chortled. Mud-faced Jenny gawked at her oppressor. "Mouth the mud, missy," Jan taunted. In a fast move Jenny retaliated, returning the mud-hold charge. Slipping and sliding, they nose-dived into the muck. Jenny popped-up with a cakey mud grin, "What a ball!" Jenny proclaimed, actually enjoying the bout.

Jan winked a mud-filled eyelash, " Wish I had a mom like you."

Overhearing the remark Helga stepped over to Jenny. "That was good faking. You have a young attitude and energy. But youth is owned by youth." Patting Jenny on the back, Helga smiled. "Moldy-oldies have to think faster, reserve and conserve."

The two-day boot camp was winding down. The last phase of training included mastering the use of surveillance technology devices. Teams assimilated a school riot, a political rally, and a panty raid. Each team utilized night goggles, listening devices, hidden cameras, and deterrent sprays to defuse the rioters.

Each cadet got his or her chance to riot or feign security. Jenny excelled at rioting, rebelling, and yelling, releasing years of pent-up angst. Retaliating with outrageous threats and behavior, sticking out her tongue and shouting profanities, she finally screamed, "SCREW YOU!" Her fellow cadets tied her up and tied her down.

Before sundown, the grand finale, filled with pomp and circumstance, arrived. It was graduation time. The cadets, dressed in crisp security uniforms, saluted their master, Helga. "You gut-starved babes cleaned-up nice. Serve and wear your Security Badge with pride. You are programmed to dominate, regurgitate and annihilate." Helga walked the line, awarding each deserving cadet a Security Badge. Jenny beamed as Helga pinned the coveted prize on her uniform. Gathered together they sang the Cadet Anthem: "We are the campus security. Here to preserve a coed's virginity."

Jenny loved the slogan. Now more than ever committed to her duty, she whispered to Jan, "Maybe I found my new life's calling."

Jan answered in a smart-ass manner, "And maybe you didn't, wuss-face."

In a surprise reaction, Jenny smiled. "Why fight it, wunderkind? I'm on an adventure and there are no guarantees."

That night, feeling exhilarated by the boot-camp experience, high on top of the bunk bed Jenny studied the Campus Security manual. 'Hipster slang'? Are they serious?"

Aggie croaked from the lower bunk, "In your case I'd add 'desperately need.' "

Jenny read aloud. " 'A no good creep' – synonymous with 'Slime back wonker', 'Dong-creeper', 'Shot wanger'."

Aggie, worn and tired, griped, "Give me a break and read to yourself. My head hurts."

Jenny closed the book asking, "Are these terms what the kids use or what we say?"

"Get a few oxy-moronic comebacks down, so they don't suck your brains."

" 'Suck your brains.' That's a good one Aggie," Jenny chirped.

Noting that snoring sounds were now emanating from the lower bunk, Jenny set the book aside, pulled the starched cotton top sheet and scratchy wool blanket over her and fell asleep, images of little dancing cadets wafting through her head. A few hours later, however, nightmarish dream images of little dancing Samantha's in sexy underwear brought Jenny back to waking reality. She scrambled down the ladder, hoping not to wake Aggie-the-Terrible. Another punch and Jenny would be in a hospital ICU.

Practice makes perfect. It was a peculiar sight. Over the edge of her balcony Jenny hung upside down in space-boots. At eye level with Samantha's window she had a clear view inside the dorm room. Samantha sat in bed, her back propped with pillows, gobbling a bag of pretzels.

Jenny muttered, "Ummm...better than chips."

Tanya zipped on a windbreaker. "Sam, I won't be too long. Whatever you do, don't call my cell."

"Why not? Have a hot date?"

"I'm turning it off...can't take a chance it might ring."

"That is hot."

Jenny watched Tanya leave. "It's way past midnight. She's a curfew buster." Flipping her heels over the railing and pulling the weight of her body upward, she landed back on the balcony, lifted out of the space-boots, and headed into her room. Once inside, she slipped on her sneakers and a camouflage jacket and tiptoed out the door.

Chasing after Tanya, she spotted the lone figure heading toward the Science Building. Cloaked in the shadows Jenny watched Tanya jimmy-jam a window. Elbows on the sill, Tanya lifted and managed to crawl inside. Jenny waited a moment then approached the window.

Attempting the elbow lift, she slid downward. "Damn! Not enough strength." Trying to hoist herself up again, she struck a heel on the window, causing it to rattle. As she once again slid to the ground, she uttered to herself, "Damn these Pygmy legs!" Just as she began to stand up, someone grabbed her in a chokehold from behind. "Ohmigod, don't hurt me," she rasped.

The voice demanded, "Last resort. Use the master key." The hand released her. It was Aggie.

"Did you have to creep up like that? I thought you were asleep."

"Gotta work. Creeping up, by the way, is just procedure. You're on your own."

Up for the task Jenny's eyes gleamed like a battling warship. "I'll get the vermin-sloat." Sneaking to the front of the building Jenny unlocked the door, and quietly moved cat-like into the large hallway. Small amber night-lights were positioned every few feet, flickering a golden glow along the corridor. She aimed a flashlight, ambling down the hallway, quickly opening closed doors, toe first, nose next, peeking inside each room. Ghost-like indistinguishable shadows darted, scaring her wits.

The old wooden floorboards creaked, echoing danger in the air, possibly a warning to her prey. Jenny stopped by a doorway to listen. Behind a slightly ajar door, the sound of ruffling paper alerted her. Gently pushing the door open, it squeaked like a frightened mouse.

Tanya searched in a file cabinet for a test. She retrieved a paper. Satisfied that she had the right one she turned directly into the flashlight's glare, blinded. Jenny seized the moment and grabbed the evidence. "Caught in the act. Stealing a test? Big time infraction! Expulsion looms."

"Prove it." Tanya tried to get away.

Jenny put a foot out, tripped her. "Make me."

Tanya looked up, pleading. "You mean like 'On the make. Make me'?"

Jenny looked intent, "Are you dealing tests or drugs?"

"Get real."

"You get real!"

"Well then, I'll get real." Tanya looked down at the floor, avoiding Jenny's eyes. " It's the only way I can ever pass. I'm too stupid to do it on my own."

The familiar words pierced a soft spot in Jenny's heart. "On your own...that's not always necessary. I happen to be a topnotch tutor."

"Really?" With relief, Tanya looked directly at Jenny.

"Well, I was. Maybe we can work out an exchange." Jenny raised her eyebrows and smiled.

Tanya, always focused on sex, assumed it was a sexual proposition. "That's not my style...don't think so."

"How about I help you study and you give me a tip now and then?"

"Tip? I never heard it called that before."

Clueless that Tanya assumed she was gay, Jenny responded, "How about 'snitch'?"

"You mean 'snatch'?"

"I mean 'tattle-tale'."

"Oh, now I get it. No. <u>That</u> I can't do!" Tanya was adamant.

"Let's call it...a friendly informant? Reporting upcoming shenanigans around campus. It'll be top-secret'."

"Top-secret?" Tanya's eyes lit up.

"Just between you and me." Jenny winked.

"That sounds way cool."

Jenny slipped the test back into the file cabinet. Smiling conspiratorially, they tiptoed discreetly out of the building.

Alone in her room, Samantha paced back and forth. This total freedom business wasn't exactly what she had hoped for. She recalled her father saying, "Wherever you go, there you are." Suddenly it made sense. Here she was at Stanford. Every inadequacy magnified within. "I'm still an outcast! No social life! Still a nerdy two-shoes." Now she was supposed to be a young woman. Now she should be able to make a decision on her own.

And where the heck was her mother? Even she wasn't calling. "Mom!" she wailed, "Why aren't you driving me bananas?" Hadn't she promised she would always be there anytime of day or night? "So, what if it's one in the morning?" Samantha picked up her cell phone and touched the speed-dial button.

The machine answered. "Forrest residence. You got me."

"Okay, Mom. Pick up. Come on. I'm scared...I won't make it into Kappa Kappa." Stopping herself from continuing, she hung up. "I'm not dissing myself on a recording. Who knows who'll hear it?" Samantha was quiet for a moment and then began to pace again. Unable to bare the tension, she punched the redial button. "Okay, you win, Mom. Now I know what it feels like. Please pick up." Samantha felt desperate for her mother's input. She'd be nutso-anxiety, if she had the slightest inkling- how close her Mother actually was.

The next day, several Kappa Kappa sorority sisters gathered around the recreation room at their sorority house. Tanya, preoccupied, filed a chipped nail, barely listening.

Taking an oath Samantha raised her hand. "I, Samantha Forrest, a hopeful Kappa Kappa initiate, will do all the hazing put before me. Including losing my virginity."

Tanya raised her hand. "I am Tanya Rice, a hopeful Kappa Kappa initiate. I will do all the hazing put before me...and never shall I get my virginity back."

Everyone chuckled. "To the cherry-picking-poppers!"

Sorority organizer Big Sue, a spirited thunder-thigh, formally welcomed them. Holding a pistol high in the air she aimed it at Samantha, threatening, "You are first on our list."

Samantha backed away, terrified. "What list? I don't want to be some sorority nerd statistic."

Everyone applauded. "Great original answer."

Big Sue laughed. "Just kidding. Thank you, potential newbie's. Now for the fun! May the Kappa Kappa initiation games begin!" She fired the pistol. A Kappa Kappa flag popped out, and the series of misadventures were launched.

Samantha sprayed graffiti on the Administration Building wall, then scribbled, "Take a hike. Take a peek. Who'll be in my panties this week?" She mooned a carload of kids, shaking her butt.

Abandoning her duties, Jenny hid in the bushes, envying the folly of youth and secretly egging Samantha on. "Go girl. Go!"

In a relay race Tanya and Samantha tag-teamed as they let air out of car tires, jumped hurdles and ate raw fish. Downing a boilermaker, chugging a beer and finally tipping a shot of tequila, Samantha trickled the last drop, gulping the notorious tequila worm. "Yucko," she cringed.

Big Sue cheered, "The chick who gets the worm is guaranteed to get the nookie!"

Jenny leaped up-and-down in the bushes. "We did it!" Samantha glanced in her direction, a puzzled look on her face. Realizing that she had almost blown her cover, Jenny quickly slipped away from sight.

Booze-tipsy Samantha slurred, "Fungus-monster. Mommy and me...that WE voice rattling my skull."

On the way back to the dorm Tanya listened to Samantha obsessing over her mother. "It's been way too long without a phone call. I'm worried...not really worried...more rejected and abandoned."

"Maybe you should call your father," Tanya suggested.

"But...she wouldn't be talking to him, right?" Samantha pushed buttons on her cell phone anyway.

Richie was dining alone at Fishy Franks, a favorite eatery at Watonga Gambling Casino. He slid a twenty-dollar bill in a miniature slot machine on the table. Pulling the lever, Big Bird, apples and pears spun in a dizzying flurry, clanking. The motion stopped. Four Big Birds with flapping wings quacked at him. Bells rang, lights flashed, alerting everyone nearby that Richie had hit the jackpot.

Unfortunately for Samantha, the hubbub drowned-out the ringing tones of his cell phone.

Aware of sneering patrons, some hangers-on types that were snickering and signaling, "Give me some of that dough, jerk," Richie responded to the threatening vibe by shouting, "Lobster for everyone!"

Within moments a waiter placed a full red lobster in front of him, dutifully tying a babyish bib around Richie's neck. "I'm Jim. At your service, Mr. Forrest," the waiter announced with a toothy smile.

Richie peeled off some bills. "Take the night off, kid. Have some fun on good ol' Richie." Saucer-eyed and grinning, Jim slipped the cash into his pocket. "Thank you, Mr. Forrest," he bowed. Within seconds he disappeared into the crowd.

The cell phone rang. Richie clicked on the speakerphone as he cracked the lobster shell. "Richie on the horn."

With spurts and stutters Samantha reeled, "Dad? Dad, it's too weird. Mom hasn't called me even once to check up. Catastrophe, that's what it is."

"Well, I know why she's not calling _me_. And she's mad at Brian. So..."

"So? Something awful could have happened."

"She's probably fed up. Went on strike."

"Or went missing. She could have been abducted, gagged, taped-up and is pounding to get out of the trunk." The sound of Richie using the lobster cracker smacked, crackled, and popped in her ear. "Not funny farting in the phone, Dad."

"That's just a lobster shell, honey."

Belching a hiccup, Samantha slurred, "What lobster? What's going on?"

"Calm down. Have you been drinking?"

"I got the tequila worm." Samantha caught herself. "I mean, uh, no...er, it's no such biggie, right? Especially to you." Richie was silent. Samantha continued, "Dad I'm worried. Do something, please. Find Mom."

A bead of sweat dripped from his brow, "I'll take care of it, sweetie."

"Good. Gotta go, I'm way nauseous, bye." She quickly hung up.

"Take care of yourself," Richie said into the irritating buzz of the dial tone.

What next? Now his once-innocent daughter was drinking, partying and...? "Stop it Richie, don't go there, she's almost grown," he muttered to himself. Not taking Samantha's concerns lightly he skyrocketed emotionally, hitting a brick wall. Shifting mental gears he wondered, "Who knows what Jenny could be up to?" Feeling almost obsessed like his now-precious Jenny had been, Richie knew he had to take action. He paid the bill, took the lobster to go, and headed to the house. Once there, he discovered that his garage remote-clicker worked. "Surprised she didn't change the code," he mused.

The lights were out. No sounds! The silence was alarming. Richie proclaimed, "Jenny, it's me!" No response. He began checking all the rooms. Raiding the closets. There was no visible sign of life. Holding his breath, anticipating the worst, he flung open the shower curtain. "Thank God, at least there's no bloody body." He scoured the kitchen, climbed in the large pantry. "Jenny, I know you hate me. But if you're here, please talk to me."

He checked the answering machine. Most of the messages were from Samantha. "Mom, pick up. Mom, what should I do? Mom, help me! <u>Mom</u>!"

Perplexed, he slumped in a greige satin-covered chair, stroking the Jacquard weave pattern. "It's nice...I mean, beautiful." Clutching a matching pillow close to his heart, he spoke gently. "You did a great job decorating." His knees weakened at the sight of their wedding picture on the mantle. "The once happy couple." He downed a jigger of gin. Then another and another.

One hour later, totally blitzed, Richie reminisced, speaking to the wedding photo. Both he and Jenny were young, innocently hopeful. He rubbed his finger over her face, slurring, "Soft curls frame that perky, pixel pixie face." Rubbing her breast, "Your falsies puffed those little boobs."

He moved closer, eye-to-eye with the photo. "It's like yesterday on the wet sand mingling under the boardwalk, making out, hot and heavy. Remember how excited I got...and told you to look up at the cracks in the wooden planks at the people walking by? How they couldn't see us. I nabbed a falsie; I admit it now. I stuck it in my pocket and showed it to the guys the next day. They were stoked. 'You touched her boobs?' I was 'cool man Richie' from then on. And, you were 'pancake Jenny'." Feeling no remorse he laughed a mouthful of sillies.

Holding the glass up, he toasted the photo. "I know you are a little schist, daffy. So what! You're still my girl."

Jenny's red lips seemingly pursed into a pout. The mouth moved and appeared to speak to him. "It's your fault, you crazy-making schlmeggie-schlemazal."

Richie scooted closer. "Wait a second. That sounds like me. Not you!"

"Oh ya'-ya'. You lying buffoon. Assanova!" Jenny's apparition spewed green goop on his face, streaming down his hand, dripping on his trousers. He reluctantly licked it. "Mmm...Apple Betty, my favorite." Fervidly lapping it up, he looked at the picture once more. "It is you. Forgive me. I was crazy making. Oh my Jenny. Where are you?"

At Stanford, thrilled with her new career and dressed in full combat garb, Jenny crouched under a stairwell. Using a listening device she detected groans and girlish squeals in the room next door.

Static crackled over a man's voice saying, "Well done. I'm down to my skivvies. Who'll be the lucky little lassie?"

Girl's voices overlapped. "Hold on." "It's my turn." "No, it's mine."

Jenny clumsily picked at the door lock with a special tool. She wiggled and joggled too hard, causing the pick-tool to break in two. Muttering with irritation, "Gee whiz!" she spun on a dime, pulled a hairpin out of her wig, stuck it in the keyhole, gently jiggling and praying, "Give me one tiny little break. Please open."

Inside the room Dean Chase played strip poker with two nearly naked undergrads. Turning their cards over, one girl proudly stated, "Pair of jacks." The other announced, "Two fours."

Dean Chase applauded. The girls focused on his hand. Sardonic, yet smiling, he spread his cards on the table. "Three aces. I win again." One girl removed a necklace; the other one unfastened her bra.

Stomping in the room storm trooper style, Jenny busted up the ruse. Screeching full volume into a megaphone, she targeted Dean Chase. "Why you lecherous, crotchety pedophile. Get down on the floor!"

Sauntering out of the bathroom, barely dressed in only a bra and panties, another girl emerged on the scene. It was Samantha! Jenny's nightmarish dream had come true! Suddenly light-headed, Jenny immediately lost her composure. Her voice shouted into the megaphone, "Samantha! Put your clothes on right now and get back to your room!"

Samantha looked at her in disbelief. "You know me by name?"

Thinking fast Jenny motioned to the other girls to leave. She belted into the megaphone. "All of you out... or immediate expulsion. I want to deal with this aberrated scum-bag...in private."

Samantha shot Dean Chase the evil eye. He quivered as she boldly raked in not only her winnings, but his winnings as well. "Not your day, slime-ball."

Protecting her guise Jenny wittingly flattered Samantha. "Pretty savvy move, Ms. Forrest."

Samantha was taken aback, not used to compliments from strangers. "Ya' think?" she asked.

With the mark of an amateur Jenny fumbled the handcuff latch, failing to subdue Dean Chase. She reached for him and her fingers slipped off his weather-beaten baldhead. He escaped her clutch and started to bolt. Sticking out a combat boot she tripped him, wrestling his muscle-sagging body to the floor. Rolling on top, pinning him down, she growled. "You no good wretch of a man. You know what I should do to you?"

"This could be interesting," he cooed. Anticipating something sensual, he totally relaxed and closed his eyes.

"I'll show you interesting," Turning to Samantha affecting a Hallbally gruff tone, she snarled. "Come on, get with it girl. Let's incriminate and decimate the old lecher."

Disgusted, Samantha flung one of Brian's insulting comebacks at him. "Eat my grits." With gusto they dragged him into the dorm hallway. Megaphone to mouth Jenny shouted, "Dean Chase on display, dressed-down to his skivvies."

Doors flew open. Girl's heads poked out. Giggles, sneers, jeers aimed at Dean Chase resounded through the hallway. "Dean's got a teeny-weeny." "Old smelly crotch." "Down with Dean Lecher!"

Jenny scorned him. "Now look who's the embarrassed spectacle."

With trembling hands Dean Chase covered his 'privates'. "Hallbally, you are fried. One pork belly roasting in hell."

The next day Jenny was reprimanded for her actions. Helga clamored over her, shouting "I am the inquisitor, the judge and the jury."

Panting heavily Jenny did penance push-ups for her infractions.

Helga spit-fired, "What's a subordinate?"

Breathless, Jenny answered, "Bottom of the totem. Lowest dreg on the food chain."

Hovering like a stealth bomber Helga barked, "Bottom-feeders don't invade the privacy of a superior! Got that, Hallbally?"

Out of steam, Jenny slammed flat-faced to the floor. Looking up, earnestly trying to understand what she'd done wrong, she asked, "What about our cadet song? Protecting the virgins?"

"You don't attack the shark that feeds you."

To make her point Jenny sang, "We are the campus security. We protect our coed's virginity."

"That's it, Hallbally. Freeze your lip." Helga grimaced tight-faced, fighting an impulse to slug her.

"I did the right thing. I saw that pedophile in action."

"No excuses! The roof could fall in. A rhinoceros could attack. No insubordination! Get to the blackboard." Jenny crawled to the board. Helga handed her a piece of chalk. "Now write, 'What you didn't see. Didn't happen'."

Forty-five minutes later, dizzy and worn, Jenny repeatedly wrote the slogan on the blackboard. Beyond coherence she jumbled out loud. "What you did see. Did happen. It didn't happen. Did you see it happen?" She wrote in giant letters, "WHAT I DID SEE HAPPENED". In a fit of exasperation she tossed the chalk against the wall; white dust splattered up her nose. Sneezing and wheezing she blurted, "This is crap. I saw what I saw." Uttering the statement repeatedly, she collapsed in a fetal ball of exhaustion.

The next day was business as usual. Jenny recouped her lowly status. Aggie tried to console and inform her of the trials and errors of past rookies. "There was this zealous security rookie assigned to P.E. – you know, physical education? Anyway, she was always checking, peeking, listening to male toilet trash, graphic bragging conquests. Eventually she blew. Gang banged the entire football team. Got suspended and ended up in hellfire...which means she was locked-in with Helga for a torturous week."

Thinking of Brian, Jenny felt the blood suddenly rush out of her. "The football team? They're not even safe here?"

Aggie shot a quizzical look at Jenny's pasty-white face. "You're worried about a football team that released tons of pent-up semen? They were so stoked by her they won every game after that and the championship to boot. What about the rookie-nympho? You're not curious what happened to her?"

Unable to conceal her prudish judgment Jenny replied, "Not really."

Revolted by Jenny's self-absorption Aggie tossed a smelly rag at her, "That's really cold."

"Not cold, more like icecaps in a freezer." Jenny was consumed by a perilous thought: What if a pack of horny hussies pummeled, seduced, and devoured Brian? Unable to reveal her son was a football candidate apparently in lethal jeopardy, she solemnly endured a double-trouble existence. Taking it to heart she whimpered, "Bite the bullet."

"'Bullet? This is major. It gets ugly. Helga tied floozy-slut-mama to a chair. Made her watch bondage porn for days. Wouldn't let her sleep, eat or drink."

"Guess life's an unfair bitch." Nonplussed, Jenny smirked.

Shining her boot, Aggie snorted in disgust, "What's with you? Post-traumatic brain-lock?"

"Go ahead, slam the nail in the hole. I'm interested, okay? What's the punch line, what happened?"

"A miracle. Helga turned her around. She left chaste and obedient. Works in a strip joint rehabbing ladies of the night."

Fed up, Jenny rapidly wiped black paste on her shoe. "You think 'tall-tales', lies, made-up stories are a magic cure? I'm here to tell you when the smoke screen tricks are over, so are you and I. Our brains are already jacked-up with nonsense running out our ears."

Aggie polished her boot, faster and better. "I'll pretend you didn't just blow smoke up my britches. You owe me."

As rumor had it Dean Chase got his just dues. In closed chambers Judge Hickey, a tyrant on the side of the security babes, had castigated him. "You are dean in name only. A mouthpiece for the higher good." By day Dean Chase smiled and followed strict orders, closely monitored by security. By night his penance was custodial duty: Spit-cleaning the Administration Office latrines with toothbrushes.

Aggie wanted to prove a point to Jenny. "You'll believe the rumors, the 'tall-tale' stories. You'll know we mean business and don't mess around with sleezoids."

Leapfrogging to the graveyard shift, Jenny trolled the Administration halls. Turning a corner into the custodial area she stopped – cold. Dean Chase was scrimmaging through a trash dumpster. Resisting the urge to push him in she perked-up, "Heard you were on cherry-flavored steroids?"

He reached his hand toward her, pleading, "Please help me. Can't you just get me a live hand grenade...and pull the pin?"

"Right on! Then we can hold hands and sing 'Kum-By-Ya'." She handed him a fresh supply of toothbrushes.

"I know I was shifty and lost control," Dean Chase said remorsefully. Hitting himself on the head with the toothbrushes, he grimaced, "Why, why, why, I keep asking myself...<u>why</u> did I kick the little babes to the curb when I could have pulled them to the height of decency, respecting their chastity vows?"

His delusional rant didn't deserve an answer. Jenny left him scrubbing a latrine on hands and knees. Holding fast to the rumor that proved to be true, and helped to fire her pride as a rookie security babe.

The philosophy class was filled. Samantha glanced at the syllabus and realized that she needed a dictionary to interpret it, "Another dropped class," she thought dismally. Raw emotion rattled inside her like a blender concocting a smoothie. She prayed that she and Brian wouldn't end up in the same classes. Detesting the comparison, the twin jokes, she always ended up on the short side of the stick, grade-wise and in the popularity game. As she found a seat in the auditorium-sized room, it was clear that she didn't need to worry anymore. There he was in all his glory. Brian was sitting two rows in front of her.

Samantha's view of his note-taking or doodling, or when he answered a question or shot a cute girl a glance, sent her rolling into catatonia. Impossible to concentrate when he was around. He was the life of the party, the leader – everything she aspired to be. Why did she care so much? Why couldn't it just end? Why couldn't she just be Samantha, a solo act instead of a twin?

Conversely, Brian liked having his sister around in class. He knew someone was close by that really cared about him, instead of needy jerks wanting information about the next party or how to score some booze, or how to score high grades on a test. He often repeated, "I admire my sister for not dabbling in social nonsense...for her restraint to sit on the sidelines with high-minded values."

Brian had been a social director since kindergarten. Settling squabbles about first batter-up, he'd champion a kid, who could barely hit the ball. "Come on Billy, give it the old one-two try," and then follow the poor loser with a slammer. It was amazing to him that no one caught on. Perfecting his strategies over time he knew the 'ins and outs' of working the crowd to his advantage

Samantha fidgeted in her seat, twirling her hair. Philosophy professor Dr. Ron, a flamboyant ex-Berkeley graduate, posed a query. "What is the primary destruction of creativity and individuality?" Clueless, the class stared blankly at him. Not anticipating an answer, Dr. Ron continued. "It lies in the concept of 'Normal'. The 'Norm' is society's number-one crippling disease. That mean-average lowers the bar of human potential. Dumbing-down a person's expectations and concept of themselves."

Samantha drifted into 'Neverland', imagining the cute guy sitting in front of her turning around and kissing her with passion.

Dr. Ron elaborated. "Normalcy predicts a group can be hypnotically manipulated into a mass-think state." On the chalkboard he jotted a list: "It curtails the ability to think creatively. Dissolves critical thinking. Inhibits solving complex problems. Agreement of ideas controlled so individual actions can be fairly predictable."

"Okay class," he challenged. "Let's hear some examples of normal."

Students answered, "Checking in on My Space." "Boring, average." "Digging JJ Cool?"

Jax, a smart-ass clown-type stood on his seat and spun around to face the class. "A cat chasing its tail?" The student's 'hissed'.

Dr. Ron tapped on Samantha's desk, awakening her stupor. "What do you think is normal, Samantha?"

A little humming bird had been circling outside the window; its "Hum" seemed to say to Samantha, "Kiss the teacher's ass." That's exactly what she absent-mindedly blurted. The class cracked-up, laughing.

"Laughter insinuates agreement. So most of you agree?" Dr. Ron skillfully baited them.

Freaked by her airhead insult, Samantha recouped with, "Sheep-like, maybe?" The class laughed even louder.

"Sheep-like! Very good," Dr. Ron confirmed. "Absence of creative thought, stuck in a box mind-set. Normal's end game wipes out hope of cutting-edge inventions, cures for disease. It stamps out genius."

"How is it?" Samantha stuttered, "Why...wwwhat happens that some of us are dummies?" The class roared.

Dr. Ron nodded, "Sounds like the dummies were listening." Dead silence prevailed in the room. He continued, "It's a conspiracy!

Governments, world religions, big corporations control the masses. Info' is manipulated. Vital education is prohibited, and guarded."

"Sounds hopeless, like doomsday." a concerned student commented.

"Not so," Dr. Ron quipped. "Human salvation lies in what society at large considers aberrant behavior. The unpopular stands taken by renegade activists, the free-thinkers like Buddha, Socrates, Martin Luther King." He turned to Brian, "Can you describe individualized free-thinking?"

Brian had a teasing grin. He paused, calculated, waiting until all eyes were on him. "Dr. Ron it's not my intention to upset the norm's apple carts. However, I think it happened in the sixties when students marched against Vietnam. Protestor's were tear-gassed, clubbed by cops. The world was watching. They warned, 'Don't trust anyone over thirty'." Rising to his feet he drove home his point home. "Hippie crusaders brought down the establishment. Mutiny paved the way to freedom of thought. They were leaders, true believers in free speech, free love. They taught us it's our birthright to hail sex, drugs and rock and roll."

Stunned by his speech, unsure of the meaning or how to respond, the class choked. Sheepish eyes turned to Dr. Ron waiting for a cue. He fixed his gaze on Brian, recognizing that his prize student had spoken. Amazing to find a kindred spirit among the many idlers. No need to break Brian's balls like his egotistical professors had done to him. Brian would feel comfortable here. He'd grow and sow his oats in Philosophy class. Dr. Ron chose his words carefully. No praise, no shame was a necessary tactic with a bright student. Barely audible, forcing everyone to listen carefully, he uttered a perfunctory remark. "I knew that."

Samantha couldn't help herself, mesmerized by his charisma she jumped up from her seat applauding. "Yes!" The class followed suit. "Dr Ron's the bomb."

Slightly bowing his head Dr. Ron accepted the applause as his own. "Remember, a paper's due next class. The subject is something or someone uniquely unique." The bell rang, ending class. As the students filed out Dr. Ron shot an affirming nod to Brian who returned a sly grin. Clearly a camaraderie signal, they both knew this would be the first and last time the professor would publicly take credit for the student's genius.

Samantha waited for the room to clear. With a quirky little skip, she approached Dr. Ron. "Ah, I want to thank you." staving back tears, "for not making me look ditzed-out, even though I probably am, but I can't help it. I'm not like my brother, smart, that is. You got that. What I'm trying to say...I never wrote a paper on my own before. I aspire to C's, not much I guess. Maybe you could give me a clue what you want..." She gazed at the blackboard, reading, "Like what 'uniquely unique' means to you?"

Dr. Ron stopped shuffling papers. He knew the downside, the struggling student with no confidence, wallowing in mediocrity. Why? Because no one believed she could do one ounce better. Grades were always the dominant concern. Learning was the second priority. Weighing the little waif, doe-brown eyes, probably close to anorexic and most certainly tethering on teen heartbreak, he decided to take the upbeat, 'you can do it yourself' approach.

"Brave of you to step up like that. Most kids slink into the woodwork and get low grades, if they don't completely flake and flunk out. You won't because you don't want to. You already said you were up for passing, right?" She nodded. "You already questioned what is unique, that means you want to know, to learn."

She giggled, "If my brain worked better I probably could learn more."

"Good start. Your brain is working or you couldn't have 'thought' to come up and ask me a question, or wait for an answer. So that's rubbish, you are thinking, right?"

"Right, it's just not real deep."

"Nothing wrong paddling in shallow water, practicing until we plunge in the deep."

"What does that have to do with writing my paper?"

'Probably nothing, except what you make it" Barely resisting the attraction and a desire to touch the tiny erect nipples under Samantha's skin-tight tee, Dr. Ron continued. "You're uniquely special, you know."

She blushed. "Ya' think?"

One flimsy come-on remark and he got to her, sensing the familiar vulnerable weakness. No way did he dare to tread that tempestuous path again – the innocent flirtations leading to an illicit affair with a student. His intellectual prowess slipped away as his mind rewound to last year as a teaching fellow. "Ahhh, sweet Teresa," he recalled. She was an Italian exchange student with a tight rump, legs touching her chest, a virgin on the verge of prostitution. How could any horny guy refuse a wild-colt who arrived at his door in the middle of the night, dropping her coat, lusciously naked underneath, her hard-burning body begging "Take me."

He should have known better when one-by-one she sent the other little Italian maidens on campus to him for that brief six weeks. Giggles mixed in English and Italian. "Ma fagule. You are a good cock." Seduced and blackmailed into a male sex slave, he was forced to service them at their bidding or they threatened to expose him to what seemed to be the Italian Mafia, their father's, brothers, and uncles and cousins.

If it hadn't been for B-12 shots, protein powder, and vitamin E boosts, he surely would have succumbed, folding under the nose of the faculty, potentially costing him his life's purpose, creating his demise, losing the right to teach. No way! Not this semester!

As Samantha squirmed in her girly imagination and raging hormones, he remained focused, on track, punching. "I'm unique too. It doesn't matter what I think is special. It's your call. I'm not you, couldn't be if I tried or vice-versa. This pencil is unique," he instructed, holding up a red pencil etched with little teeth marks, "I chewed on it, not another one in the world like it."

She took the pencil, relishing it like a trophy, "Wow! That's really interesting."

"Great – now you're interested. That's how to start your paper. Interested in someone or something. Just write it, don't think, don't edit, just write."

"Just write, I'll write, right?"

He jotted 'Brain-Joggles' – a tutorial requisition – on a notepad. Handing the paper to her he said, "Check this out, it's right here on campus. I was their prize candidate. I wouldn't be who I am without them."

Samantha was impressed and excited. "Wow. That's some recommendation." Unconsciously licking her lips, she lifted up on her tiptoes, planting a wet kiss on his lower cheek, very close to his lips. "Oh, Dr. Ron, thank you for caring, most teachers dismissed me like a lame-duck flunky."

Dr. Ron cleared his throat. "Ahem...keep me posted when the light bulb goes on and your brain explodes with blasts of ideas and purpose." While Samantha skipped her quirky step out of the room he touched his cheek, smiling; yes, he had reached some part of her, maybe her brain, but most certainly penetrating that jailbait female heat.

Crossing the campus on her way back to the dorm, Samantha sailed on a new cloud of faith and lust. Entering her room, she found her roommate in bed. Tanya had ditched Philosophy class, ill with the twenty-four hour stomach flu, and had been knocked-out on painkillers most of the day. Now awake but very groggy, she asked how the class had gone. Whirling in a tizzy she learned that a paper was due. "Write something uniquely unique about someone or something," was all Samantha repeated, but she couldn't stop raving about Dr. Ron. "He makes you burn to learn, like you want to breathe free or make love."

"Big confusing deal," Tanya had quipped. She'd be hanging out with Brian and it was a blast, but asking for help from him would signal she was academically challenged. She believed that at a college like Stanford, a dummy translates to "not sexy." Even Tanya knew that cleavage and plunging necklines had a shelf life. Her only hope was Hallbally. Who knew if the dyke really could tutor? She set-up a private rendezvous to find out.

Meeting in the laundry room at 10:00 P.M. was a natural ruse. With the clanking-swish of the washing machine and the click-clack of the laptop keys, Jenny was doubly at home. "Homework on a laptop and doing laundry." She chuckled at the absurdity of her current situation resembling her former life as the "Oh-so familiar dormant house-frau."

Tanya was on edge. "I should drop out now and save a year's tuition."

Jenny loaded the washer. "Sad-sack's give up before they start. How about the old college try?"

Tanya handed her a jug of "Mighty All" detergent. "Try this – it's good stuff."

Jenny laughed as she pulled the exact brand out of her bag. "Good choice. Gets the grime out without fading colors."

Relaxing with the affirmation Tanya said. "I should do hair, nails, shop, something fun. Something I'm into."

"That's easy, let's write about something you're into."

"They want us to write about something or someone unique. "Rolling her eyes, Tanya poured a cup of detergent into the washer.

That was the opener Jenny was waiting for. "Ah Hah! Your roommate's uniquely a twin, right?"

"You knew that?"

"That's my job. Now what is so special about her?" Jenny held her breath as she put coins in the washing machine.

"Nothing much. Boring, plain, sort of a sub-zero."

Jenny swallowed her disappointment. Poor Samantha, no one ever appreciated her. Impatiently she prodded, "Come on, there must be something. Like, is she having sex?"

"No surprise you'd go there." Tanya was amused that Jenny was such a 'perv'.

'No surprise you wouldn't answer. Well, is she?"

"No, she says no, which is usually a lie. But, in her dork-case, virgin-bound as she is, she probably goes down, doing the knee-bending fellatio tricks. Doesn't deny it. It doesn't count anyway." With a vapid expression, Tanya asked, "Wasn't it Congress or some judge that voted that sucking wasn't technically sex?"

Rubbing her knuckle raw, wanting to punch the little brat-teen piffling, Jenny batted her eyelashes curiously. "Not exactly how it went. Now think! Think. Think. What is unique or special about her?"

Smiling with a twinkle in her eyes Tanya replied, "Okay I'll tell it jet straight. Having a way-cool twin brother. That stud-jock makes me so horny I can't wait to get into him."

Holding back the growing impulse to strangle the little tart, Jenny bit her tongue. "I wouldn't rush into anything with a twin. What one does the other one feels."

Tanya's forehead wrinkled in confusion. "You mean if I did it with Brian...Samantha would feel it?"

"Most likely. Sort of like kissing cousins. She'd feel it real good," Jenny leered at Tanya.

"That may be way happening for you. Being a 'Security' babe and all that. But, I'm totally not into it."

Jenny still didn't get the homophobic drift. "Into what?"

Tanya sighed. "Duh. Oh come on. You know. Females! Bullies! Always flexing."

Jenny flexed a semi-cut bicep. "I am. Hard bodies are great." She laughed, "Especially at my age...I mean...stage."

Crestfallen, Jenny felt the mission had misfired. Typing a fast, ninety-words-a-minute, she didn't look up for a second. Thoughts of disdain for Tanya lingered. "Why bother to teach a damn thing to this shallow dumbskie?" A twinge of guilt singed through her for judging. She wouldn't have thought twice if Tanya had reamed anyone else other than Samantha.

Heaving wet clothes into the mouth of the dryer, every dripping uniform reeked as a reminder that she was Lucy Hallbally, not the obsessed Jenny Forrest. Hallbally was on task, on a crusade. With determination she backed-up the assignment to a disk, waving it at Tanya. "Before I hand over this little gem of a paper, remember our deal. What little campus shenanigans are worth busting?"

Tanya hesitated. She didn't want to snitch. However, when a girl is down she has to come up fighting. Beaten to earthbound necessity she came up with a smiling face. "Rumors are flying..." (Blah, blah, blah.) She went on to elaborate secrets, along with some shoddy details of upcoming campus escapades.

It was a balmy Friday night at 11:30 P.M. Barbecue flames danced a glow on Brian's face as he sat around the fire with a group of horny jocks. The smell of sizzling marshmallow's, the crunch of their creamy delight, cranked their testosterone levels even higher.

Jax, the clown frat boy from Philosophy class, wearing designer horn-rimmed glasses, grilled Brian. "How can you be so sure the girl's are in the dorm and not out partying?"

"I have my sources. Either you're in or out."

Jax dropped his jaw. "What do you think, man?"

Brian elaborated, "We need a decoy just in case we get spotted."

Jax twitched as the guys singled in on him. "What kind of decoy?"

Skeeter, a seven-foot freckled-faced giant, pulled a lavender lace dress and a wig out of his bag. He tossed them at Jax. "This kind, sweetie boy."

Jax decided in a nanosecond that Skeeter was no one to mess with. Quickly, he pulled the dress on over his clothes and then stuttered. "Purple? Like plum. I like plums."

Brian plopped the short-cropped Three Stooges 'Curly' wig on Jax's head. "Good choice picking Jax, the bravest of us all."

"Since when?" Jax shuddered.

Brian patted him on the back, "Since now, good man."

With raised arms, waving clinched fists, the group let out a pumped-up, "Hya'aa! To Jax the brave!"

Getting into the spirit Jax flexed his biceps in a Mr. America pose. "Bring on the girls."

Brian gave the awaited go-ahead. "May the panty-raid begin." Carrying sheets, racing on skateboards, they sailed across the campus.

The guys hid behind trees, amazingly still and quiet. Waiting for the attack cue they watched as Jax, tentative and clumsy, climbed a tree. To keep him moving, Brian stayed close behind, pushing him up the tree's edge. Hanging onto a limb Jax held on for dear life. Dizzy and scared out of his wits he waffled, foiled by the cement below. "I could plummet, squish, splat and mangle."

Brian slapped his hand over Jax's mouth and whispered in his ear. "Or you could climb to the top. Be a hero. And get laid sooner than never."

"Right. I could. Get laid. Couldn't I?" Less afraid and eager to go Jax ambled up the tree, moving closer to the target. They reached the second story of the girl's dorm. Brian opened a window and anchored a sheet on the ledge. One-by-one the jocks held onto the sheet and hoisted up the wall, making entry into a hallway.

On the lookout for security, Jax sashayed ahead of the pack of teen wolves. He waved to them and mouthed. "Coast is clear."

They crept deeper into the hallway. Then all hell broke loose. Like banshees they cruised the halls, knocking on doors. Busting inside, they shouted, "Aiiiee, mates!" playfully surprising the girls.

Shrill screams rang out amidst the bedlam. Girls tossed shoes, soda cans, and anything they could get their hands on at the would-be assailants. One girl clunked Skeeter on top the head with a shampoo bottle, while her hefty roommate mounted his back, riding him to the ground, taming the heifer.

Using his cell phone camera a zealous frat boy snapped photos of the riled pranksters wrestling girls, trying to strip them of their panties and thongs. "Smile," he chortled.

Left to his own devices (which meant not many), Jax was subdued by three girls. Easily overpowering him, they stripped him of his dress, jeans and skivvies. A cute girl nuzzled on his ear. "Having fun, sweet thing?"

Jax, overcome with excitement, succumbed in her arms. "I'm stoked." A buxom blond grabbed a broom handle and stuck his prized pair of red Speedo's on the tip, waving the red flag of conquest proudly out the window. An alarm sounded on campus. Security babes in full battle gear were deployed to the area. "Annihilator's attack!" blasted over the dorm intercom.

Someone shouted, "Let's bail!" Another boy yelled, "We're out of here!" The jocks clamored out of the rooms, following the planned escape route. Like pirates on the run, some scaled down the building on sheets. Others jammed out the front door. Attempting to divert the attention of the charging Campus Security guards, the guys separated in formation, scattering in different directions.

Defiant and over-zealous Brian waved a flimsy thong in the air. Dressed in full-blown battle gear, Aggie spotted him as he ran down a stairway. She pursued him in a madcap chase into the dining area, through the gymnasium, and across the tennis courts. Jenny, huffing from exhaustion trailed close behind, screeching, "Don't hurt him!"

Brian made a zigzag turn, just missing Jenny. He circled the swimming area. Aggie remained on his trail, gaining ground. "I'll tar your sweet ass," she bellowed.

"Over my sour ass you will," Jenny threatened. Attempting to protect him from Aggie's brutish assault she blocked Aggie like a fullback, plowing into her and taking the hit head on. Winded and off balance Jenny tumbled, then belly-flopped into the Olympic-sized pool. Weighted down by her heavy gear she sank to the bottom like a rock.

Aggie responded swiftly. She ripped off her helmet and heavy jacket and dove in, swimming to the bottom. Jenny was floating along the sidewall. With all her strength Aggie tugged her by the waist, paddled hard. Finally lifting her to the water's surface.

Brian hung over the pool's edge until Jenny emerged, and then dove in, heaving her out of the water. Aggie pulled herself out of the pool by grabbing the rim and rolling out onto the concrete. Standing up, she dashed over to Jenny. As Aggie leaned over to remove Jenny's headgear, she unknowingly blocked Brian's view of Jenny's face. "She's not breathing," Aggie said before she performed mouth-to-mouth resuscitation.

"One, two, three...push!" Brian counted, pressing his hands on Jenny's chest to assist in the procedure. He had no idea it was his mother's life he was attempting to save. Aggie's large head was planted over Jenny's face.

The frat boy with his cell phone camera watched in awe, snapping their photo.

Still unconscious, Jenny was caught in a rapturous wild fantasy: A male stripper was humping a lap-dance on her. Tongues entwined, they kissed passionately. Jenny regained consciousness, moaning.

Relieved that she was revived, Brian took off like a bat out of hell. Running for his safety he yelled, "Glad I could help out!"

Jenny cogitated, tongue-mashing Aggie. "Oh...No. No! This can't be." Jenny coughed, spewing water at Aggie. "Hanging out with you, everyone probably thinks I'm...I'm a..."

Wiping the water drops from her face, Aggie asked, "A what? Just say it."

Pursing her lips, Jenny forced the words, "I'm gay. A dyke. A Butchie girl."

High-fiving Jenny, Aggie exclaimed," So you're a Lesbo! Way to go!"

Jenny recoiled. "I need a drink."

"Congratulations. You're coming out!" Aggie beamed at her.

"Out where?"

"Out of the closet.""Out of your mind. Can't you see I'm a judgmental, certified homophobic?"

"Certified for sure. Or maybe you're just in denial...that you really want me big time." Aggie's big smile registered a seed of desire.

Jenny backed away, "Not funny. Get real."

The next morning, in the Campus Security Office Aggie gloated as Helga chastised Jenny. Leaning over her, Helga raised a baton. "So you're a sexual discriminating goody-two-shoes." Terrified of being clubbed, Jenny scurried under a desk like a gofer racing to its hole. "I said I was sorry."

"Aggie saved your life, dimwit. She's your partner. Your sole back up. You're glued at the hip."

"Glad you said at the hip, not at the lip," Jenny quipped.

Humiliated, Aggie sank to the floor eye-level with Jenny cowering under the desk. Aggie confided. "I just wanted a friend. Nobody ever likes me. Since fifth grade I've been the six-foot pre-pube, bed-wetting dufus."

Helga commanded. "Cut the cry-baby crap. On your feet! Pronto, Sergeant!"

Aggie rose to her feet, standing at attention. "Yes, ma'am!"

"Go for your dignity, your muscle-power, your orb."

Aggie altered her stance. "My orb...like orbit-uary?"

"Like orbit, your sphere, your influence. Zing it."

Standing erect Aggie towered like a flagpole. "You pathetic sniveling rookie get the hell out of that pothole and face the fossil-fuel-burning Aggie."

Jenny crouched, sweat dripping, breathing heavily. Not knowing what to expect she crawled, inching out on all fours. Stopping at the toe guard on Aggie's big boot, she whimpered, "Yes, ma'am! Sergeant Aggie, ma'am, I'm ready for," covering her head with her hands, "my premature demise!"

"You ungrateful, tight-ass holier-than-us, ritzy-titzy sex-starved bigot." She lifted her boot placing it next to Jenny's mouth. "Kiss my boot."

Jenny looked up bug-eyed. Aggie stared her down. Jenny grimaced. SMACK-erino! She planted a walloping kiss on the shiny spit-shined boot.

Helga nodded to Aggie. "Bull's-eye! That nailed her."

Aggie paced around Jenny, who groveled meekly on the floor." On your feet, Hallbally."

Jenny automatically popped-up, "I'm up, Sis...I mean, ma'am. Sergeant."

Helga intervened and snarled, "Step up, Hallbally." Jenny moved closer. They were nose-to-nose. "Now's your opportunity to thank Aggie for her guts and vigor to bare the truth."

Jenny registered the significance of the moment, the humiliation she may have caused Aggie. "You're the first person who ever..." Jenny struggled to finish the sentence as tears welled-up, probing to find the right words. To ease the tension Aggie came through with a touch of humor. "...spit truth bullets in your face?"

"You could put it that way. Thank you Aggie...for trusting me."

Aggie nervously shuffled back and forth. "I'm sorry I razzed you about liking me...all I wanted was a friend."

Jenny smiled, "I hope so. Thank you...you saved my life. Hope you are my newfound friend."

"Me too." They shared an elaborate handshake similar to the college kids they patrolled.

Helga looked on with the pride of a mother duck whose squabbling chicks hadn't discovered that one of them might become a swan.

The disappearance of Jenny was no longer a probability, a question mark or a laughing matter. It had the makings of an unspeakable crime, a possible tale of devious plotting, crafty revenge.

Baby-faced detective Gritty, with a 1930's gumshoe attitude, was on assignment to investigate Jenny's seemingly untimely departure.

He descended upon the Forrest household aware of unanswered questions and possible motives of wily deceit.

His presence in the Forrest foyer made Richie edgy. Gritty puffed a cigar and made it a point between coughs to blow smoke rings in Richie's face. He followed Richie into the living area, sniffed through a pile of stacked packages. "Anything unusual about your wife?"

Richie shrugged, "Just a normal fanatic, neat-nick homemaker. She wouldn't even let a maid touch the house. Pointing to a pile of unopened packages Richie blathered on, "You can see that Jenny's a super-shopper."

"Little early for Christmas?" Gritty pulled a hockey stick from a box and examined it.

"My son didn't want it, "Richie explained.

"A Wayne Gretzky. Is he nuts?"

"He's into football."

Gritty 'stick handled' an imaginary puck. "Maybe she was planning on moving. Leaving you, maybe?"

"I'm the egghead. I left her."

Gritty's eyebrows rose in a knowing manner. "For the little secretary? The wife away from home?" As he swung the hockey stick, a vase crashed to the floor.

"Hey, that's Limoge." Stunned at the lack of respect, Richie picked up the shattered relic.

"Most likely priceless in a divorce settlement," Gritty remarked with a tinge of sarcasm. "Did Mrs. Forrest have any other enemies?"

"Bambe isn't an enemy," Richie responded defensively.

"Witness's claim Ms. Bambe verbally assaulted your wife in public."

"What?"

Gritty body-checked Richie into a wall. "Called her a 'troll-mama'?" Richie was breathing hard, but didn't answer. Gritty squashed him tighter like a nail driven into the wall.

Richie moaned. "That was my nickname for her."

As if on ice skates detective Gritty slid along the floor, bending his knees, turned, and aimed the hockey stick at Richie. "So, you're the enemy."

"That's preposterous," Richie said as he ducked, avoiding the swinging stick.

"Where were you the day your wife disappeared?" Gritty swung the stick overhead. Richie dove to the floor.

"You aren't insinuating I had anything to do with Jenny's disappearance? I loved Jenny!"

With reverence Gritty put the stick down. "'Loved' is past tense, Mr. Forrest." He inserted a DVD into the player. Footage of the Cheater-Eaters confrontation appeared on the screen.

Richie got up off the floor and turned off the DVD. Miffed, he faced Gritty, "That's an assault. An invasion of privacy! I could sue. I..."

Gritty interrupted, badgering. "How much insurance did you have on your wife?"

"Not your concern."

"Hiding something?" Gritty smirked, as he jotted a note on his tattered legal pad.

Richie clarified, "I have a quarter of a million on her. She has a million on me. Women tend to live longer, so we made an adjustment."

"Can you explain fifty-thousand dollars missing from your joint account that was – coincidentally –withdrawn two days after her disappearance?"

Visibly rattled, Richie stated. "I can't. Isn't that your job, Detective Gritty?"

Gritty nodded, as if he was on to something. He paused, stuck a match and lit a thin cigar. "We'll be back with you, Mr. Forrest," he garbled. Then he inhaled a deep puff and rudely blew a humongous smoke ring in Richie's face.

Richie waved off the smoke, "Get out you crude...ape. "Richie held back verbally annihilating Gritty, sputtering, "Jenny doesn't allow smoking in the house!"

With a clear intent to intimidate, Gritty cocked his head, "I'll remember you said that." Then, he left without waiting for Richie's reply.

Shaken by the ramifications of the interrogation, Richie removed the DVD from the player and smashed it, stomping on it with his foot. The weight of the implications didn't look good for him: "Husbands are always a prime suspect, he acknowledged with bitterness." In spite of this awareness, his tenuous situation was secondary in his mind. "What could have happened to Jenny?" was all he could think. His heart twisted. His brain baited and boggled, envisioning a warped maimed body tossed like a sack of potatoes in the back of the SUV.

He recalled Jenny's fears. "I've been worried, waiting up at night for you to come home." She would say, "Morgue's. I had every horrible thought going through my head. Bodies on cold slabs." Unable to handle another awful thought, he bawled. "Oh no. Please don't let anything happen to you." He paced. Thought and paced some more. Then it dawned on him; maybe she had gone back east to her mother's. He mumbled to himself, "Why the hell didn't I think of it before?" On tenterhooks, he called Rita.

"Hello?" she answered half-asleep.

"Hello Rita, this is Richie."

"It's one o'clock in the morning." The receiver banged in his ear.

Richie thought about it. He could wait until 8:00 on the East Coast. Nevertheless, time was of the essence. Finding Jenny was all he cared about. He called back. To his amazement Rita picked up the phone.

"Richie, what do you want?" With a pen and pad in hand she jotted, Tuesday 1AM, the jerk called.

"Rita, please don't hang up. I'm worried about Jenny. Is she there?"

Mistrusting his motives, she asked cautiously, "Why would she be here?"

"Look, I know you hate me. You have every reason to. If Jenny's there please tell me. No one knows where she is and we're worried sick." Richie sniffled, wrapped himself in a blanket, covering his head.

"She isn't here. Get serious Richie." Disgusted by his audacity and sudden concern, she rammed, "Why in the world would she want you to know where she is?"

"But, she hasn't even called the kids."

"Thank God, she's giving them a break." She removed her front partial, dropping it in a glass of water.

"Aren't you worried?" His tone reflected his frustration.

Slightly lisping without her teeth, "Mother's know when to worry. I'm not worried. Good night, Richie." She hung up.

Richie was totally stupefied, wanting to believe Rita. Was he relieved or not relieved? He didn't know. Needing resolve, he called his mother and babbled his anguish about Jenny.

Mrs. Svartznegger complained. "I'm an old lady. What do you want with me at one o'clock in the morning?" After a minute of her verbal thrashing he burst out, "How could her own mother not worry?"

"Avoiding the worst. Everyone denies, lies, hides." Her tone was convincing.

"Maybe Rita was right... for sure everything was over the top, a chaotic hellish mess. Maybe Jenny is taking a long, needed break."

"You deserve what you get." In Ruskie gibberish she warned, "Putz ein. Schtup putzen fried-en." English translation\\\: "Play, you pay."

Richie sputtered a hyperactive tirade. "But why the detective? And then there is the missing money. Her cell phone?"

"Too many questions!"

"No answers! What the hell is going on?" Rapidly tapping his fingers on his forehead, trying to make sense of it.

"Go to bed already, Richie. You're giving me a feh-cockta headache."

Richie's analytical mind was going berserk. He needed evidence, details. Unsure who he could trust he placed a call to Brian.

Crashed-out on the couch in his apartment, Brian was groggy and incoherent from a night of partying.

The cell phone ring woke him from his stupor. With his head tucked under a throw cover he flung an arm out and picked up the phone.

Richie babbled a mile a minute. "Your mom? Where is she? You saw her last."

Brian held the receiver away from his ear. "Blah. Blah. Blah." It was hard to recall his father being so out of sorts. "Dad, are you okay?" Squinting at the green illuminated dial on the alarm clock, Brain jolted up. "It's 2:30. Morning or afternoon? I've got football practice, don't I?"

Richie grew impatient. "Are you deaf? Think, you imbecile."

"What's up?" Brian rubbed his eyes trying to stay alert.

"The last time that you saw her...did she say anything different?"

"She was pissed at you for getting me an apartment."

"Any other clues? Did she say she had plans?"

"Plans?" Brian paused trying to remember. "Uh, like a torrential storm was coming. I told her to be careful."

"Anything else?"

"Well, she thought I was trying to get rid of her. I said no one was trying to banish her."

"Why the hell would she think you would get rid of her?"

Unable to conceal his resentment Brian scorned, "Maybe because that's what you did."

Richie prodded, "Brian, did you have an inkling...or a feeling that something awful was about to happen?"

"Not really."

On automatic Richie interrogated, "But you did say 'Be careful' as well as 'I'm not trying to banish you.' You must have had a feeling about something?"

"What feeling?" Brian lowered his head, "You're making me feel guilty."

Richie hammered, "Are you?"

Feeling whipped and misunderstood Brian pleaded, "Don't be a lawyer. Just be my dad."

"I am your dad. Lawyers solve cases with gut feelings."

Brian challenged, "What happened to 'no assumptions'?"

"Assuming means you don't have the facts and you should. Gut-stalking means you follow the leads. Ask the questions. Get the facts. Capiche?"

The nature of the probe clicked in. The blood seemed to drain from Brian's face, "Dad, this is serious, isn't it?"

"I hope not. We have to work fast. Do whatever it takes to find your mother. In the meantime, I'm calling a contact at a TV station and get the word out."

Going on all eight cylinders Richie took over like a pro and set up a TV interview in search for Jenny. The local news van pulled into the Forrest driveway. Nerve-wracked, Richie waited out front to make a plea on the evening news. Jittery and hot, he fanned himself with their wedding photo.

The news anchor, Kat Moran (a Gloria Alred clone) was noted for defending the underdog, approached Richie with a camera crew in tow. "Mr. Forrest, sorry about your wife. If she's out there, we'll find her." Her tone changed to short of accusatory, "That's what you want, isn't it?"

Avoiding the desire to lambaste her media- hyped innuendo he displayed their wedding photo. "Of course, that's what we all want." He glanced lovingly at the photo. Jenny's left eye seemed to wink at him. He dreaded what else it might do. Trembling, he guided the interview. "Let's not waste time – every second counts."

Kat faced the camera. "Everybody's ready. Let's roll tape." Facing Richie, she turned- on an expression of concern and began the interview. "Mr. Forrest, your wife Jenny has been missing since September 2nd ... disappearing mysteriously. Can you show us her photo? In happier moments, this was taken on the loving couple's wedding day."

Richie held the photo in front of the camera lens. Inexplicably, another hallucination flashed before his eyes as he saw green goop dripping from Jenny's face. Trying to cover his shock at the vision, Richie composed himself and began to plead, implore, and beg on camera, "If anyone has seen my wife, my sweet dear Jenny, please come forward. No questions asked. Just bring her back safe and sound. If you can hear me Jenny, be strong. We want you home."

Meanwhile, in the Campus Security Office, Jenny, Helga and Aggie munched popcorn balls as they watched Richie on TV, Aggie joked, "Another suburbanite bites the dust."

Jenny rattled to herself, "Same old, same old. Always going for his image." Losing control she shouted, "You lying philanderer. Acts like he's the victim. Traitor! Using our wedding photo."

Both women glared at her accusingly. Helga laughed, "Hallbally, are you busted or what?" Aggie smirked, "Did we just tag-ID you?" They motioned to Jenny for a high-five, but she didn't respond. Quickly recouping the blunder she created a cover story.

"That's kind of what happened to me. See, ah...my guy was a big...big..." She spaced her hands a foot apart. Both women waited in suspense for her to complete the sentence.

Helga asked, "A big what?"

"A big...a...mist!" Jenny blurted. "That's right...he was a rotten bigamist. He banged this nympho-bimbo... who burned a raspberry on his butt with an iron while she was watching Martha Stewart. And then..."

Aggie was bursting with curiosity. "And then what?"

Jenny's voice lowered into an overly dramatic tone. "He wanted to mess around...no trust between his legs, he wanted to share his testy, flabby raspberry with everybody."

Aggie shook her head. "How disgusting."

Helga wasn't sure what was true and what wasn't. Something didn't feel right and she hesitated to believe the whole story. Nevertheless, she realized that Jenny was far more than a fledging loser. "So, you were an abused, battered little hussy?"

Jenny laughed. "You could put it that way."

Aggie added with conviction, "I knew it. Never fooled me with that goody-sissy act."

Helga nodded in agreement. "It's about time to give this little lady some overdue respect." Out of her usual ball-busting character, Helga began to sing; breaking into an Aretha Franklin riff, "R-E-S-P-E-C-T." Aggie and Jenny joined in. Bonding for the first time like girlfriends, they danced, sang, and laughed together.

At the same time, in her room at the dorm, Samantha waved her Philosophy class paper at Tanya, boasting, "I got a whopping 'C '. Not bad for whipping it out on my own."

Tanya jubilantly waved her paper. "I got an 'A' would you believe? This is the first 'A' I've gotten...since like soccer in middle school."

Trying not to show envy Samantha bit her fingernail down to the quick. "Ouch!" she squealed, rubbing her tender fingertip. "It's totally amazing how two super-dummies could pull above a 'D'." Casually prodding, she asked, "What's yours about?"

Embarrassed to admit it Tanya faltered, "You, kind of."

Flattered and intrigued Samantha exclaimed, "No way."

"Want to hear some of it?"

Playing it down, Samantha uttered a blasé, "Sure, I guess."

Tanya read to her, stumbling over a word or two in the process. "My roommate is a twin. I have been captivated by her other half. Her brother, the handsome, brilliant, most popular..."

The familiar words grated Samantha to the bone. "Give me that. Sounds like my Mom's rap. You wrote this crud?"

Tanya hesitated, "Not exactly. I was tutored by a security-bully."

"Unbelievable. Who?"

"Hallbally."

Samantha broke out laughing, "That spazz storm trooper?"

Rolling her eyes Tanya reflected, "Actually, she kind of reminds me of your mom."

Indignant, Samantha crossed her arms," My mom's not gay."

"Dah!! Well, she does have a militant vibe."

Wanting to set her straight, Samantha explained, "She was raised tough – an Army-brat by Gramps who was a four-star general, I think."

Tanya wasn't buying into it. "So that gives her the right when she meets me to bully, bitch and diss on me?"

"On you? Try night and day for eighteen agonizing, dissing years. Me, the underachiever. The dyslexic, dreary dumber twin! The one egg that never ever deserved to pop out of her golden vagina...so I didn't."

Misconstruing the revelation Tanya beamed, "Wow! That explains a lot. She's not your birth mother?"

"I've wished that too. That my real parents would be someone like Brad and Angelina and would come out of hiding and rescue me."

"Gee, I imagined my parents more like Jay Leno, so I could cruise in a rad car every night."

"Why not just pick that president, Bush junior...or be a triplet. Get your drunken self in the Inquirer."

They giggled at the thought. Samantha continued the rebuke, "Spill it. What indecency did you perform for Hallbally to write an 'A'?"

Tanya defended herself. "That's like...confidential. Top secret stuff."

"Please. Let's not even go there."'

"Then we won't." Tanya took a deep breath, hoping she didn't give away too much. Still needing Hallbally's help to pass a few classes, she couldn't afford to blow their secret arrangement.

On the other hand Samantha had revealed a very personal piece of herself, issues far from being resolved. She felt closer to Tanya. "I hope you won't use this info' trash against me."

"Right! When you've got cheating over my head."

Tanya glanced at Samantha's paper, reading it aloud. "My roommate is so cool. She's ever so popular. Hanging-out with her is the best thing that ever happened to me." Embarrassed, Samantha ripped the paper from her, tearing it into shreds. Gathering scraps from the floor Tanya admitted, "I'm really taken. That was really nice."

Samantha sniggered, "So who says I was talking about you?" Trust issues were up for both teens. Learning to trust their inner gut was a challenging quest, let alone learning to trust each other.

The 'C' grade lingered inside Samantha like a whiplash, a big pain in the neck. She was hooked on becoming smarter, wanting more. Pushed by the desire to get it on with Dr. Ron (maybe someday) or, at the very least, go to a movie with him, she entered Brain-Joggle, armed with the requisition in hand. At the sight of Samantha, Hadley, a fuzzy-fro'-haired man wearing a beige knit J. Crew sweater, freaked-out, verbally attacking like a screaming mīmē.

"Quick change, huh? You're in all blue one minute, now you waltz in mocking me with last years' J. Crew beige knit." Samantha touched her sweater, amazed that it was identical to his. He ranted, "Trying to mess with me? Don't do it, Grace. I can't take one more mind-trip."

Samantha looked over her shoulder to see who else was there. No one! "If you're talking to me...I'm not Grace."

"You wish. Let's stop the games. Our grants are being pulled unless we can get some beefcake numbskull in here that completes the program or we're history." His teeth rattled, typing info' into a computer.

She turned her back to leave, tossing out a closing remark. "Good luck with whatever's bugging you. I'm Samantha, not Grace, by the way."

Hadley spotted the paper dangling from her hand. "Wait, wait! What's that, a requisition?"

"Guess so. Dr. Ron from Philosophy class sent me. You know him, right?"

"Chess freak Ron, the Berkeley flunky who thinks he's Neitze or is it Karl Marks this year?"

"Why rip him, he had good things to say about you."

"Really? Like what?"

"Like he wouldn't be who he is without Brain-Joggle."

"Oh brother, that's a scary thought. I personally never went through it, but look at you, I mean Grace –pure genius."

His words became muffled as Samantha transfixed on her mirror image standing before her dressed in blue. She lifted her arm, checking to see if it was an odd mirror trick. Nothing moved except for Grace's lips,

"I knew you would show up eventually, Samantha Forrest. Born August 8 at Cedar's hospital, 3:00 A.M. Social security number 622-53-5554."

Stunned, Samantha gaped at her. "Guess I entered the 'Twilight Zone'. What was that all about?"

"I was paid to forget Jenny Forrest, but she was too stupid to add forgetting you. So I didn't and I won't."

"Oh, hell freeze-out. You're that menses girl?"

"Mensa," Grace corrected with a slightly superior attitude. However, she didn't want to make Samantha feel too terribly stupid. "What's past is past," she said in a friendlier tone. "The question is, what are you doing here now? Do you want to raise your basic IQ? Emotional IQ? Popularity Q?"

Tingling from head-to-toe Samantha mumbled. "You can do all that?"

"And more. How are you doing in math?"

"You could say its doing me in."

Conjuring the perfect enticement Grace shared, "The perk is Brain-Joggle can count as a math course, if you need it." Reaching in a desk drawer, she handed Samantha a form. "Sign here and you're on math-track."

"Amazing. Sure. I can do that." Hands trembling with excitement, Samantha signed the paper.

Firmly putting her arm through Samantha's, she gently coaxed, "Follow me, I just happen to have a cancellation."

Hadley rose to his feet, exuberant. "Grace, you are total genius. Yes! We're back in biz."

Tossing the signed paper at him, Grace sneered. "Go whack off for five minutes, Hadley. Then call Central and update our stats. Samantha Forrest is here on math-track."

Grace and Samantha entered Brain-Joggle's inner sanctum: A sparse white room, white desks and carpet - very sanitized. Outdated computers sat on each desk. A small sound booth was in a corner. "You like computer games?" Grace asked.

Samantha's leg jittered up and down, "Sort of. Not really."

They sat in front of one of the computers. Grace turned it on, explaining the procedure. "Let's start by ramping your imagination skills, pretend you love playing, win or lose." Grace reached in a box, selected some electrodes. "We hook you up first, so I can monitor you from the booth." She squirted gooey gel on the electrodes, strategically placing them on Samantha's head. "Oh, that's cold," Samantha cringed.

"Don't worry, it'll warm up."

"You can't get electrocuted, I hope."

"Juice only comes out of your brain, none goes in."

"That sounds just as scary. Like a brain-suck, or what?"

Grace assured her, "Dr. Ron got rewired, look at him. And, so did I, Samantha." Flipping on a computer, little critters, trolls, lady bugs, and buttlerflies lit up, moving speed-bound on the screen. "You play. Make mistakes, have fun. Just don't stop until I tell you."

"That's it? I heard just the opposite – that computer games wrack or whack your brain."

Pleased by Samantha's educated concern, Grace confirmed, "Some, maybe...violence begets violence." Grace continued explaining with strong conviction, "For starters, the repetition in our skill-based games reprogram areas in the brain like the frontal lobe, the executive think-tank decision-maker. It's simple. You play videos.

Bingo!" She snapped her finger at Samantha, who was mesmerized by her look-alike. "You'll be smarter and will get a world overview and work it, baby."

With a big grin Samantha replied, "Wow...this is awesome. Let's play."

Grace headed into the booth. "I monitor the session from here. Have fun."

Little yapping trolls blasted on the screen gobbling numbers, flashing into equations. Samantha quick-fingered the joystick, battling, breathing hard. "Zap you! Yay! Oops, I'm dead."

In the booth wearing headphones, Grace plugged into Samantha, shooting white flaring lights into the mix, rewiring, re-circuiting worn or unused synapses. Little trolls and numbers were dividing and multiplying as the skill level incrementally increased. Samantha blinked several times, slowly building endurance, not giving up until she screeched, "My head hurts!" Calm and calculating Grace adjusted dials; a meter lowered from red level to green. Samantha was 'in the zone', basking in a pleasant euphoria. "Don't you just love it?" Grace remarked.

At the end of the session Grace handed Samantha a box. "This contains vital brain boosts. Vitamins, minerals, amino's, fish oil. Take it religiously – that means everyday. It's part of the program."

Samantha was eager to please, "Cool. Can do."

Grace wanted a definite commitment. "<u>Will</u> do!" she ordered.

"Done." Mentally alert Samantha left Brain-Joggle's building floating on air. She was like the Scarecrow in Oz, skipping, rather limping, down the yellow brick road chasing a Menses, or was it *Mensa,* brain?

The Warehouse Dance Club was off campus. A large dingy hangout with planked floors, pool tables and a raised strobe-lit dance floor. Students flocked to it like homing pigeons on weekends, paying a hefty twenty-dollar-plus cover charge. Inside, multi-colored strobe lights flashed a hypnotic rhythm timed to the DJ's tunes.

Disguised in her retro look, Jenny entered the packed 'Rave Party'. A metal nose, tongue, eyebrow-pierced waiter approached, greeting her with a breezy "Hello, Mama. Want a taste of brew?" as he handed a smoking-hot reddish foam liquid to her. Almost dropping the glass, Jenny spilled a few drops on her dress.

Trying to appear ten years younger she snickered a tiny voice, "Thank you, brew master." He used a napkin like a come-on and wiped the drops off her dress. Gazing at her invisible cleavage, he crooned, "With pleasure, my moist Ho'dunk."

Protecting her cover and wanting to blend in she toasted a couple of Dred-locked mangy-looking guys. "Here's to the drinky stink." She downed it straight away, completely unaware that the concoction was spiked with a bona-fide 'Love Drug'.

One of the guys shouted over the music, "Wait until the brewsky kicks in. You'll be all over us."

Within minutes Jenny was dancing wildly to a throbbing Metallica tune. Egged-on by the out-of-control guys who were shouting, "Take it off, retro-mama," Jenny seductively unfastened a button on her jacket, revealing a skimpy black waist-to-breast body bra underneath.

Taunting them one button at a time, the guys encouraged, "More skin." "Tease me." Strip it, babe." The "Love Drug' kicked in. Joining other wild exhibitionists, Jenny danced around a cage pole, sliding up-and-down while strobes flashed, adding intrigue to the mad-dog flurry.

Outside the party a patrol car screeched to a halt. Two burly police officers, heftier than the club's bouncers, ambled out of the squad car. Toting Billy clubs and pepper spray, guns drawn, they made a garish entry into the club, shouting, "Bust the lust!"

Bright house lights flickered on. The under-aged crowd dispersed like trapped mice at the sight of the officers. Mayhem broke out: pushing and shoving, bottles flying, drinks spilling, the punks tripped over each other, scattering in all directions, and racing out the front, back, and side doors.

Caught-up in her own world Jenny danced her little charade on stage. "I love rock and roll!" she raved.

A cop bamboozled her. "You're coming with me."

"Oh, you want to fraternize, big boy? I'm part of Campus Security."

"Right. And I'm Godzilla." He tossed a flailing Jenny over his shoulder, carrying her outside.

A crowd of rowdies shouted, "Go home piglets. Grunt. Grunt."

In the midst of hecklers Samantha and Tanya, who had also been at the 'Rave Party', were leaning against each other to keep balance, tipsy from more than a few drinks. Samantha tossed an empty whisky bottle at a cop. Slurring her words, she baited, "Get a five-cent-cent return, you grumpy muff-trainer."

Responding brutishly and overly reactive, "Oh yeah, Ms. Jailbait!" he yelled and pepper-sprayed Samantha in the face. She went down on the concrete yelping like a wounded pup. "Ouch! Aauuug! My eyes, I'm blind, I can't see."

Easily subduing her, the cop hiked her over his back. "Hope you like bars and chains."

Tanya shouted, "You hairy toad, let her go." Attempting to free Samantha, Tanya held tight to her legs, dragging along the ground like a bumper-body. "Stop, you animal!"

Corralling them next to a wall the burly cop commanded. "Arms over your head." He frisked the flaming felines. Tanya kicked at him. "Nasty to get 'touchy-feely'!" Samantha blubbered, "Get your slime paws off me." Cops wrestled them into a Paddy Wagon. As the vehicle whisked away, Samantha screamed through the wagon's cage, "Burned-out donut-suckers!"

The women's holding tank had a pungent odor. Rudely intoxicated Jenny sulked in the jail cell corner, blustering, "Now look at the mess Jenny's in. Nah, a security babe locked in jail cell overnight. Doomed. No one to call for bail."

At the police station, Samantha, Tanya, and Trish, a rowdy brunette, were jostled through the jail cell door. Jenny crouched in corner, with a glazed look on her face, watching them. Clinging to the cell bars, Samantha's nose poked through. "Let me out of here!" she demanded. "My father's a frickin' lawyer. He'll sue you grouch-bags 'til King Kong comes marching through the rafters."

Trish pulled her off the bars. "Shut your preppie face or we're in here for life."

Samantha was baffled, still not making complete sentences. "Talk it up, girl. The one night we're carded, supposed to jam to the crack of dawn."

Tanya bragged, "Wait until this sex-kitty-scandal gets out, Kappa's will just die with envy."

Samantha drooled, "They hate virgins. This was my night. My 'Rave' party! My chance to prove to the world I'm not a dweeb, a second-rate twin."

Tanya mused, "I wish I had a twin."

"Let's trade places," Samantha slurred. "You be the smothered child of a harrumphing freako mother."

Tanya put her fingers in her ears. "I know...please don't tell me again. She stole your childhood. Lived your life for you."

"Sucked the breath out of me." Samantha held her breath like she was suffocating. Trish grabbed her from behind, snapped a fist around her waist thrusting a Heimlich maneuver. A wad of Samantha's gum spat across the room. "Gross me out, idiot!" Trish yelled. Samantha's breath released.

Appalled by Samantha's admonishment Jenny wheeled in-and-out of a stupor, "Guilt me," she muttered under her breath.

Whether it was inborn intuition or just chance Samantha turned to Jenny, plaintively admitting, "I'm a virgin. This was going to be my 'pop-the-cherry' night."

Still affected by the date-rape drug Jenny declared, "Me too."

Samantha looked questioningly at Jenny. Her vision was a blur. Jenny's face waffled; morphed into her 'Mom-look', then back to the retro-look. Samantha stared even harder. The moment stretched. It appeared that Samantha recognized her and moaned, "She haunts me like a festering zit ready to pop. Like I think she's everyone, staring at me."

Tanya knew it was Hallbally. She winked, not revealing they were conspirators.

A jailer called out, "Ms. Forrest? You got bail."

Jenny and Samantha simultaneously answered, "That's me." Catching her mistake, Jenny turned away.

Samantha shrieked, "Get me out of this echo chamber before I kill myself!"

Upon hearing the threatening words Jenny, feeling wounded, took an emotional blow, doubled over, clutching her stomach. "I'm going to be sick."

The jailer returned, nodding at Tanya. "Ms. Rice. You got bail."

Tanya answered. "That is I...or, is it 'me'?"

Jenny responded weakly. "It's you!" I'm me. Or am I?"

Sensing Jenny's distress at being left behind, Tanya reached out and whispered. "Your job is way tough. You're everywhere, all the time for everyone." Tanya tried fixing her hair, as she headed out of the cell.

Tanya and Samantha entered the holding area where Brian was waiting for them. He had bailed them out. "Well, aren't we looking good?" he chewed-on his words.

Tanya nuzzled up to him, rubbing his masculine chest, "How did you know we were here?"

"Followed the Paddy Wagon. My dad posted bail." Boasting, he smiled, "He'll get you off, no sweat."

Mortified, Samantha quivered. "Dad knows about this?"

"Ah... he's way cool with it. Proud you finally rebelled."

"Go figure. If I'd known that, I wouldn't have waited so long", Samantha said as Brain he led the girl's outside the room and to the waiting SUV.

Shrinking in the cell corner, Jenny dropped her head between her legs, holding the back of her head with both hands, feeling lost. "I'm destitute. No one knows me...the real me, anymore. I've got nobody."

Trish scooted close and snaked an arm around her. "Don't worry, babe. It's worth it. You'll just love the pancake breakfast."

"Not pancakes, please?" Crushing her face on bent knees, Jenny said, "I'm no flat-boobed...pancake."

"Got it. Think more strawberry mush."

Swatting at a fly on her cheek, maniacally driven, Jenny's eyes rolled, tracking the circling fly. "There's nothing left to hate. I hate my life. I hate everything."

Swatting the fly against the wall with her palm, it bounced on the floor. Trish encouraged, "Good start. Now just find something you like."

"Oh, go smoke a bong, Pollyanna. That's what I preach." The fly's wings fluttered one last time before succumbing. Jenny felt sick. "Ugh, geez...its life's gone. All over in an unsuspecting second." The thought sent her deeper into questioning her own temporal existence while her inebriated and drugged brain checked in and out.

Brian drove the girls back to the dorm. Tanya nibbled his ear, practically climbing on his lap. No question they were staying together. Dropping Samantha off at the front of the dorm building, Brian said, "Sam, you're still sloshed. Are you okay to be alone?"

"Didn't know you're running a 'Child Care' thing. I'm a big girl, Brian." Blinking, trying to get him into focus, slurring a word or two Samantha rattled on, "Night-Night. Go ram-rod your brains out," she waved as they sped off.

Shivering in the brisk night air, Samantha buttoned her sweater, mumbling under her breath, "I failed to 'pop-the-cherry' night. Of course there's tomorrow night, next year, or before I die, at maybe at ninety-five." How pathetic, she thought. In a loud explosion of laughter, she burst into tears. "Damn, am I a drunken fool? Nope, I'm not drunk, this feeling is exciting, different, mischievous." Something had snapped inside like a rubber band. "Daddy's little girl doesn't have to be perfect." She felt the absence of repression; replaced with wild, free, and careless abandon.

"Thanks for bailing me out, Dad," she murmured to herself while unlocking the dorm door. Not fully understanding plea-bargaining, she was certain that he was sure to do it. Growing-up she always heard him shrieking, "Cooked books, questionable gifts, money laundering – no problem. That's my job – keep you out of jail and the tabloids." She had become numb or maybe, jaded. The constant questions, statements, all the drivel she heard over the years, haunted and taunted her mind while she whipped into the closet and stripped down to her bra and thong. Tossing on a black London Fog raincoat, she smeared on bright red lipstick, kicked off her espadrilles, strapped on Tanya's high-heel 'do me' shoes. "You owe me one, girl," she smirked

Escaping into a full moon night, Samantha arrived at Dr. Ron's apartment building.

Amazing luck, she located his apartment, taking on the challenge of the stairs. In painful teetering heels she hobbled three stories, reciting quotes from one of her 'How to Seduce a Man' books: "Give him honey, don't mention bald-spots. Tell him he's nice." Pumped for love, she tapped on the door.

Dr. Ron wasn't expecting company, but at 2:00 A.M. he couldn't risk not answering – it had to be an emergency. He opened the door, and to his surprise, there stood a beauty, his physical fantasy, a specimen he so desired to deflower. She giggled, "I was thinking, a first, for sure you're hot, not bald, no-no bowling balls, you're drop-dead gorgeous."

"Samantha, are you okay?" Dr. Ron asked. She brushed past him into the apartment. He left the door ajar. "Ah, what's up?"

"That depends on you." She dropped the trench coat to the floor. There she stood in all her spender ready, willing, way overdue, and able. He didn't budge. "Déjà vu" whimpered from his lips, a haunting memory of the lovely Italian seductress. Before he could say another word, a woman's voice cut in. "Samantha? What the hell?"

Looking spent, yet luscious in silky bra and thong, stood Grace, her double, her other mentor. Samantha hyperventilated and grabbed her coat to cover herself. "I had no idea. The two of you, my favorite people, hooked-up. Geez, I'm so stupid."

"No. No. No, not stupid," they both said in unison.

Grace showed modesty, self-wrapped a throw from the couch. "Must have been a rough night," she said.

"Want some coffee, need to sober up?" Dr. Ron stammered with concern.

"No thanks, I'm as sober as I ever want to be. Sorry. Wrong bald guy. See ya'." Samantha fled the apartment, ambling down the three flights of stairs, not looking back or stopping for the ardent calls, "Samantha, come back!"

There was no going back. "Ride the road forward, onward, upward," she recited in her mind. Wandering back to the dorm, she greeted the starlit heavens, "Let it rip, Mama!" There was no stopping her now. Once she settled back in her room, she pondered the night's events. She felt an uncanny aloneness. Unbeknownst to her there was no spy that night peeking or leering in space-boots from the room above. Samantha was clueless about how free she actually was, or how imprisoned her mother, the phantom room-spy, literally was.

She clunked down on the bed, undressed from a prone position. Tossing the 'do me' shoes on the floor, it occurred to her, "My life never worked as a dork-ette, it clearly won't work as a slut, so what to do?"

Couldn't her guardian angels take pity on a bumbling wallflower? Toss her a red bling-bling magical slipper? Help speed the growth into naughty-girl buoyancy? Finally, she nodded-off to sleep with the last line of a childhood prayer, "I pray the Lord my soul won't bleep."

Lucid dreams engulfed her; life in a nunnery, humbly serving, sacrificing, and growing thin and frail. Miraculously, a man's face flashed, unrecognizable, 'blurry'. Falling out of an apple tree, smacking her on the head, they were lip-to-lip. Then what happened, did they kiss or what? The dream abruptly ended.

Facing the consequences for her actions landed Jenny in front of a judge. The boisterous courtroom was jammed with student 'Rave Party' offenders. Judge Hickey, streetwise and stern, chastised Jenny, who looked like death warmed-over and freeze-dried. "Ms. Hallbally, you are one dysfunctional disgrace. Your pity-poor example is demeaning. A below-the-belt blow to our coveted Campus Security."

Roars of raucous laughter spilled from the gaping crowd. The judge slammed the gavel. "Order in the court."

Jenny percolated, frazzled and embarrassed. Feeling guilty, she lowered her head, staring blankly at the floor. Judge Hickey instructed. "Hung-over? Stand up and face the court." Jenny threw her shoulders back, standing upright.

Judge Hickey's piercing cobalt-colored eyes amplified her directness. "Do you have an explanation for attempting to sexually molest a minor?"

"I didn't *touch* anyone, intentionally. It was innocent slam dancing. People sort of bang your boobs, hump-ride your tush."

"That's enough trash-talking. You respect this court." Judge Hickey raised her chin, looking down at Jenny.

Jenny bit her lip, "So sorry. How would I know? I was on a date-rape, sex drug."

Waving her hand, Judge Hickey dismissively hissed, "Ridiculous, defiant, deviant. Ms. Hallbally, your professional duties are suspended. To evaluate the extent of your exhibitionism you are hereby reprimanded by the court." She paused, running her finger down a list. "The court finds a depraved infraction and hereby sentences you, Ms. Lucy Hallbally, to behavioral modification with the 'Grunge Group Rehab.'"

A bailiff bellowed. "The court calls Helga Schmidt." Helga stepped forward. Judge Hickey slapped her on the wrist. "Sgt. Helga, the rookie crashed on your watch. Prime her or else there will be tough justice for both of you." Judge Hickey tapped her gavel, staring at Jenny as if she was the devil incarnate. "Let's hope I never see your degenerate debauched flagellating face in here again, Ms. Hallbally." She nodded at Helga. "That includes you, Sergeant."

Not flinching Helga took the reprimand with professional stride. As she escorted Jenny out of the courtroom the spectators jeered and cheered.

Jenny frothed in expectation, "Okay, rip me to shreds, torment, torture me for my whatever she called it...'depraved infraction'."

Helga related, "We all faced the judge."

In a moment of relief, Jenny was stunned. "You did?"

A first for Helga, she let her guard down and opened up, "When I was sixteen, Hickey awarded my parents my...out of wedlock son."

"I'm so sorry. I didn't know."

"No problem. We're still tight. He's still family."

Crinkle-faced, holding back the tears, hiding a mother's pain, Jenny's cover-up plight became transparent to Helga. "Mom's have to stick together," she said with compassion.

Drizzling in a dim glimmer of hope, Jenny's mouth flew open, "Who said I was a mom?"

Helga grinned. "Everything about you says 'Mom'. Trying so hard to make everything right, for everyone. Now's the time to make everything right for yourself."

"Well, we know I can expertly mess up."

Helga wrapped a reassuring arm around her, "Don't we now." She added to ease the strain, "We all mess up." No doubt the two women would share a bond that only estranged 'Mom's' could know...and seal.

Paying her penance, Jenny drove to the therapy group. Her heart sank, as the impact of her circumstance engulfed her. Inhaling a breath of courage she entered an alcove at the Comic House, that read 'Grunge Studio'. Resembling an amateur theatre more than a rehab center, playbills plastered the walls with old-time comedy stars from the Marx Brothers to Mel Brooks. The décor and accessories were odd, ranging from life-sized Laurel and Hardy plastic chairs, to a Lucy wind-up doll that crossed the floor, repeating, "Ethel, where's Ricky?" Hesitating, she wondered if this was the right office.

An eccentric looking woman flaunting a top hat and a skin-tight black jumpsuit greeted Jenny as she entered the waiting area. "Hello. I'm Kara Hanes," the woman said, extending her hand. Jenny awkwardly shook hands with Kara, and then politely asked, "Is this the Grunge Group? It said so on the door."

"You must be here for an intake or a retake?" Kara laughed heartily. Jenny held up the court order for the mandatory session. "Not exactly a laughing matter."

Kara affected a professional air. "As I previously inferred. No intake! No out-take!"

Shaken by the insolence Jenny stammered, "What double-talking jive are you talking?"

Kara's lip curled, "No Grunge! You end up on the cutting room floor."

"Whatever. I'm ready." Jenny tried to appease her.

"Ready for what?" In anticipation, Kara waved her top hat.

Jenny placed the mandatory court order in Kara's face. "For your edification I will read it aloud. "Ms. Lucy Hallbally is ordered by the court to attend 'Grunge Group Rehab' for behavioral therapy."

"I could see that. You're hyper, rude and very pushy." Exuding distain, Kara tossed the court order in a trash can.

In shock, Jenny retrieved it. "Who do you think you are?"

"Don't throw your nose up at me. I'm Kara Hanes, ex weed-head, partying up-all-night honky-gang-banger, getting my well-deserved second chance." Motioning to the jumpsuit. "So, I wear all black, mourning, not 'living-it-up'. There's no shame in that." She once again extended her hand to Jenny. "Pleased to meet you and your dirty laundry."

Trying to maintain her composure, Jenny stated, "No fraternizing! I didn't come here to make friends. Now can we get on with the intake?"

"Somehow this feels more like," Kara tipped her top hat as if bidding an adieu, "an out-take."

"All right. Out-take." Jenny fired back.

Kara seemed confused, "Or maybe a re-take?"

After five more minutes of excruciating mumbo- jumbo. similar to a warped rendition of the 'Who's On First' routine, Jenny's patience

evaporated. "I want to see Grunge right now."

Kara smiled as if she had just accomplished the greatest feat in the world. "That's really good. Now you're here voluntarily."

"No I'm not." Jenny brandished the court order at her.

"Yes, you are. You just said you wanted to see Grunge."

"That's why I'm here."

"Good. Then we agree."

She escorted Jenny through metal flanked medieval crested doors. Not knowing what to expect on the other side Jenny hesitated, "What's in there – a dungeon with vices, steel restraints, a torture chamber?" Upon entering, it turned out to be anticlimactic to see a bare room with several chairs, mats on the floor, and a large leatherette Bozo-the-Clown punching bag hanging from the ceiling.

Ruggedly handsome, ex-con Max Grunge, a stand-up comic turned therapist, facilitated the behavioral session. A group of misfits took turns punching the bag. Rank Rhonda, a whacked-out ex-stripper, and

Howdy, a red-bearded ventriloquist, watched Willy the Worm, a contortionist. Willy twisted on his back, slapping Bozo's bottom like it was a little kid. "Bad Willy is overdrawn fifty-dollars again."

Howdy punished, "Shame, shame on you."

Rank Rhonda yawned. "Boring! Why is your problem always about a few bucks? Do you like the attention?"

Willy flipped to his feet, puffing his chest out, "Why is your problem always about a few fat pounds?"

"Fat! I'll give you a fat head." Incensed, Rank Rhonda took a killer stance, preparing to attack.

Willy rolled into a little ball, tucking his head under his knees. "Don't knock my head off. I got a few brains left."

She inched closer to Willy. Grunge commanded with hypnotic authority. "Rank! Rank Rhonda! Breathe. Inhale <u>now!</u>" She inhaled like a snorting horse, nostrils flaring, upper lip raised, and teeth gnashing.

Grunge ordered. "Focus, realign the target. Now!"

Viewing Willy rolled-up like a doughnut, she flew into the air, and with aimed precision her foot gently touched him, then followed through with a high-kick, striking the Bozo bag smack on the nose.

Grunge sighed. "Good anger control choice. How did that feel?"

"Not bad," Rank Rhonda replied. Jabbing a fist toward Willy, she continued. "Maybe better than a crunched skull."

Grunge encouraged, "Let's give it up for Rank Rhonda." The group applauded.

Grunge's steel blue eyes landed on Jenny. Her teeth chattered, fearing she was trapped in a chamber of horrors filled with mad people, drowning in limitations, hauling emotional baggage. "Please pretend I'm not here," she said to herself.

Grunge greeted her with a disarming smile. "And you must be Lucy?"

Caught off guard she stammered, "Jenny."

"Ah! You prefer Jenny to Lucy?"

Correcting her mistake, she quickly answered, "I am Lucy."

Howdy remarked to Willy, "Probably a little schizo, eh?"

Grunge took over. "Come on over and meet Bozo, our friendly punching bag. Using him helps us to tell the truth, get the anger out and feel good." Jenny reluctantly stood in front of the clown bag.

Grunge asked. "Ever punch a bag?"

Willy wiggled, throwing a fey punch. "Are you a punch-board-hotty or a bag-hag?"

Turned off, Jenny folded her arms across her chest, "Are there no civil, humane rules here? What is behavior training anyway? Insults, slams, and hurting someone?"

Howdy added, "You'll get immune. Then fine-tuned."

Watching the group dynamic Grunge let it flow. Demonstrating for Jenny's benefit, he instructed. "Now here's the stance. Plant both feet firm. Lift your arm up. Raise your heel. Toe solid. Twist at the waist. Power from the ground up. Follow through." He punched the bag. "Feels good. Take a go."

Jenny's knees wobbled, imitating his position. Holding her hand he folded it into a fist, and then right-angled it. "Never punch dead-on. A little English, a bit to the side. Won't break a knuckle."

Rank Rhonda stepped up, jabbing and slashing the bag. "Then you beat the ka-jeebies out of it," she growled. "Let out every little pain, shame, and blame. Everyone you wanted to slam and didn't!" Double-fisted, pounding hard, she snarled, "But wished you had."

Jenny vibrated with a rush of adrenaline. "Everyone, huh?" She clenched a fist. Twisted it straight on, then sideways.

Grunge complimented her. "Not bad. Just hold it closer to your chest." She tried. "Higher up."

"I'm supposed to remember all that, while I'm angry and screaming?" Jenny complained.

He prodded, "Now Lucy Hallbally, why are you here?" Grunge prodded.

Jenny slugged the punch-bag, rambling as a video camera inconspicuously hidden on a lamp recorded her actions. "I am here, because...I have to be."

"Take responsibility...why are you here?"

"I don't have any delicacies...I mean deviancies...that anyone else doesn't." She grimaced and threw a hard punch. "Ouch!" She pulled back and rubbed her hand.

"It's not about them. Who are you!" His eyes locked on her, penetrating her cover.

Uncomfortable in her skin, she looked away, "I'll pass. No answer."

The group shouted out to her. "Splito." "Jenny or Lucy?" "Defecto." "A wilted daisy."

"I'm a tyrant. I wilted my daisy, Samantha." She punched the bag harder, low jabs, low kicks, high-kicks, pounding. Breaking down in tears, Jenny confessed. "I'm a shut-out, an outcast of...of..."

Grunge commanded, "An outcast of what? Say it."

Jenny slipped to the floor. "The 'Soccer Mom' society."

The group badgered. "Boo-Hoo." "Break my heart."

Grunge signaled, pointing to the door. "Everyone except Lucy – get out of here. Take five." The group filed out. Grunge continued processing with Jenny. Steadfast, unrelenting, piercing her defenses, excuses, going for her truth, he said. "So, you lost your identity. You lost what made you want to get up in the morning. You lost your dream job."

Jenny wailed a deep sob. "You have no right. You don't even know me."

"It's not important what I know. It's what you know. Do you know who you really are, Ms. Hallbally?"

Her resistance wearing thin she pleaded, "Stop prying. It's none of your business."

"True! You're the one who needs to get down 24/7. To care about you, to be happy with yourself and your life."

Unable to pull away from the action, the group eavesdropped from the doorway. They joked and poked at hope, generating positive expectation for Jenny, and themselves. Finally they burst back inside calling out to Jenny, "Rewrite your script."

"Life's not a script," she lamented, 'It's a random...mess-up."

Howie put his arm around her and wiggled his nose, "Take-two, mummy."

Rank Rhonda added, "Why so heavy? It's a second chance. Take it and smile."

Jenny waffled, thinking, really wanting to make a shift. "I always believed in second chances."

Willy scooted across the floor, bumping into a wall, chortling "Life's just a rehearsal".

With a smile of relief Jenny acquiesced. "Rehearsal, huh? That's it? Is that all there is?"

They nodded. Jenny broke into a thunderous roar. "Then I'll just keep on dancing!"

Intake day became Jenny's debut. She discovered a platform for Richie harangues. During lunch she went on and on. "My marriage crashed and burned. He was the bas-turd. A shallow good-for-nothing nincompoop! I was the laughing-stock of the Burbs."

Rank Rhonda suggested. "Even the score. Rent a male hooker."

"Why me? Such an offer, getting the clap or worse is a sound solution, " Frustrated, she smacked the punching bag.

Willy yawned, bored. "She's a recycle, rehash."

Rank Rhonda made a motion, "We're checking out, dearie." They ate lunch, blabbed among themselves, basically oblivious to Jenny's wretched rap. Then, back on the firing line Grunge grilled Jenny.

Grunge coaxed her fixated viewpoint. "Come up with one new thought. Now!" Jenny went still, stiffening with a vacant expression. "Any thought?" He waved his hand over her vapid stare. Her eyes blinked. Diagnosing the symptom he muttered, "Synapse glitch. No thoughts at the moment." Grunge took a more positive approach. "What's your desire, in your heart-of-hearts?"

In a most unusual gesture, Jenny cracked her knuckles and chewed on her bottom lip. Suddenly she was alive, alert, stimulated "Oh my God, I forgot about my 'heart-of-hearts'. I wrote a whole BLOG on that one. Everything's changed...I don't know anymore."

"Change is good. Go on," Grunge pumped her to say more.

Pressured to say something she dribbled an incredulous speech. "My heart and soul longs to be a change-agent of truth. A reformer, a reclaimer of lost ethics, morals. Of cheaters...infidels, mainly."

The group heckled. "Blah-Blah-Blah." "Take a hike." "Cut the bully-poop." Intentionally making grotesque faces, loud arm flapping farts, burping annoyances, the group seemed like a crew of monkeys at a zoo.

Rejected, Jenny moaned, "Even my spontaneous dream sounded stupid."

Grunge kept fueling her. "Get over yourself. This is the world taking a crap on your parade. Get past it. Tell us what you love."

She snickered, "Love? Would you mind spelling it? Not in my vocabulary."

Rank Rhonda threw up her arms, "It's the 'Nobody Loves Me' syndrome cop-out."

Examining her truth Jenny spouted, "My kids. Okay, I love my kids."

Unrelenting, Grunge grilled her. "Who's your hero, someone you admire?"

"Ah, maybe Martha Stewart. She's like a friend. Shows up every day. Never talks behind your back."

Amused by her childlike reasoning Grunge challenged, "A felon's your role model?"

With sincerity Jenny defended, "She bravely served railroaded time. I got off. She is my domestic hero."

In a dramatic exhibition, Rank Rhonda did a full-out split. She raised both arms overhead pointing to Jenny. "Grunge's felon club welcomes 'Miss Wanna-be Loved'."

Willy squeaked, "Master-minded by the number one lewd-dude-felon, Grunge."

Taken aback and bewildered, a distorted thought crossed Jenny's mind. How could the legal system send her to a criminal? Not hiding disapproval, she blurted, "Grunge is a felon! Some credential! "

Willy scooted apelike across the floor, dragging his knuckles. "Get with the program. Grunge is a world class hacker, a CIA despot, our comedy shrink."

Jenny scowled, "Very funny. Make me laugh."

Howdy took her to test with twisted, warped facial expressions. Folding his lip under his nose, wiggling his ears, Jenny burst into a belly laugh. Howdy milked it, stayed on a roll, performing, contorting wild hand gestures. He pointed at Jenny, moving lips without words. Interpreting his intent, the group shouted wild guesses, "Yo' talk is a somersault." "Spin Queen?" "Trapped in Bullshit!"

Rank Rhonda went face-to-face with Jenny. "Let's see you rock your talk, Sister Gloom."

"What talk?"

Howdy screeched, "No more talk. Pleeeease!"

Rank Rhonda challenged. "How about charades. Sixty-seconds to show us your life, girlfriend."

Jenny always loved charades. From ten-years-old to a teen, her family and friends jumped up to act out the silliest of the sillies. Reluctantly, she stood in front of the group. Within seconds she mimicked her life's misery, delight, and hilarity. She pounded the mat and rolled on the floor, pumped her butt up-and-down, acted-out macho cop antics, and slam-danced the punching bag.

The group taunted, "Go Lucy, Go!" "Pump it." "Grind it, prissy-muff!"

Taking the jeers lightly rather than as perceived assaults shifted Jenny's oddball world. "I love you guys...too!" she yelled back at them.

Grunge smiled to himself. Jenny had joined the group. Masterfully aware, he knew that every action between teacher and student has the power to heal or to damage. The vote was still out on Grunge. His background spoke to his ability to 'control and annihilate' at will. Yet, his comedy-antics lightened the spirit of his student's. Jenny found a place to let it all hang out, to gain an upswing in self-esteem instead of struggling to revive a disintegrating image. She could risk losing control in this safe haven. She was busting out of the confines of the 'do's and don'ts' of suburban life, or being squelched under the strict guise of the security babes.

Agitated, Rank Rhonda paced back and forth asked, "Hey, can somebody give me a lift to work?"

Howdy razzed. "Face-lift or tow?"

Willy belted, "Greasy-spoon – calling all waitresses!"

Jenny offered. "Come on, I'll get you out of this loony bin." Rank Rhonda didn't hesitate and followed Jenny out of the studio.

Howdy yelled after them, "What's two tunes leaving together? A durge."

With the Caddy's top down Jenny and Rank Rhonda cruised Main Street. Students hung out in coffee shops, skateboarders whizzed by, and bikers wove in and out of traffic.

Rank Rhonda shared, "Call it a sad-sack life. I was orphaned at eight. My parents just up and disappeared. I hopped fences and crawled through doggie doors just to get a meal."

"How horrid, you were homeless at eight?" Jenny swallowed hard by the mere thought of a little girl alone.

"Hit the foster care system. My caseworker said, 'She needs a rabies shot or a mother'."

"That's criminal."

"Dun-da-dun-da. Try nine abuse-pads. A crack house, eleven foster kids piled in a pigsty trailer, a church belfry with a backed-up cesspool. Gag me. So, I drank myself to sleep. Did some drugs. Some jail time. Grunge saved my sorry butt."

"I thought changing schools was bad," Jenny felt indulgent, You had a rough go. So sorry."

"No need for croc-tears. You're the powder puff that needs tough lovin'. Grunge-man's the expert in that department. He'll tame you."

"You mean S&M tough lovin'?" Jenny slammed on the brakes to avoid a swerving car in front of them

"Try mortal combat, heavy duty CIA, the paranormal woo-woo division. Grunge was trained to leave his body whenever, escape mangling and Sumu torture. They had him prisoner in an enemy camp. He'd zap into someone's brain, make them trip-out, croak, faint, do whatever."

"Are you serious?" Jenny cringed, rolling down the window to catch a breath of air.

Rank Rhonda lit a cigarette, inhaling deep. "Imagine what he does to the babes."

Waving off the thought, Jenny answered, "No...no...not a clue."

"He can vibe-in anywhere on the planet and 'remote-view'."

"What's that?"

"He can actually be there. See what's going on. Trippy, huh?"

Jenny laughed, "Way too trippy to imagine."

"Start imaging, girl. Your roller coaster ride hasn't even started. Better get rid of commitment issues; learn to kick it like a Marine or Grunge will have his field day." She pointed to an alley. "I'll get out here. We trainee slaves use the back door of the restaurant."

A myriad of incomprehensible impressions whizzed through Jenny's mind as she swallowed the lump in her throat. She saw the courage, vitality, and spunk woven into the waif. She gushed, "I admire you, Rank Rhonda. Trying to better your lot. Showing up for your 'Self'."

Rank Rhonda smiled. "Thanks...for the ride. It's been real...kitschy and bitchy."

For the first time in fifteen years Jenny felt she had finally found a place to play and just take a moment to find and be herself. Like a clipped-winged bird set free to bumble, recoup and explore her wacky-newness, Jenny believed that she was on the road to recovery.

However, for the first time in nineteen years Richie was 'home alone'. Clothes were strewn about. He munched Chinese food from a take-out carton. The phone rang. Juggling chopsticks, he glibly answered, "Richie here. Don't ask. I don't know."

"Mr. Forrest?" A male voice asked.

Chewing and talking Richie garbled, "You got me."

"It's Detective Gritty. We found your wife's cell phone in a ditch."

A chill swept through Richie's body. "Her cell? Oh no. Where?"

"Forty miles from town...on a desolate road."

"Jenny would never leave her cell alone."

"Sorry, it doesn't look good. Smells like foul play."

Fearing the worst, Richie braced himself. "What does that mean?"

"Open your front door. I'm outside." Before he finished the sentence, Richie quickly opened the door.

Gritty held a box, fixing on Richie with compassion. "So sorry, my condolences are forthcoming, Mr. Forrest."

"Condolence's? You aren't giving up the search?" A sinking feeling in his gut prompted Richie to offer, "Please come inside."

"I can't, sir. The case is too hot to waste time." Gritty handed the box to Richie.

Relieved that the pursuit wasn't over, Richie patted Gritty's back "Yes, the case." Richie peeked at the cell phone in the box. A tear trickled down his cheek.

"Until we find the body, this is your beloved wife's remains," Gritty said, avoiding Richie's tearful eyes.

Richie gasped, "Oh my Jenny."

Gritty eyed him suspiciously, "We'll keep you informed. Might need you for questioning. So, stay in town." His tone was firm.

Adamant and raw to the bone, Richie stared Gritty down. "I will aid in the discovery. I'm not going anywhere."

With a lilt of suspicion Gritty stated, "Good. No botching, blunders, or bungling on our team." Apparently in a rush, Gritty turned away from Richie and abruptly walked toward his car.

Reeling in a wasteland of regret Richie cradled the cell phone in his arms. Holding it to his ear, he spoke gently, "Jenny, we <u>are</u> a perfect fit."

Exiting the premises, Gritty smiled sardonically, whispering into his cell phone. "Bait delivered."

The clock read 1:00 AM: The once pristine Forrest household was a mess. Clothes, newspapers and general litter was strewn everywhere. Richie compulsively unpacked boxes filled with Jenny's online purchases. He tried on new clothes that were stuffed in shopping bags; some from two season's past.

He examined the "WipeyWipes", reading the label. "Cleaning clean cleanest cleaner." Using the wipes he shined mirrors, scrubbed windows, dusted furniture, and mopped the kitchen floor. Several empty packs later he collapsed, mumbling with pride. "I am the cleanest cleaner."

A barrage of phone calls from Bambe torpedoed a reminder of his unforgettable, unforgivable ways. He refused to pick up, letting the answering machine do his shameful bidding. His cell chimed repeatedly. Checking Caller ID he saw Bambe was call-stalking. Voicemail would take her message.

2:00 A.M.: On TV a psychic hotline touted, "Feeling lost? Out of sorts? Has your life turned to Jell-O? Want to bring back the dead? Call 'MiaTia Psychic Channel'. Only ninety-nine-cents per minute."

"Bring back the dead?" Richie felt hooked. Typically logical and analytical, a doubting naysayer of the occult, he felt a desperate urge to call. The need for advice and consolation overpowered him. Throwing practicality aside, defying logic, he frenetically called one of the hundred (unbeknownst to him) so-called MiaTia's.

In a white-trash trailer, a toothless two-ton Tessie stuffed in a Hawaiian muumuu, lisped into a speakerphone. "MiaTia here. Stop thinking, it hurts my brain."

Finding her remark preposterous, Richie retorted "then how can you read my mind?"

"I have no intention to. It's all garbage in there."

Ready to hang up Richie barked, "I'm paying to listen to this crap?"

"No, you're paying to listen to your crap."

Agitated and nervous, Richie popped a chocolate truffle in his mouth. "Okay, lay it on me."

With a MiaTia manual in hand, she turned to the pitch section marked, "Smart-Ass." Proceeding, she read directly from the script, pausing in-between for the client's question or comments. "Denial has its pay-off, doesn't it, bud?"

'What do you mean by that?"

"Aren't you the basic spoiled guy? A triple threat. Uncouth, self-absorbed, a virility-challenged finagler?"

He winced, "Somewhat true."

"That's sucky! You didn't ante up – take responsibility when you had the chance. Didn't alter your hoakie-hoax ways or face the music when you were under the gun."

Stunned by her accuracy, Richie stammered, "Uh…sort of."

Leaning over a small propane camp stove she dished hash and beans onto a plastic plate, and continued to read over the clanking and banging sounds. "Your self-destructive fickle tricks backfired, didn't they?"

Popping two more truffles in his mouth Richie muttered, "That's an understatement."

"Not even your family can forgive and forget or ward off the doom, the consequences of no scruples."

Nervously gulping and munching the truffles, sticky chocolate glued to the roof of his mouth. Richie garbled, "That is probably true. A never-ending cycle inventing lies, fraught with…menacing deception."

MiaTia shoveled beans into her mouth, chomping and slurping like a beached whale. She raised her voice in an amateur bravado. "Covering up your naughties won't spare you. You're blitzed in uncertainty. You don't have a comfort zone!"

Dumbfounded he murmured, "You're right. I need Jenny."

Feigning crocodile tears, the so-called MiaTia said, "So sad. You're spiraling down a dark rabbit hole of oblivion. Like Rip Van Winkle waking up with a long white beard and the guilties." Slumping over and burping, she licked the bottom of the bean pan.

Richie muttered. "It's all so bleak."

"Just punish yourself. You'll feel better soon."

"I will?"

The lights in the trailer began to flicker on and off. Squinting, she read, "Guaranteed! Chart your course like a ship's persnickety captain. Remember to spin on a dime when the perfect storm hits." Slamming the book shut, she ended their session. "Good luck, hoboman! MiaTia signing off." Like a giant walrus she mounted a sloshing waterbed, clutched a pack of Twinkies, and stroked a purring Cheshire cat curled-up on her bountiful chest.

The phone clicked in his ear. "Hobo? Try a donkey's tail pinned to the wall." Richie felt a belly-button umbilical twitch. "There's this primal connector to my sickly glum, lowdown blues-stricken life." Looking for relief he held tight to his solar plexus. "Punish myself. Yes! I would feel better...or worse?"

Gazing at the answering machine, he grasped his pointer-finger forcing it to push the "Play" button. "Feel the guilt. Bare the pain." Tortured and mind-twisted he strained his senses listening to Bambe's banal phone messages. "Richie, miss me?" "Remember your massage at three." "Got the tickets for Maui." "Call me." "I know you're listening, lover-boy-toy."

At his wit's end, he couldn't take it anymore. Irritated by the invasion of reckless idiocy he changed the out-going message. "I don't live here anymore. Don't call me. We don't fit."

At 3:15 A.M. the phone rang, awakening him from a dead-sleep. Dazed, he snatched it from the cradle. Bambe seductively whimpered, "You'll go crazy if vee don't talk. You need to be leestened to, pampered, devoured."

Perking up on the word "devoured," it triggered a startling tender-hook stand. "Leave me alone! I am a married man."

"You are a widower," She taunted.

His face toughened. He raised a fist in the air. "Try a scared rabbit in the hole of oblivion, devoured by skanks."

Concerned for his well-being she implored, "Stay right there. I'm coming to you."

"No! You, ahh...harebrained predator." He pulled the telephone plug, tossed the base unit and cordless phone against the wall, smashing all of it. The plastic splintered like a chopped log getting ready for the burn.

Not willing to take 'No' for an answer, Bambe left her apartment in a huff. Wearing a silken Japanese kimono with hot pink marabou feathered slippers she slithered into her Lexus and headed to Richie's.

Driving senselessly around and around the cul-de-sac, Bambe recounted the last year of her life. "I was his devoted personal assistant, catering to his every whim. Forging checks, buying condos, cars, jewels, and furs. It wasn't exactly stealing. I brought in clients.

Call it a commission, a finder's fee, a bribe." She pulled the car under a giant spruce tree, hiding in the shadows. "It's true vee never had an intimate relationship, until one night when I poured triple shots in his vodka martini. He screamed 'Jenny, Jenny, Jenny' when he climaxed, rolled out of bed and went home."

She wiped a tear, and then blew her nose with a tissue. "We French adore love affairs, especially with married men. How could this adolescent American woman make it so unnatural? Raving on about betrayal, lying, deceit." Whimpering a confessional, purging her soul, Bambe carried on. "It ees true. I prayed, lit candles, stuck pins in a voodoo doll hoping Jenny would slip on a banana peel or fall in love with zee pool man."

Gazing in the rear-view mirror she pouted, her lips curling vamp-like. "When she went missing it became obvious - I am the one destined to end up with Richie." Then she sniveled, "Who would have dreamed he would spit childish regrets, ignore me, and even worse, cast me aside like a stinking old shoe?"

She started the engine and within minutes Bambe's car pulled in front of the Forrest estate. Determined, resolute and unwavering, she ran to the front door and pressed the buzzer. No response! Richie scrutinized her on the security monitor. Bambe's distorted image looked like a shrieking shrew. Tears streamed down her face. "You'll regret this, Richie. We do fit."

Richie watched her leave. Tears at night seemed the plight of women: first from his mother, then his wife, and now his ex-mistress. Trying to erase the night's misery he clutched Jenny's cell phone. "Jenny, you are the love of my life, where are you?"

Funny Mummy

The clock read 2:30 A.M.: Jenny had been frolicking with Rank Rhonda, Howdy and Willy the Worm._Everyone formed a circle, massaging each other's backs. Grunge rubbed Jenny's back. She melted at his touch, "Oh that feels so gooood."

Grunge beckoned, "Rub deeper, trust. With passion, lust."

The behavioral session ended. The transformation was quite obvious. Jenny was in the first flush of feeling utterly smitten, swooning like a schoolgirl. Grunge gently held her hand. "Congratulations. You survived a Grunge Group intensive."

Jenny beamed, "I loved it."

"We need to set up a solid program plan for you. How about dinner?" He made the encounter seem so natural. Yet Jenny's heart pounded. She could almost hear it thumping. New excitations arose within her, sensations that had been buried, percolating, longing to emerge.

She managed a shy grin. "You are the leader."

He liked winning her over. But he felt compelled to warn her, "Watch who you follow, lest it be yourself."

Jenny felt the familiar alarm-twinge in her belly. His words struck a truth. A touché trickled from her lips. "Watch who you lead, lest you be forsaken."

Brian ran track daily, pressed weights, went to practice scrimmages. For the first time in his life, he was vying for second, or even third-string on the football team. "Say, man, who has it in for me?" he challenged the team captain. The 245 pound captain came nose to nose with Brian and sputtered, "Don't whine-ass. Play harder ball, dude." At Brian's core, there was no way he could handle second-best. Striving, he pushed past limitations, driving toward his goal. Heavy class loads expanded his interests and for once he did the minimum required. Philosophy class became his focus. Notions of helping the "little people," the unfortunate, the downtrodden, had inspired him to become a cause-driven advocate to dismantle the establishment, creating a better way.

Dr. Ron upped the class learning curve. He switched gears, using the class forum to serve a thesis he was writing. The basis was individual potential vs. groupthink in a controlled environment, affected by variables and unpredictability.

The platform was an outdoor chess game – a humongous chessboard. Students served as human chess pieces. Wearing colored symbol hats some were Knights, Rooks or Pawns. King and Queen wore flimsy paper crowns. Samantha cracked-up laughing when she and Jax were chosen King and Queen for the day. Earlier they had been chatting and flirting with each other. Among the last standing in a beleaguered game, dizzily falling into his arms, Samantha dramatized, "Save the Queen, I'm out of here."

Initially the players were Dr. Ron and Brian (no other student could play well enough to compete). Kids squabbled, "No, it's the Rook that goes sideways." "No man, you're sideways, the Rook goes up one." Some games timed-in as little as ten seconds per move and required full attention to leap, jump a couple of spaces, get out of the way, or be trampled. Twisted ankles, wrestling and touchy-feely experiences kept them laughing and participating.

Other games went on forever – a 'free-for-all'. Kids were eating, sleeping, watching TV shows or videos on their BlackBerry's or talking on their cell phones. The only rule was, "Stay in your spot until you're moved or removed from the board." Being a Knight was fun: leapfrog over a player and talk to a new kid. Being a Pawn with its side and front moves promised hanging-out, sharing a snack or exchanging a CD, enjoying real camaraderie with the other players.

Sometimes, when Dr. Ron and Brian were just staring at them contemplating a move, the students would settle, focus on the board as if one thought – the myriad of possible moves – floated amongst them. They would yell out, "Save the Knight!" or "Take the Queen!" Often that was the best move. Proving Dr. Ron's point, subliminally they were in 'groupthink,' learning the game by osmosis or mere physical exposure, perfecting it by watching.

The moment of truth arrived. Students became chess players. Apparently through random selections, no one knew the process of elimination. Eventually, Samantha found herself pitted against Brian.

Jax joked, "Suck it up, girl." He rallied the class to place bets, spotting ten-to-one odds favoring Brian. Tanya, the most primped girl in class, collected the money.

Maybe it was Brain-Joggle's effect because as the game heated, Samantha could see moves well in advance. Combinations whizzed through her brain, as if she was on the Brain-Joggle computer, gobbling up the numbers – chess pieces, in this case. She could see checkmate.

Brian sweated bullets. Samantha was firing them. All she had to do was knock the little sucker Knight and – boom – she'd have him. Dead, checkmate. "It's about time," she thought. Hadn't she waited her whole life to be first, to beat him, instead of lurking in his shadow? Other ideas flashed; the dignity of knowing glory for herself and not having to prove it to anyone, or live up to bullshit expectations, or live down to them. Maybe the smart move was to lay back, punt, and throw the game. Protect her brain-smarts. Keep them concealed, all to herself.

Brian could visualize the moves from the top. He knew her advantage. She'd have to play the perfect game. One false move and he'd shred her; the game would be his. No one would have believed she could be a viable opponent, at least not Brian. In the final moments he secretly prayed, "Come on little Sam, you're so close. Don't blow it."

Samantha made the smartest move of her life. She moved the bloody Rook. "CHECKMATE," she called-out. For once in his life, it was Brian's fate to be the loser. She was the winner this time. No one, including Samantha, could deny it.

They shook hands in protocol. Then Brian twirled her around. "Congratulations, you just leveled the playing field, little sis."

Grace had stopped by that day, sharing Samantha's victory, jotting notes. Witnessing the bloody Checkmate kill, she yelled to her prize student, "Bravo!" Placing the only bet on Samantha, she raked in her winnings. Everyone thought they were sisters or twins. Except

Samantha already had a twin, which would suggest a triplet. Grace explained that one away to the class. "Only eight basic face types exist - whether Chinese, African or whatever, the features are fixed. You're bound to see similarities every day and will hear 'you look like so-and-so'. But looking soooo identical stymied me." She pulled out two very similar baby photos. "That's me, this one is Samantha. I admit, I checked out the hospital where Sam and Brian were born. Was there another Forrest baby not accounted for, stolen from the nursery? No trace of a phantom infant, of course!"

Samantha relished her brilliant input and boasted to her cohorts, "Grace is for real. A living, walking, breathing, 'Ask Jeeves'. Like a talking encyclopedia. She knows everything. Ask about condoms, minks, mascara, she'll tell you the varieties. Ask another question, BANG! You'll get the answer. It's like flicking the TV remote on to a new show. What a hoot."

With a candy-ass smile, Grace revealed Dr. Ron's sordid dossier to Samantha. "He's basically neutered, sort-of celibate since those Italian sluts used him as a sex-slave. Then his tragic soul-searching meltdown, as he called it. Hopefully he's still on the amino-boost."

"Poor Dr. Ron, he's soooo potentially delicious, totally strong-minded," was all Samantha could muster, wishing she was his sex-slave or maybe that he was hers.

Romance was definitely in the air in and around the Stanford campus. The patio at a local café exuded an air of sensual ambience.

Tiny lights flickered overhead, private nooks and quaint tufted booths gave the patrons a sense of privacy. Decked-out in retro-garb Jenny watched Grunge pour a Cabernet Sauvignon taster into his wineglass. Expertly, he swished it around his mouth, staring into Jenny's eyes. He filled her glass. She swished it around in her mouth, rolling her tongue gently across her lips. Flirtatiously, she held up her wineglass for a toast. "I feel tongue-tied."

Grunge seized the moment. All sugar he sweet-talked her, "To our first personal encounter."

His breath so close sent a chill down her back. Blushing, toned-down and demure, her eyelashes fluttered, "I'll admit it this is my first so-called date in nineteen years."

He moved even closer, his nose gently brushed hers, "And our first ever."

As fate would have it, in a far corner Jenny spotted Brian and Tanya. Maneuvering a huge hamburger to Tanya's lips, Brian fed her a giant bite. Wiping dripping juice from her mouth, Tanya chewed and giggled. He laughed. Jenny nervously wondered, *"How can I get through the dinner without having a heart attack or losing my wits."*

Brian seemed to look directly at her. To avoid being seen, Jenny blocked her face, wiping it with a napkin. Grunge refilled her wine glass. She took several big gulps. He moved in for a kiss. Skittish, Jenny kept one eye open. Afraid to move she pressed her mouth on Grunge's. Clearly turned-on he kissed her with a gentle passion. When their lips parted he sighed. "That was heavy."

Jenny positioned herself behind Grunge's head to avoid Brian. When she chanced to peek again, Brian and Tanya were gone. With a smile of relief she uttered, "Now maybe we can relax."

Grunge refilled their glasses, pouring the last drop into Jenny's. "We broke the ice."

Music throbbed from inside the restaurant. Snuggling under his arm they joined a few couples on the dance floor. Grunge whisked Jenny into his chest, held her close. His feel was strong and masculine, comforting. Melding into him, Jenny rested her cheek on his shoulder. It felt like a first-time dance on prom night, swaying together with expectation. The rhythm switched to an upbeat tune. Grunge held her tight, leading her in a swing-dance. Gliding across the floor with ease he twirled her around, expertly keeping her on balance. A seduction of eyes meeting, body's touching, teasing, sizzling, energized each moment.

In one intricate move she pranced away from him. Spinning out of control like a wind-up doll she landed in the arms of a man – a very young man – none other than Brian. Stunned, her mouth gaped open. "Oops!" she exclaimed. They stared for a brief moment into each other's eyes. Intentionally letting out a squeal, she quickly vaulted away from him, gracefully landing back into Grunge's arms. They continued dancing. Brian and Tanya left the dance floor. Jenny's mind dizzily chattered over and over, "What a close call."

At the end of their dinner and dancing delight, Grunge and Jenny, quite inebriated, zigzagged toward his van in the parking lot. Bright letters on the side panel read, "Grunge Mobile". Nearby, Brian's SUV rocked 'to and fro' like a 1950's teen-scene at a drive-in movie.

Jenny recognized the license plate number. 'BF Junior'. That's Brian's steamed-up windows, rocking like a boat." She wiped moisture off the driver's window. Banged on it. A head popped up. It was Samantha.

Jenny cried, "Oh, my God! Incest!"

A young man's head popped up. Samantha's date was Jax, her nerdy friend from Philosophy class. "It's a shakedown." Jax yelled.

Jenny wailed back at him. "Wrong call. Date rape, huh?" She pulled on the locked door. "Samantha, come with me."

Jax fired. "Who the hell is that?"

Samantha started the car engine. "That hag, Hallbally."

Grunge pulled Jenny back. "Discretion, sweet-thing. Save it for private." Covering his tracks, not wanting a bad rap, he yelled to the couple. "We're not really swingers. I'm a one-on-one kind of guy." Opening the panel door of his van he lifted Jenny into his arms and slid her inside. Jenny flopped onto a tufted-velvet bed. "I'm not tired." She declared. No longer starry-eyed, seeing Jax and Samantha sobered her mood. Obsessing, she turned-off to Grunge, for the moment.

Still flying high, Grunge smiled and said, "Good," believing 'not tired' meant 'playtime'. "Welcome to the Grunge Mobile. A love chamber on wheels." Fuming, she stared out the window as the SUV peeled out of the parking lot.

Jax flipped the 'bird' at them and shouted, "Peeping perverts!"

Grunge closed the curtain. "Why you little voyeur. Grunge here will provide. Want your own super-duper peep-show?" He dimmed the light, flicked on Salsa music, and popped a bottle of champagne.

Showing off his machismo tricks, he gyrated. Peeling off his shirt he unzipped his pants, cavorting, tantalizing. It was possibly a most revolting striptease, had she bothered to notice.

Oblivious, Jenny crunched in a corner obsessing. "The look on that kid's face. First it was kill. Then lust turned to porn. He's dangerous."

Totally into himself, Grunge bragged, "You bet...I'm dangerous."

"He's a rapist. Maybe a serial killer."

"I'm a love-bug. A lap-dancing fool." Grunge the seducer moved closer, bumping and grinding in Jenny's face.

At eye level Jenny stared at his crotch and squealed. "Deja vu! Already had this nightmare. Let's try a K.G.G?"

Grinning from ear-to-ear he asked," What kink-trick is that, my sweet?"

"K.G.G. means 'Knee Grungie's Gonads'." Showing no mercy she swiftly lifted her knee, slamming it into Grunge's groin. He yowled, kneeling to the floor, grabbing his stinging crotch.

On a crusade she promised, "If I can't save Samantha, I'll save myself."

He glared up at her panting, his tongue hanging out like a whipped pup. "My little Dominatrix. A teaser! You play insecure so good."

She glared at him with conviction, "Lots of practice."

Lying there like a beached whale he begged, "I'm waiting...come to Daddy."

"Daddy? 'D' stands for Dominance. I didn't get my Security Badge for nothing."

With the stealth of an 'Action Mama' she charged at him with a "Yeeehai!" Holding him in a headlock, she walloped him into a back crunch. As the undisputed champion she raised her arm overhead. "And the winner is Jen...ah...Lucy." Spent, she rolled off him. "What a release! I waited years to get that out. Only it should have been on Richie. Not on you Grunge, I'm sorry."

Gently rubbing her head, Grunge murmured "No sorry needed. I gladly accept the transference. I've been waiting to be spoiled and you did it, Lucy. You spoiled me."

She jerked her thumb at him, "Sick, sickening, sickest, sicker." The lights flickered in the van, an electrical malfunction that seemed to emphasize each syllable she uttered.

Destiny sometimes moves at a lightening fast speed. Jenny could barely keep tabs on her new life. She and Aggie scurried into the restroom at a retirement home. Aggie helped Jenny slip on a tight sequined retro dress. "You're on in five minutes."

'"How about in five years?" The zipper caught on her back. "Ouch, you're slaying me."

"Save the blabbing for your audience."

"I'm not ready for a live audience."

"They're not exactly alive, more like dead, or let's say half and half."

Jenny pouted, "What if they don't like me?"

Aggie soothed her. "Don't worry, they'll love you."

"What the heck was Grunge thinking? I'm not ready to do stand-up." Jenny's teeth chattered.

"Then sit down. It's community service. The old folks you're performing for won't remember if you were here or not."

"Yah! They probably don't know they're here either. I feel better."

Jenny hit the stage, rattling off comic bits. Octogenarians were slumped in wheelchairs, gazing at her.

"Just got my hormones checked. The doctor says to me, 'I've seen more estrogen-action in a corpse'." Jenny laughed at her joke and then waited for the expected laughter. Instead, there was dead silence – a performer's kiss of dread. A stiffened old lady bolted up, screaming, "Shut up and feed me!"

Jenny scanned a cue card, shuddered and stuttered. "What did the ninety-year-old man say to Saint Peter when he got to the pearly gates? 'Wouldn't join a club that would have me as a member'. Saint Peter laughed and said, 'Me neither, that's why I'm up here'."

The geriatrics' glazed over, stiff like cryogenic's. An ornery female crankster broke the monotonous routine. "Bugger out, you hayseed hooch."

A dainty lady tossed a pillow at the crankster. "Go back to bed. Why bother to get up?"

Putdowns and scorn rained down like torpedoes on an anthill. "Asinine nymph." "Poppycock fiddle-faddle." "You suck." Discarded snacks from apples to Gummy Bears were flailed at Jenny. Booed off-stage, she tripped and landed on the lap of a decrepit codger. Senile and befuddled he leered at her, "Is that you, Lorraine, coming for me?" Releasing his bony grip she raced out of room. They cheered, "Old folks rock!"

Back at the Grunge Group Rehab studio, Jenny was beaten down, awry and askew. "They badgered me like a worthless handmaiden." Grunge, Howdy, Willy the Worm and Rank Rhonda, shot a series of remarks her way. "Bone up, girl, or bow out." "You blew it, a dish of taboo." "Get a decoy, you bottleneck flunky."

Crushed, she blustered. "I bombed. A unanimous, 'I stink'."

Howdy agreed. "You'd put a jumping-bean to sleep."

Willy the Worm contorted his head between his legs. "Send out the hooker."

Grunge interjected, "Reality smashed the expectation bubble. No love!"

"Okay, pay me back. Be the sadist." Jenny whimpered.

Howdy wouldn't let up, thrusting his chest out, strutting around Jenny, "Keep grinding the loser."

Rank Rhonda clapped in rhythm. "Give it up for the chest-thumping poseur."

Willy the Worm slithered across the floor. Wiggling a face-painted sock-puppet on his foot, a matching one on his hand, the sock-puppets bantered back and forth.

Willy's hand said, "Who's paying? Flip ya' for dinner."

Willy's foot answered, "Let's be fair. Heads I win. Tails you lose."

In spite of herself and Willy's silliness, Jenny let out a scream. "Will someone please talk like a real human being. I'm sick of this crazy-making bantering nonsense." Grunge put his arm around her. "To choose or not to choose?"

The group indulged philosophy quips: "Afraid to live or die. Laugh or cry." "Freedom versus booooring "

Howdy responded in rote, "Nudey-undies caught on the fence."

Jenny finally smiled, "I get the drift. I know I'm sitting on the fence."

Grunge replied, "What you resist. Persists."

Jenny regurgitated. "Resist it. Then it persists. Of course, I get it, Grunge. You finally made some sense."

"Just go for it." Became the unanimous vote of approval.

The thought, "Go for it," continued to resonate as Jenny returned to the dorm. Filled with expectation and possibility she strolled onto the balcony. In the moonlight, gazing up at the star-filled sky, she contemplated her fate, understanding a promising turning point loomed, another chance to claim her life. She wondered, "*Will I finally go for it?*" Familiar voices on the balcony below broke her train of thought and stirred her curiosity.

Brian held Tanya's hand in his, pointing to the twinkling constellations. "See the bright one? It's the North Star."

Jenny sighed, "I taught you that." Immediately realizing that she could be heard and possibly seen from below, she ducked out of sight.

He looked up toward the voice. "Get out of my head. You slay me."

Tanya assumed he was talking to her. "You are so radically...unique," she said.

Brian guided her finger like a marker tracing across the sky. "Move to the left...the Big Dipper. Down right...the Little Dipper. See the little handle?"

Jenny 'mouthed ' his exact words and 'mimed' where he pointed.

Tanya looked at him adoringly. "You blow me away. So sweet."

Jenny puffed-up with pride, pleased at the chivalrous young man her son had become. "I taught him everything I had to give. Now's time to give...him space." She quivered at the realization. "Mommy-hood is kaput, kaplunkt, finito!"

Going back inside, she viewed her face in the bathroom mirror. Stroking the skin under her eyes, she studied her facial lines. "Earned them all! This one's definitely Samantha's appendicitis attack. That one has to be Brian's drug-bust or maybe my botched tummy-tuck." She pushed her thumb between her eyebrows. "That little crevice is crater-bound. The sucker means total pandemonium. Nursery, elementary, middle and high school."

Teary-eyed she ran a fingertip down the length of a laugh line, stretching from nose to lip. "That baby is for all the good times, the fun, the hugs, the love." Sighing, she turned away from the mirror and walked back into the room. She stole a quick glance through the window. A foggy mist filled the air and seemed to sparkle under a full moon. There was a big world out there - she felt a promise of a new life. An opportunity for growth confronted her. A first! "Let go of pestering, meddling, foxy-moxy, allow privacy." She hyperventilated. To steady her balance she leaned on the side of the bunk bed. Gaining composure, she courageously closed the drape.

PART THREE
HIGH-KICK STAKES

The Grunge Group Rehab studio filled with laughter and witticisms as the group jokesters worked out new material and comedy skits. Willy the Worm coached Jenny. Attempting to loosen her body moves, he exhibited belly-dancing gyrations. Jenny stared at the uninhibited slim-framed man in wonder. He snickered, "Ya like? Follow me. Here's how a star struts her stuff. Chin up, chest out, tummy in." Stiff and uptight as a broomstick, she tagged along behind him.

He goaded, "Come on, undulate, roll that tummy up-and-down. Fannies up and out. Squeeze one cheek, then the other, both together. Add a figure-eight, hips rolling all around." His buns and tummy jiggled like a belly dancer charming a snake.

Jenny did her best imitation, "Dig in your pocket, funny man. I've got a big surprise."

Joking he grinned, "Not bad for a 'yes-yes-yes' dame."

Slightly offended, Jenny sat down on the floor like a spoiled brat. Drawing her legs up to her chin, pouting her lips, she said, "I'm not a mindless 'yes-yes-yes' anything."

Staring directly at her, he duplicated her baby-like pout, "Then you're a 'no-no-no'." He contorted into an N-shape.

"Cut the bully-shtick, Willy. Did you grow up in a carnival or what?"

"I wish. Being triple-jointed, I tried to join when I was nine. Slammed me a turndown. So I turned 'Rat Whisperer.'" Blasting a loud 'squeak', Willy continued. "I'm the kingpin rodent finder. I squeak, draw the prey, contort in a hidden spot, terrorize, immobilize, and pounce. I collect the dirty rats and sell 'em to pet stores."

Jenny gaped with her hand to her mouth. "That was the truth, wasn't it?"

Nodding like a cat had his tongue, Willy blushed pink. Having copped a tad of reality, he earnestly offered, "Back to the improv', lady. Let's get your would-be, should do, court-ordered, community act down."

Funny Mummy

Jenny experimented, diving into a wealth of funnies, sporting costumes and masks teemed with zany outrageously fantisimo-frolics. She bounced from a shy 'House Frau' to a hippy-hep mom. Dipping into history she captivated the black humor side of Medea. "Who the heck didn't want to strangle a screaming kid?" She went over the top with a sacrilegious Virgin Mary ala' the Da Vinci Code. 'VM', as she called her, was preggie and lactating at the Last Supper.

Flopping big-time, the group booed Jenny to tears at her insipid Barbara Bush interpretation, prompting Big Daddy George to buy the Presidency for little Georgie W. Jenny recouped, assimilating giving birth to a sixteen-pound infant. Moaning and groaning, she inhaled long then blew out a hissing,. 'One, two, three' Lamaze style. In agony, she writhed on a make-shift cot screaming, "This sucks. Epidural, pleasssse! No big heads coming out of my vagina."

Within seconds she flipped characters to a tribal-mama giving birth, simply squatting in a sugar-cane field when delivery time came. "De Baby mine you just popped. No bigge deal – just drop." She reached down, picked up the imaginary newborn and swaddled it. Rank Rhonda shuddered, "It doesn't get much worse or sore-eyed than that crap-ola."

Not giving up, this was Jenny's time to get her act at performance level. The group and Grunge coached, tweaked her act as Jenny found her style. She took on a Bette Midler bawdy delivery and rocked. Prancing up and down stage, she got into a 'roast em and toast-em' rhythm, letting out her life woe's. For once the group was into it, captivated by her harangues.

"That's one funny mummy." Howdy applauded.

Grunge stepped up and put an arm around her. "Congratulations, you've got a ten-minute act", not able to stop from smiling, he teased, "No need to go AWOL."

Jenny stepped back and skewered them with an untamed glare, "Are you crazy, I can't go up there as me...and be seen by the world."

Rank Rhonda spun around, "Hey, show up as me."

Jenny shot back, "Scary thought, nail me to the wall."

Willy scrimmaged through a prop and costume bin. He retrieved a strange looking headdress. "Hey, the unknown comic wore a bag over his head. Our funny mummy can wear this."

Jenny giggled, "What the heck is that mop?" With great affection, as if he were crowning the Queen, Willy offered, "Your crown to fame." He put a gauze mummy headdress over her head. It covered her face, with slits for eyes. Her emerald beauties stared back at them, as they witnessed "The amazing 'Birth of Funny Mummy."

Richie's SUV pulled out of the Forrest driveway, crisscrossing over speed bumps through the cul-de-sac. He was heading out of town, traveling north. The coastal view was overcast and dreary. Winding through the wine country, meandering through hills and canyons, the gloomy day reflected his state of mind. This was the trip he dreaded. Lost in thought, the same old drill, 'would of, could of, should of' haunted him. Wracked in apprehension he missed the turnoff, whipping the wheel, swerving onto the road's edge. Straining to decipher the directions scribbled on a map, "Go a tenth of a mile past the Medville sign," he made a U-turn and circled back. Watching the odometer he determined the exact place to stop.

Clutching a multi-colored orchid flower bouquet in hand he stepped out of the vehicle. "It should be somewhere around here," he said to himself. Walking along the road's dusty soft shoulder, he could see a yellow police crime tape ahead. A sign posted "No Trespassing" was on the soft-shoulder. A red evidence-marker was stuck in a ditch. "This is it. My poor Jenny." He dropped to his knees, placing the wilting flowers on the marker, wailing, "It's all my fault. I brutally maimed you. Like a defenseless deer in the headlights." With folded hands he bemoaned in prayer. "It was supposed to be 'til death do us part'. Not part. You died on me."

A red Mercedes SUV pulled up beside him. Behind the wheel, Festus, decked out in a Stetson hat, spoke out. "Need some help, mister?"

Overcome with emotion, Richie threw himself on the marker. "I'm a drunken coward. A cheat! A hot-blooded murderer!"

"Say no more, sinner. You have come home, to be saved." Without hesitation Festus sprang from the Mercedes, tossed a rope overhead, lassoing Richie like a runaway maverick. "Hee-Haw! Yippee-Aiiee-Yay!" he shouted. Richie struggled to get free. "Help! AGG!" Festus hooked him behind the Mercedes and started slowly up the road. Richie ran behind keeping pace, gritting his teeth, huffing and puffing.

Nightfall covered the Barton house sequestering the new visitor. Richie hunkered down on the sofa. Elma leered over him. "Just nailed you! You're that suffering wiener on TV, wanting your wife back."

Seemingly suspicious Festus squinted an eye. "We was wondering, if you cared so much, why you never offered no reward?"

"Elma backed him. "Right. You just said, 'no questions asked'. Never mentioned a reward like a decent man would of."

Richie was taken aback by his instant notoriety. "It's unbelievable I made such a lasting impression. It must be my stage presence. All those highly visible trials! Winning tons of court cases.

"Festus mocked him. "You impressed us, all right."

"What'll it take to heal that broken heart of yours?" Elma cut to the core of the matter.

"If only Jenny was safe. All in one piece" Tearing up, Richie's voice cracked as he said, "If she could ever forgive me for being a lying, no good..."

Elma cackled, "A crumb bum? A stud bad boy?"

Richie wallowed in shame. "I never knew, I mean, never thought I was doing wrong. I was just worried about getting caught.

"Elma ranted excitedly, "Holy Moly, Festus. There's a disbelieving evildoer among us.

"Lifting his arms in the air Festus exclaimed, "The rapture is upon us."
Dramatically placing her hands over her heart, Elma pronounced, "I hear the calling.   "In unison they cried out. "He needs purging."Elma gave Festus a sly wink, and then placed her hands on Richie's head. Festus presided as evangelist, spellbinding Richie. He laid hands on him, pushed on his chest, exorcising him. In a fervor Festus declared, "Devil be out of this sinful-sludger." He yanked Richie's hair, pulling his head back.

Richie howled in pain, "Oh holy baloney!"

Festus stuck his fingers in Richie's eyeballs, then down his throat. Richie gagged. His head appeared to spin around. In a surrealistic moment, as if the 'uncanny-spirits' were being released, Richie spewed multi-color light balls firing like cannon balls, ricocheting off the walls he garbled, "Aggh. Aga. Moo-Moo...Goopers."

Festus ducked the flying ball barrage. Gaping, his mouth hung open. A ball popped in his mouth, holding his jaw open, stuck between his teeth. He pried it out. His false teeth anchored fast on the ball. A toothless Festus commanded, "Give up your wicked, vile, vulgarly ways. Repent."

Richie's eyes glowed a shimmering reddish hue. "Shove it. Slime-wonker."

Elma screeched, "Devil be gone!"

Richie squatted, reaching for her leg, "Rot in hell, you gold-toothed hag."

They stomped on him. Elma demanded, "Say it. I repent'."

Richie's eyes bulged. "I repent."

"Prophecy is given for this reborn man. Love will re-bloom in a waking kiss,"

Elma seemed enchanted. Festus poured a jug of water over him. Richie's dripping head bobbled, "Yes. Yes. Yes." Festus smirked at Elma, "Can trim a sheep lots, but you can only skin it once." Holding him under each arm they tugged Richie to his feet. Hopping in a wild jig the threesome spun in circles, twirling faster and faster in a heated flurry. Richie held tight for dear life: there was no contest for the old odd couple.

A bit later Elma mothered Richie, "Nothing better than a good ol' fashioned down-home exorcism to bring on the snooze's," Elma smiled. She tucked Richie in the little trundle bed, where Jenny had slept securely swaddled in a couch potato robe and pointed nightcap. Singing a soothing a lullaby, Elma crooned, "Go to sleep, little creep. Dream of dudgeons and gallows. La... dee...dah...lah...lah...lah." Curled up, comforted in a womb-bound state, Richie drifted off into slumberland.

The shrill squawking of Caruso, the rooster, didn't bother Richie. It was sunrise at the Barton's and soon to be Richie's initiation into 'life on the farm'. They had make a work-exchange agreement and Festus primed him with instructions. "No egg gathering for you, boy. You'll put in a real man's workday. Dawn-to-dusk without complaint."

Over a big breakfast of ham and chittlin's, Richie was his usual demanding self. "Chittlin's did you say? This mushy-gush is hellish chittlin's?"

Festus answered, "Hell,' did you say? Thought we pulled you out of hell."

Elma was on her feet. She grabbed a bar of soap from the sink and stood in front of Richie. "No swearing around here, city boy. Now go wash that filthy mouth out." She handed him the soap.

Not believing what he heard Richie stammered, "You want me to do <u>what</u>?"

Not waiting for another insult, she pried his jaw open and scraped the soap bar on his teeth. "Take that."

"Yuck" he cried. He dashed to the sink and turned on the faucet. Twisting backwards he stuck his face under the nozzle. He gulped, swigged, sloshed water, and rinsed his mouth.

Festus roared with laughter. "That'll teach you. Now's about time you learned some cow-poking."

Showing no mercy, the blistering sun beat down on the men. Festus put Richie to task shoveling manure. Huge gobs of dark and light brown mush stuck to the shovel. He tried to knock it against the dump barrel, which turned out to be a maneuver that sent blobs of muck splattering all over him. His nostrils, cheeks, and lips were caked. Crumpling his shirttail he attempted to wipe it off. "Damn, I mean...darn shit...I mean crap." He corrected himself for fear his mild profanity would be heard.

Festus guffawed and roared. "You are shit-faced."

"Oh, so _you_ can swear? Say 'shit' and get by with it?"

"That ain't swearing. That's natural, boy. Wasn't you raised to know the difference? Some things is right and some things is wrong."

Richie tied a bandanna around his face to block the smell. "Yuh. And this stinks."

Festus kicked his boot on the shovel, chastising him, "Only sissy boys don't know the power of dung."

Richie bit his lip and kept his mouth shut: a new survival tactic for a most verbose manipulative lawyer. Festus took charge and shoved him into the bull pen. "Now for the super-duper droppings. Let's see how you handle Big Bull."

Richie panicked as the barbarous Big Bull stared him down. "A clear death warrant," he said as he squirmed, backing away from the beast. The bull lowered its head, kneading razor-sharp horns on the ground. He edged closer to Richie.

Festus motioned, "Grab 'em by the horns."

Richie continued to back away from Big Bull. "That could be dangerous."

"Coward!" Festus reared the bull through the gate. He pointed a pitchfork at Richie. "Get on him."

Richie tried to buy some time. "Maybe you could show me how?"

Festus gave him a light poke, forcing him to mount. "Cut the gabbing and excusing."

Richie climbed into the entry box. "Hope you're insured," he remarked as he threw one leg over the animal. The clumsy effort slid his butt off Big Bull's back. Clinging to the chute's door, he hung upside down. Big Bull's gonads were dangling in full view. Richie gasped, clearly intimidated. "Super-endowed."

As if understanding, Big Bull stomped his hooves. To avoid being kicked Richie grabbed the wooden chute, struggling to lift himself upright. He managed to scoot back and mount the angry beast. Not sure what to hold onto he leaned forward, tugging its ear. "Let's be friends, okay, Big Balls?"

"It's your balls at stake here, boy," Festus laughed. "Take back your manhood, your pride, own those balls." Festus lifted the chute lever. The chute opened and Big Bull bolted out of the cage, thrusting, bucking up-and-down. Richie bounced a couple of beats, flew off, landing on his butt. He reached for his crotch, checking for damage. Smiling in relief he said, "Genitalia...still intact."

Big Bull kicked up dirt, challenging Richie. "You tub of lard," Richie grimaced. Mustering a newfound strength he flexed his jaw. Foisting himself at Big Bull, he grabbed the horns, twisting and turning. They didn't budge. Big Bull raised his hind legs, shuffling dirt in a dustbowl behind him.

Richie headed for cover, clinging on the edge of the fence. Festus tossed him a red cape. "Fix on Big Bull's eyes. He'll follow the red."

Time slowed down. From a deep memory within Richie, he flung the cape in front of him like a seasoned matador. Big Bull stampeded head-on. With the grace of Zorro Richie whipped the cape in several directions: On the ground, up in the air, in front, in back. Turning sideways the cape angled in front of him. Big Bull kept on charging. One thousand pounds headed directly at Richie who remained fixed on the black bulging eyes of his adversary.

Distracting him, Richie shifted his torso in the opposite direction, flipping the cape. Big Bull followed the cape, skidding on all fours, inches away from Richie. The creature froze in his tracks, mesmerized. Richie jumped up and grabbed his horns, tackling him to the ground. Locking eyes with his 'tons of death' opponent Richie gloated in triumph. "You're down, boy. Way down."

The word "victory" just slipped from his lips when a strange rattling sound echoed. Out of one eye he spotted a rattlesnake slithering toward him. "Holy wicked doomsday!" he shouted.

The snake reared its ugly head, staring at Richie. Holding Big Bull by the horns, he wondered, "What can I do?" On impulse he tickled Big Bull's stomach. Wriggling and letting out snorts, the beast rolled over on his back, all four legs sticking upright in the air, content and tame.

Richie didn't falter. Multi-tasking, his eyes glued on the rattler, staring the sucker down. A crow flew low, dusting the snake's path. Richie remained fixed, holding still. Lowering its head, the rattler seemingly nodded at Richie, then it slithered away.

The sun slipped below the horizon. Festus and Richie trudged back toward the house in silence. No words were needed after sharing a solid day's work. Famished, they downed a big dinner that Elma prepared. Richie ate six pork chops and polished off a mound of mashed potatoes. "Delicious," Richie complimented several times.

Festus remarked, "He eats like a darn horse."

Elma gleamed, "Just like Finster, huh?"

"Who's Finster?" Richie asked. Before they could answer, his cell phone rang. He saw Bambe register on the caller ID. Elma quickly confiscated it. "No rude gabbing at my dinner table."

"Sorry about the interruption. I'll turn it on vibrate. Reaching his hand for it, "Then you won't hear it."

She laughed, handing it back to him, "Vibrate, eh? Sounds good to me."

He seemed both relieved and grateful to remain out of contact with the world.

Elma was 'all ears', attentive to the day's tomfoolery. She sized-up Richie, "Sounds like you're choosing to be a man's man. Ladies love a real man."

With a glint of hope he said, "Maybe I can win my Jenny back."

Elma challenged, "You think she's like a prize at a raffle drawing?"

Putting a thumb up Richie bragged, "First prize."

Elma cackled, "She's no trophy. She's a woman. You don't win her back. You woo her back."

"How?"

"By learning what a woman wants."

"What does she want?"

Elma shrugged, "You know her. You figure it out."

"How about a little clue. Give me a break, I'm not a woman!"

Festus blurted. "At least the sissy knows that."

Richie appealed to Elma. "Come on, you're a woman...what do you want?"

"Now you're catching on. Women are different than men."

Festus chimed, "And the same, too. A good woman wants plenty of hot lovin'. Isn't that right, Elma?"

Blushing like a schoolgirl, she laid a sweet peck on his lips. Festus cooed, "Whoopee!"

Richie didn't get the scoop why 'Women are from Venus and Men are from Mars', but locked in his jaded once decadent and immoral soul was a first-hand glimpse of a loving couple, respecting, supporting, and whooping it up.

Nightfall descended on the Barton farm. Richie yawned, nodding-out watching an "I Love Lucy" rerun. Festus' uproarious laughter jolted him awake. "Where do you get all that energy?" Richie asked. Drowned-out by laughter, he joined in the nightly 'Lucy' rerun ritual.

Something had shifted in Richie. Stepping up to the plate, he had stretched his limited view of himself. What he liked or didn't. How things should be or shouldn't be. What he was capable of or afraid of. The day's activities pummeled through his mind. He envisioned Big Bull's giant balls as his own, prancing and dancing, feeling honor and pride. He laughed out loud. "Richie, you're a new man." Both exhaustion and satisfaction overwhelmed him. He slipped into a fuzzy couch potato robe and crawled into the trundle bed. The clock read 8:00 P.M. His eyes closed. Within minutes he was gone; out like a light – zonked.

At 8:00 P.M. the Comic House was jumping with college kids and rowdy locals. Saphro, a legal near-beer brew for minors, overflowed.

Backstage, Jenny experienced a bout of fright. Shaking from head-to-toe she looked like she was in a juice mixer. Squeezing into a skimpy dress, Aggie once again caught the zipper on Jenny's skin. "Ouch! You butch-ery sadist," Jenny exclaimed as she slid to the floor.

Aggie held tight to the zipper, sliding down with her, muttering, "Hold still, will you?" One last yank and Jenny's skin was free and the dress was zipped.

Jenny cried, "Get me out of this torture chamber! I'm too young to die!"

Grunge subdued her jitters. "It's your chance to knock them dead. You were reborn for this moment."

Making a dash toward the exit, Jenny yelled, "I'm out of here, Grunge! Thanks for everything!"

Aggie wrestled her to a chair. "Chill. Or I'll cuff you."

"Help!" Jenny screeched.

Aggie held a hand over her mouth muffling the plea. "Not so fast, girl. You didn't come this far to ditch yourself back in the clinker." Aggie picked up the mummy headdress that was wrapped in twisted yards of cotton cloth, affecting a mummy. She wiggled, twisted, and pulled it onto Jenny's head. Mummified, it covered her face. Only a gleam of her emerald green eyes stared out.

Grunge admired his protégé. "Too gorgeous for words," he gave her the 'thumbs-up' sign, and then slipped through the curtain.

Grunge took the stage, facing the crowd. "Good evening, you yellow-belly laugh-trackers. Welcome to knock-your-socks-off, pee your pants, shake-a-booty night"

Several 'hoots' rang out from the audience.

Grunge continued. "Behind these curtains lurks a potential felon with twin melons." With both hands cupped he mimed a couple of bouncing boobies.

"Bring it on," someone shouted from the crowd.

"All right!" Grunge enthused. "Let's give it up for our unknown comic-babe. The haughty, bawdy, naughty, 'Funny Mummy'!"

The crowd let out a few uninspired claps. On cue, Aggie pushed Jenny through the curtains.

The clock read 8:30 P.M. 'Funny Mummy' debuted on stage.

Jenny faced the raucous crowd that was talking loudly, drinking, mostly unaware of her presence. Startled by the bright key lights she squinted at the hazy audience. Stepping-up to the microphone she said, "Can't see a damn thing." Her emerald green eyes bulged, piercing through the slits in the flimsy headdress.

A drunken heckler tossed a book of lit matches at her. "Lookie here, if it isn't Frankenstein's bride."

Quickly reacting, she zinged the burning ball back at him. "Burn, lard head."

Batting flying sparks off his jean jacket, the heckler grunted, "Mangle the Mummy."

Jenny fixed on the exit sign and made a dash for it. "Try it, skunk-breath."

Too soused to make chase, the heckler tripped over a table landing on his face. "Let me at her," he growled.

Assuming the pratfall was part of the act, the audience roared, "Go, 'Stunt-Mummy'!" A muscle-bulging bouncer detained the drunken customer, neck to wall.

Jenny bolted outside into the chilly night. Removing the headdress she squiggled it onto a fire hydrant, commanding the red-looking dwarf, "Go get 'em 'troll-mummy'. Set me free."

Aggie chased after her. Stopping to pick up the headdress she chuckled, "Now that girl is funny." Jenny ran for her life, lively and reckless, disappearing from sight.

Later, in the dorm room, Aggie and Helga placated Jenny. She fretted, fumed a loose fuse, "Lucille Ball would plotz, roll over in her grave, and slap me silly for being such a bomb."

Helga consoled Jenny. "You did your act. Followed the drill."

Jenny continued to berate herself. "How dare I use her namesake? Its sacrilegious, probably a peccadillo sin."

Funny Mummy

"Don't bother explaining that one. Spare us. No graphic details." Aggie asked.

The clock read 2:00 A.M. Still consoling Jenny, Aggie and Helga's eyes blinked open and shut, rolling like a turnstile. "Look at the upside. No jail! No suspension! You're clean in the eyes of the law."

"Who cares about the stupid law? I'm a disgrace. A sinner in the eyes of the 'funny-ladies'," Jenny's face crumpled, as a lone tear streamed down chin.

When he slipped into bed earlier that evening Richie naively believed the workday was over. As the clock struck 2:00 A.M., Festus and Elma converged like bats in the night. They shook the trundle bed, jostled him from what he remembered to be a wet dream. "I need your lovin', too," he mumbled.

Festus pulled the comforter off, "Up and at 'em. Get dressed you lazy critter." They hog-tied, then wrangled him into the back of Festus' old pickup truck. It seemed like miles traveling over bumps as Richie's body smacked and whacked into the metal backside. The truck stopped in a desolate and barren wasteland. Brush and cactus covered the high desert.

Festus untied Richie. "Get going, you lazy varmint," he ordered. Richie tried coaxing, "Not a good day to die, don't you think?" Festus informed, "Yep."

Richie squirmed, "Yep-yes? Or yep-no?"

"Yep's 'Yep'. Now's time for a 'Vision Quest'," Festus announced."

'Vision Quest'? Thank God! I'd thought you'd 'tar and feather' me."

Elma handed Richie a piece of paper. "Follow these 'Vision Quest' directions. And don't blow it." Then she prophesized, "By the next dawn, when a black crow flies overhead, you'll find out who Richie Forrest really is." Turning away from Richie, Elma and Festus climbed into the pickup, leaving him to fend for himself. Desperate and frightened Richie chased after them, howling, "Don't leave me alone out here..." he fell to his knees, "...to die!"

Sneaking under the clouds, the moon cast very little light. Richie had been plopped in the middle of nowhere and felt chilled to the bone. Elma's last words stuck with him. "You will find out who Richie Forrest really is." Scrounging around in the darkness he found two sticks and a rock, gathered pieces of wood, and then crisscrossed the chunks into a pile.

Wracking his memory he wondered how to start a fire with sticks. Even as a Cub Scout he conned other kids to do the dirty work. He was the leader with the ideas. They were the worker bees doing his bidding; manipulating them by bribery, "Make the fire, I'll get the burgers." He never watched Jimmy Watson with his shirtsleeve full of Scout badges actually light the fire.

It was too cold to doubt his abilities. Fast, slow, soft, hard, he rubbed the sticks together. No luck. The wind railed through him. Panicked by the thought of freezing to death he rubbed again with vigor. "Hypothermia, frozen toes, amputated feet – only hours away."

Finally, a boon presented itself. A golden glow emerged with the delicious aroma of smoke! Quickly tearing Elma's paper in half, he held it to the sticks, capturing a spark, igniting a flame. One by one the sticks sizzled into fire. In gratitude he postulated, "Richie, you have joined your ancient brothers, the Cro-Magnon ape-man, wild Tarzan, every whacked-out pyromaniac. What a scary thought that we all share the same DNA."

Warming his hands over the campfire, witnessing the crimson flames dancing in the wind, gave him a sense of serenity. He read Elma's instructions aloud by firelight. "Four easy steps for a 'Vision Quest'. 'One: Be alone in the wilderness. Done that. Two: Light a fire. Done that. Three: Find a sign for your direction.' Haven't done that yet! 'Four: Be on lookout for black bears.'" He jumped to his feet and nervously looked out into the darkness. "Doing that right now."

He gazed back at the list "Find a sign for your direction." Milling about, he spotted a stone carving. Reading the inscription, "Frog hair cut in four directions. Sit in East, follow sun." Amazed at his discovery, the challenge was to figure out what it meant. "Now what is a 'frog hair'? Who knows? What 'four directions'? North? South? East? West? 'Sit in East' – easy. 'Follow sun'. That means move clockwise to the next direction. Got it!" Richie's inveterate skeptic lawyer voice suddenly entered his head, accusing, "Are you nuts? You're going to sit in the blazing hot sun all day while it moves across the galaxy?" Ignoring the mental intrusion, he shrugged. "What else do I have to do anyway?"

Mulling over the question, "What the heck is a 'Vision Quest'?" he recalled several movies with details: The map with an arrow traversing the screen in "The Man Who Would Be King" showed the journey endured by Sean Connery and Michael Caine traipsing across a continent of danger. In "ET" the little alien, sadly trapped on planet

Earth was wasting away in a plastic bubble, questing to go home. Richie looked for practical guidance in the stories. Nothing clicked. He needed something solid to guide him.

Richie thought about Native American's who sat in a circle of stones 'to find the meaning of life'. He snapped his fingers. "That I can do," he said with satisfaction. He stood up and began to gather an array of stones, placing them in a circle. After standing back to admire his work, he sat in the center, and briefly nodded-off to sleep.

A gnawing sound jarred him. In the shadows a large dark form moved toward him. It drew closer. His teeth chattered at the sight of the seven-foot black bear standing upright, two-legged, sniffing and snorting not more than three feet away.

The bear tossed his back, releasing a thunderous 'roar'. Richie hyperventilated. His body convulsed. That roar would have alerted an army. Momentarily, the bear wasn't interested in Richie, it was busily licking a paw, squatting on a nearby stump. For a moment Richie forgot the danger. Admiring the beautiful animal so carefully cleaning its paw, he began to breathe with the bear – slow, deep, and sure. Eventually, Richie fell asleep once again.

The bear came closer and looked curiously at his human buddy. After a few minutes, he gently patted Richie's head as if saying, "I'm watching over you," and then disappeared back into the woods.

Richie awakened at sunrise, unclear if the bear had been there or if he had been dreaming. Yet another surprise delighted him. He was already facing east. Now all he had to do was wait for the passage of time. He fidgeted, squirmed, and switched his leg position. Lying down, sitting up, adjusting his pained body. Richie became aware that time has its own life – it stops for no one. In addition, he realized that no matter how hard he tried he could not go back and change things. Succumbing to the 'here and now' moment, he sat cross-legged, eyes closed. Tuned-in.

The forest animals paraded by him. A squirrel, skunk, rabbits, deer – each took time to cross his path. Some nuzzled against him as if welcoming him, others busily scurried by, chasing their prey. He had become still, no longer a threat to the nature around him.

The sun continued moving across the sky. Without opening his eyes Richie changed directions. Facing south, west, and then north. He followed his instinct, a developing intuition, and changed directions at will.

Bees buzzed around him, his nose twitched. The buzzing sound grew louder, filling his consciousness. Within moments, a visualization occurred: He saw himself at a fork in the road. One way led to family, love, and happiness. The other path led to an old broken man leaning on a crutch screeching, "Feed me." Sensing he must choose his way to freedom.

The sky darkened, enveloping him in the night's womb. A flash of lightning interrupted the silence, streaking across the sky. In a crackling fury, the bolt zapped Richie in the temple. He zigzagged across the ground, yelling, "I've been touched by the force!"

Hazy images flickered before him, showing him a new way of life: He was 'Mr. Mom', dressed in an apron, mopping the floor. In a role-reversal, Jenny, plastered on vodka, mysteriously whispered and giggled into a cell phone, "See you in Rio."

Richie screeched, "Rio! What about Rio?"

"That was Cleo, rhymes with Leo," Jenny replied with a smirk.

He fell at her feet, begging, "Please don't leave me. I need you."

Jenny grew into a gigantic glistening vision. "I am near. Follow in my shoes."

Stymied, he asked, "How could I fit?"

"Carry on for me."' Her image swirled into a double helix. Traversing masculine and feminine, Yin and Yang, strands of light whirled, circling from Jenny into Richie, and then back into Jenny. Her voice inspired, "As 'WE' merge, we are one with all living things." The image faded.

Richie remained still, digesting the magnitude of it all. He had walked the razor's edge, experiencing the balance of body, mind, and spirit. Animals joined him. Richie petted a baby goat that snuggled next to him. "We are one, little Billy Goat," Richie assured him with reverence.

Billy Goat resonated a deep "BAAH."

As if sending a signal, a black crow flew overhead, "Caw-Caw", alerting Richie. He barely recalled Elma's parting words, "When a black crow flies Richie Forrest will know who he is."

Billy Goat heeded the call and head-butted Richie, forcing him to his feet. Gently, with his horns he pushed Richie from behind treading a winding trail. Climbing the hillside, Billy Goat went straight up, goat-style. Richie scampered on all fours, chimp-style. Together they crossed a stream, hopped, and straggled fences. Billy Goat guided Richie back to the farm. Amazing it was only two miles back, as the crow flies.

Funny Mummy

The next morning, at Caruso's first 'caw', Richie jumped out of bed. Hoisting on a pair of tattered jeans Elma had given him to work in, he headed to the kitchen. He was ecstatic, bursting to share his transformational outing with Festus and Elma. A shocking sight in the middle of the living room stopped him cold. Bending over a bubbled-filled tub, Elma was jaybird-naked, her butt reaching for heaven. Thin as she was, a tad of accordion fold-up skin hung off her body, jiggling in the morning air. It was as if he'd seen a ghost decaying in a horror flick.

Turning around, not batting an eyelash, she said in a deep sultry voice, "Cat got your tongue sweetie, or you just shocked to see me?" Frozen statuesque, Richie couldn't utter a word. She winked, "Hand me that towel, before them fly's get down your throat." He picked up the body-wrap towel, closed his eyes, and inched toward her. She reached for it, tugging him closer. Losing footing on a wet spot he tripped, knocking Elma into the tub. Still off balance, Richie also tumbled and rolled in, splashing on top of her, "Holy vagina!" she screeched. Both of them were yelling and shouting. "Gosh!" "Hell!" "What's going on?" Slipping and slopping over each other, they tried to get out of the tub.

The racket sent Festus darting in on the twosome who were flailing and seemingly frolicking in the bath. "I'll be a rat's ass. You no good mooch chiseler. No man's making whoopee with my babe," he growled. The old codger pulled a shotgun from behind a cabinet.

Elma wrapped the soaking towel around her, sat on Richie, pushing him underwater, forcing his head down. "Dumb-cluck fell in by mistake, was trying to hand me this here towel," she explained.

The old man's shaky arm rattled the shotgun that was still aimed at Richie. Elma stepped in front of Festus, carefully shielding the tub where Richie was still immersed, one hand still holding Richie underwater. In a gentle tone, she said, "Put the gun down Festus, I know how much you adore your Elma." She flashed the towel, giving him a peek-a-boo. "And, that's why I want you to go right up to your bed and wait for me."

Holding back tears Festus whimpered, "I'd be finished if you ever left me, Elma."

Bawdy and sexy, she commanded, "You got until the count of ten, now get going."

A single tear trickled off his chin. Resting the shotgun against a chair, he asked, "You mean it, Elma?"

"One, two, you better get going," she yelled. Festus took off to their bedroom. She lifted Richie's gurgling head out of the water. He coughed up bubbles, spraying water all over her. Gasping for breath, he garbled, "I thought I was a dead man. Shot or drowned, no way to go."

She penetrated his fearful mind, "We're all only one breath away and don't you forget it. Now hop out of these bubbles and go fix us the biggest pancakes I've ever seen. We'll be expecting breakfast waiting, toy-boy." She chuckled in a condescending way, and then dashed upstairs to chase after Festus.

Unwilling to imagine the gyrations or frigid body-locks the old couple was doing, Richie mumbled a Beatles tune, "When I'm 64"...as he flipped pancakes high in the air, grateful to be alive. Fighting an impulse to hit the road, he couldn't bail-out like a coward. Fifteen harrowing minutes passed with his conscience raging at him, "Wherever you go, there you are, fool!"

Flushed like school-kids, the Barton's finally joined him at the kitchen table. They slurped and chomped, chowing down the giant-sized pancakes.

Seeking redemption Richie spouted, "Deem this a new day, all forgiven, with any luck, forgotten."

The couple joked together as usual. "Well, nothing like a morning lovey-dovey," Festus proudly grinned.

Relieved, Richie seized the moment to explain the unexplainable. Overly exuberant, he related his experiences into the unknown. "It's my time to become a nurturing 'Super-Dad' to all the creatures in the universe."

Elma almost choked on her pancake, regurgitating. "Sounds like a hunk of that 'New Age' babble."

Festus added, "Like one of them guys on TV selling success."

Chuckling, Elma added, "And his only success is trying to sell it."

Richie was stoked, "You don't get it. I found my life purpose, my calling, why I was born."

Festus balked. "So you think one night in the boonies and you're changed. Just like that?"

Chewing a chaw of tobacco Elma spit out, "That'll take a lot of proving."

"This is the real deal. I'm carrying on for Jenny. Me as 'WE'. Get it?"

Festus scratched his head. "You get it, Elma?"

"No matter, if he does." She replied, without concern.

Downing a glass of milk Festus sputtered, "The boy's delirious, happens when you get too much sun."

Seizing the opportunity Elma ignited her sales pitch. "Maybe it's time for an identity change. It's the latest craze, you know."

Playfully, Richie rapped into a faux microphone, "Legalise Update. Tracked down ID change scammers – sentenced to twenty years in the slammer."

Disappointed, Elma tapped her foot, "Seems like I barked-up the wrong lawyer."

Festus cracked, "Can't sing, neither."

In a serious tone Richie stressed the point. "Identity changes serve the greedy, felonious, debauched wrong-doers."

Festus perked, "Felon-ious what?"

Mischievously Elma mocked, "Scammers. Rip-off artists." She nudged Festus. "Or full of 'piss and vinegar', old coot bootleggers."

"Can't you see I already had an identity change?" Richie twirled around, pointed to his arms, legs, head, and heart. "See, I'm not the old Richie. I'm transformed into the new model. Retooled, a total internal refurbish."

Festus shook his head. "Looks like the same ol' same ol' to me."

Taking charge, Elma the image-maker, went to work. "Time's come. Got something to show you." She motioned to Richie, and then pulled him up from the table. "Let's go," she snapped. Everyone traipsed down the wooden hatch to the wardrobe cellar. "Mr. 'New Boy', pick yourself a new set of clothes."

Richie couldn't believe the array of goods. "Didn't know you ran a store?" He rummaged through biker leathers, surfer-duds, and Friar's robes. In a madcap folly, Richie was on game. He tried on a spacesuit. "Ground control to Major Festus."

"You might do better on Mars, bugging some alien," Festus sputtered.

Elma put a longhair hippie wig on Richie with a beard to match. Festus yodeled. Richie made a thin-toned yodel, joining in a duet of dueling yodels. One more change and Richie had his look, settling on a 'cool' inlaid shirt, form-fit Levi's and snakeskin cowboy boots. Elma rolled her eyes in approval. "You're duds-dude."

The next morning over a breakfast piled with stacks of pancakes, ham and eggs and hominy grits, they prepared for Richie's departure. Richie savored the food and the company. He patted Festus on the back. "Feels like I was born here, reborn here for sure. You taught me real life stuff. Thanks Festus."

Festus choked up, speechless. Elma chimed in, "Yah, he taught you real good, how to be a man and not a flakey wuss."

Romping like kids they clamored outside to the front of the Barton farm. "Good-byes are never easy, even for old folks." Festus admitted. To ease the tension Elma grabbed Festus' Stetson hat from his head and plunked it on Richie.

"Seems like you're departing a reborn cow-daddy." Festus spit a chaw of tobacco clear across the yard, nailing the spittoon.

"Some shot," Richie admired.

Festus handed him a bag of tobacco. "Real men know when to take a chaw."

"What to do to thank you?"

Elma and Festus winked at each other. Elma nodded at the SUV in the driveway, "You already did. Have to admit you're the best negotiator we ever bargained with."

Richie smiled, "Come on. Let's not call the kettle black. I collected toy vintage trucks and never dreamed I actually have the guts ... I mean luck ... to own one."

"Remember the words of your old savior, Festus here. You ain't seen nothing, 'til you see one hung low." Festus clapped his hands three times in front of Richie's eyes. Recalling Big Bull's balls, he nodded.

Richie climbed into a bright yellow vintage Ford pickup. Billy Goat stood proud in the rear bed. The engine turned over, backfiring, laid a rubber trail, coughing and sputtering, cranking down the road.

Traveling down the highway, the liberated Richie sang a medley ranging from "You've Got a Friend" to "Lonesome Cowboy". Hope, vigor, and purpose were injected into his psyche. Gratitude welled-up within him as he sang, "I left my guilt on the repent turf."

Placed in the Barton's custody was his bent for wayward tendencies. All of them were to be discarded by the Barton's – his saviors or con artists – whatever and whoever they were. Richie was a professional, a seasoned discriminator who had to deal with the lawless, the tainted, and society's dregs in the underworld of criminality and so-called justice. Labels were often insignificant barometers. To Richie, it didn't matter if Festus was a con man. In many ways he would remain Richie's absolution-ist forever.

Richie witnessed the magical early evening, a golden glow bathed the sky as the old pickup chugged into Brian's apartment complex. Richie carefully tied Billy Goat in the truck's rear. Racing up Brian's steps, he felt exhilarated, ecstatic. Looking at the door, he smiled. "Number thirteen – our lucky number." He knocked. No one answered. "Brian, its Dad. Open up." He turned the doorknob. Unlocked, it swung open. "Brian, are you here?" he called out, as the door shut behind him with a quiet click.

Glancing around the front room, Richie viewed a typical teen crash pad. It was totaled, a pigsty wreck. Plates of rotting food, papers in piles, were strewn everywhere. Richie stepped over a heap of dirty clothes. "Brian? What yuck." Richie chastised himself. "Stop. No judgments! Accept. Be kind."

He entered Brian's bedroom. In contrast, it was immaculate: A fully made bed, not a thing out of place. "Safe-zone. No cooties." Richie felt the impact of the long day and stretched out on the bed, closing his eyes.

At the front door Tanya fondled Brian. He put the key in the lock, the door opened. "Warn you, my roommate's an oinker. Keep your eyes closed for fifteen seconds, promise?"

"Promise." She shut her eyes tight, rubbing next to him.

Brian led her inside. "No peeking."

"I need to go to the little ladies room. Hurry, please," Tanya implored.

Brian guided her over the clutter into the bathroom and shut the door behind him. Swiftly, he raced around the apartment tidying the mess, filling a garbage can with rotten food, old papers, straightened pillows on the sofa and hurried outside to dump the smelly trash.

Tanya sauntered out of the bathroom, stripped down to a thong and matching lace push-up bra. "Brian, got a surprise!" She peeked in the living room, and then looked for him. She opened the bedroom door. "Are you in here?"

Inside the darkened room, shuffling to the bed, she climbed in. Feeling a warm body, assuming it was Brian, she whispered, "Didn't waste any time, did you?" and began to sumptuously nuzzle his ear.

Grogged-out, Richie groped under the covers. "Mmmm. Ahhh...oooh...lah-lah."

"Shy? You still have your clothes on."

Brian came back into the living room. He saw the open bathroom door noting that Tanya wasn't there. In anticipation he headed toward the bedroom and entered the room.

In bed, Tanya squirmed, "Oh, Brian."

Brian climbed into bed. "Yes, Tanya."

She cringed, "Who's that? Your slimy roomie?"

Brian tumbled over her and flipped on the light. He whipped off the cover, exposing Richie squirming, still in a stupor. "More, baby, oooh..."

In shock, Brian shrieked, "Dad?"

Tanya attempted to cover herself as she jumped out of the bed, backing out of the room. "Dad! I was kissing your Dad?"

Brian shook Richie's shoulders. "You dirty wonker. Get your friggin' raspberry out of here." He threw a swing at Richie's face. Richie rolled over, avoiding the punch, then he stretched his arms out for a hug. "Son, my long-lost son. I worried, fretted. Almost called 911."

Confused by his Dad's behavior his anger escalated, "What's gotten into you?" With an open-handed punch, he knocked Richie to the floor. "How dare you make a pass at my girl!"

Tanya returned to the bedroom fully dressed. "Do you think I'm your girl-toy? Setting me up with your father?! Gross me out! You are one, make that two, major kink-sicko's!"

Lying on the floor, rubbing his jaw, Richie defended, "You got it all wrong."

She whipped a wet towel at him. Then she turned to Brian. "I was so stupid to think we had something special."

Brian stammered, "We did...I mean we do."

Steaming at Brian she yelled, "You're just a crotch-bitten horn-dog." Pointing a shaky finger at Richie, "Just like him."

Richie sighed. "I'm semi-relieved. Been called a hell of a lot worse."

Brian confided, "I barely know him. I'm nothing like him."

With vengeance Tanya sniped, "You are the <u>evil</u> twin, not the good one."

Brain balked at her fury, "Was that necessary? That hurt below the belt." Drawing his eyes away from her, he put his head down.

"Very funny. I'm not through with the Forrest family. Your mother abused me. Your dad tried to molest me. Wait until I report this to Sergeant Hallbally."

Brian tried to explain. "I didn't know he was here. Tell her, Dad."

Tanya snarled, "Right, like I'm supposed to believe him. Like warped father, like limp-dick son." She stormed out of the apartment. Brian wanted to go after her, knowing it wasn't the right move. He got as far as the living room and slunk down on the sofa.

"It was her big night to get down. Make love. Get into Kappa Kappa," Brian razzed with contempt.

Perplexed, Richie hovered over him. Speechless for the first time in his life, he had no choice but to let Brian rant.

Thrashing a justifiable tirade, Brian glared at Richie. "You screwed it all up. You never took any interest in me. Ever! Why tonight of all nights?"

In a shabby gesture for redemption Richie reached for his Stetson hat and put it on. Regaining his cowboy demeanor, searching for the right words, he affected a slow drawl with macho conviction. "Son, in the words of my dear old friend Festus, 'You never seen nothing 'til you see one hung low'."

"Who the hell is Festus?" Brian snapped.

Sighing, Richie replied. "It's a long story. It's been a rough day. I'm sorry about this mix-up. I'd never do anything to hurt you, son. This morning I was almost murdered when this old guy caught me in a bubble- bath with his ninety-year-old wife."

"No way! Dad, please, I can't handle your jokes right now," Brian pleaded, pulling his tee-shirt over his head.

Richie took off the Stetson, holding it to his heart. "On a more somber note, son, I have some bad, sad news."

"You mean it gets worse?"

"It's about your mother, my dear Jenny. They found her coveted cell phone in a ditch."

Brian's attitude changed from harried to concern. "What are you trying to say, Dad?"

Choking back the words Richie revealed, "She's gone, disappeared without a trace."

Needing reassurance Brian stammered, "We'll find her...won't we?"

Richie fell into Brian's arms, sobbing. "It's too late. You kids are all I got...and I'm all you got." Brian held Richie tight, wheels turning in his mind, " No, Dad. We have family. Let's get everyone together and figure things out, or least, try to support each other."

Assembling a resistant family was daunting and overwhelming to Richie. Both Rita and Mrs. Svartzneg-ger sided together and refused to attend Jenny's private burial. Richie reeled in a haze of confusion. "What happened to the 'blood is thicker than water' theory?"

Rita answered flatly, "Your lame, manipulative foul play theory is ridiculous and unacceptable."

Mrs. Svartznegger kveched, "Where's the 'proof of life...or no life'?" Wanting a sense of closure the immediate family, without the grandmothers' blessings, gathered in the Forrest backyard. Samantha and Brian dug a minuscule makeshift grave. Richie increasingly sinking in gloom clung tightly to Jenny's cell phone. Her voicemail announcement repeated like a mantra, "Jenny-Jen here...I'm listening."

Spying on the family, Detective Gritty clumsily climbed a tree.

His foot slipped. Clutching a limb, he dangled from the near-cracking branch. Bit by bit it split in two. Plummeting to the ground he wailed..."AHHUG!"

Richie looked up at the sky. "Did you hear her? An angel cry from the heavens." The sun rose, peeking through clusters of misty clouds. "Ah, her light inside makes everyone shine." Hands folded in prayer, he knelt on his knees.

Samantha and Brian glanced in Gritty's direction as he scrambled behind a hedge. "Too weird," Samantha shuddered.

Pledging his loyalty, Richie placed a hand over his heart. "Jenny, as our kids are my witness, I promise to serve as a dedicated domestic 'Super-Dad'. I vow to forever give up my depraved, unaccountable, aberrant, Viagra-bloating, lust-meister ways."

Brian pleaded. "Enough guilt-slamming, Dad. Let it go." Samantha reamed, "Dad, this is a rehearsal, kinda like a ritual."

"She's right," Brian added. "We don't know for sure that Mom is...not among the living." Unwilling to succumb to their insensitivity Richie kissed and cuddled the cell phone close to his heart.

Losing her patience, Samantha snapped at Richie. "Drop it! Put the cell in the hole!" She wrestled the phone from him and dropped it into the grave.

Gritty peered through a bush, snapping a photo of the gravesite. Whispering into his cell he conveyed, "Evidence is subterranean."

Brian sprinkled dirt evenly, covering the phone. Soon, it disappeared. Everyone stared at the mound of dirt, wide-eyed and in shock. Brian spoke with reverence, "Burying this cell gives us time to prepare for the worst, to heal."

Waving a bouquet of daisies, Samantha exploded. "Heal? From what! Mommy-oppressor who made me feel like a stupid, shriveling nothing, an incompetent bargain basement, unsexy, undesirable, second-rate twin?" Losing it, she whacked herself with the bouquet. Nervously holding back, ready to burst with anger, Brian tried to grab the bouquet. "Enough self-bashing, Sam. Put the daisies on the dirt."

"Why should I? I was her wilted daisy. You are the perfect twin. The one she loved. The love child! You popped-out first. I should have stayed in there and rotted." Samantha tossed the bouquet at him. Flowers scattered in the wind, a few petals floated, then dropped on the dirt. Brian called out in desperation. "Mom, can you hear me? I want you to know that I know the truth you knew, before I knew. I am a true Svartznegger. The 'Black Forrest'. The dark evil twin."

Samantha blathered, "No news to me. But if she knew, why didn't she let me know she knew?"

Richie escalated the confusion. "Who knew? That you knew, too?"

Brian crawled on the ground gathering petals. "You covered for me 24/7. I didn't have to deal with life. Face it, I am a spoiled, privileged, unreliable..."

Samantha interrupted, "Slacker-boner."

Brian threw himself face down in the dirt. Lifting his head, he was black-faced. "Now that I know the truth, I promise to be what you believed I could be. The best twin." Brian sanctimoniously arranged petals on the grave.

Samantha exploded, "Enough, Brian. Always about Brian! Can't you just shut your dirty face and get over your black self!"

Richie sanctioned the muddled moment. "Amen! Your mother would be proud. Her family reunited, sharing."

Samantha added, "Dumping."

Brian added, "Annihilating."

Gritty crawled out from under a thorny bush, grunting "Cripes." Pulling a sharp sucker-thorn stuck on his trouser, he whispered into his cell, "Mission accomplished."

The next day, back at Brian's apartment, Richie's day of reckoning had arrived. Caught in the throes of living his commitment, wrapped in an apron, he chopped, diced, and stewed veggies. Viewing a Martha video, he mimicked her. "You can roll the cheesy cloth wet or dry. Or pickle the peck of pickled peppers picked." After hours of meticulous food preparation there was still no hint of serving a real meal.

Brian and Samantha listened to his inane comments. She pondered, "Should we be sad or happy he's happy?"

Brian blurted, " Let's bust his obsession. Start razzing him." Brian nudged Richie's shoulder, "Dad, I'm starved. Maybe I'll just open a can of tuna."

Samantha decided, "I think I'll just fast...for a year or two."

Richie gazed up from his cheesy cloth for a second. "Is that Zen, macro or anorexia?" Samantha suggested, "Brian, how about I cook something for us?"

Brian tried to humor him, "Sounds dangerous, huh, Dad?"

With intense focus Richie hacked a pickle into smithereens. "Your call."

Jittery and confused by his knife fixation Samantha motioned to Brian, "Let's do lunch." She juggled a peanut butter jar, jelly, and a loaf of bread onto a tray. Brian followed her out of the kitchen, taking the tray from her trembling hands. "Enough of this nonsensical torture. Let's do Chinese."

"Nah, I'm not hungry. This is a sick tug of war and Dad's the rope."

"There's no noose around his neck. He's man enough to choose this, he's man enough to get out of it."

"Choose what? My mind's a blank-out...like I can hear sizzling brain neuron's..."

Okay Sam, indulge, bend out of shape. All I can hear is my stomach rumbling. Coming to lunch or what?"

Nervously pursing her lips, "Thanks anyway, I've gotta run." Without another word she ran to the garage, started the SUV and headed directly to Brain-Joggle. She jammed into the office yelling, "Need a fix! Brain tune-up!" Everything was shut down. The office was empty. She bolted into the treatment room. No computers. A worker wearing eye-goggles flogged a sledgehammer, dismantling the sound studio. The school property manager tossed files in the trash.

Desperate, she picked the files out of the trash. "Where are they? You can't do that!"

The property manager was curt and emphatic, "No freeloader ride, kid. Welch on your tab and you're gone." A studio wall crashed to the floor. She wailed, "I'm losing it...I need a treatment to hold my IQ."

"They duped you, kid. Try running track...that'll get the endorphins up."

"Brain cells aren't endorphins, numbskull." Freaked by the reality jolt, Samantha threw the files on the floor, dashed outside into the fresh air, and ran to her car. Part of the Brain-Joggle treatment included positive self-talk. Driving aimlessly, she repeated, "Self-talk, talk it up, get upbeat, high voltage." She gently patted her face, "Be your best friend, Samantha. Speak to yourself with loving care. Think about your most incredible dream." Sticking a finger in her mouth, like a simpleton, she continued, "Come on, you can remember it, you felt so good."

She smiled, "Yes. I had the same sweet dream every night...for years. I was helping the 'little people'. The rejects, overlooked, neglected, weary people. Then I saw a cool stream and I dove in, saving drowning little girls." She sighed. "Yes, you did. If you follow the loser, the 'can't do it Sam', you will loose faith and blow your dream."

She pulled up to a drive-through at Foster Freeze. "Forget that! I'm 'Strong Samantha'. I'm smart and I lead."

The voice over the speaker box answered, "Did you say tart and cheese?" Staring at the mouth-watering major-calorie's selection, Samantha salivated. Giggling with the excitement of a die-hard addict, she placed her order. "How about a double freeze, extra fudge with bananas?"

Meanwhile, Richie stayed on his maddening cleanaholic spree. Certifiably robotized he operated at a fast pace, vacuuming, scouring, dusting with feather brushes, and hose-spraying windows. Outside on the landing he fed birds, lavishing pet bowls with gourmet treats. Feral cats, skunks, possums, stray dogs leaped to the feast, lapping up water and licking his face in mutual delight.

Loading and reloading the washing machine, Richie picked up Brian's raccoon hat off a shelf. Compassionately stroking the tail he pined, "Poor 'Rocky Raccoon', hunted, skinned, mangled. Probably sacrificed your life for a gun-toting, bald-headed NRA pussy." In a state of euphoria, he tossed it in the wash, adjusted a knob. "You'll just love the gentle cycle."

Out of Richie's earshot Samantha and Brian watched with deep concern. She imitated how he dusted. Turning to Brian, she freaked, "He's a wind-up robot. At this pace he could explode" Jarred by the noise, Samantha conceded. "It's the worst scenario. Like Mom entered him and he became her."

Frowning, Brian agreed, "For sure, he's not him. He made a pact with Mom's ghost to carry on."

She gasped at the absurdity. "Poor Dad. He's totally losing it."

Brian searched, groping his erudite intellect for an answer, a cause, a reason for 'being-ness'. "I was reading about these alien 'Bod-pods' floating in space. They zero in on a human host, then zap 'em, walk right in and take over. Bang. They're history. The disguised replicate is so them, even their kids can't tell."

"Brian, your 'Bod-pod' theory will not stop me from making this call." Samantha picked up the phone,

"We have to save Dad from 'Bod- pods', whatever, or his own wacky demise."

Brian grabbed the phone from her hand. "Wait! I hate to do this. It's like slam-dunking Mom."

She grabbed it back. "Displaying rare chutzpah she placed the call anyway. Feigning an upbeat tone and attitude she chirped, "Hello, Bambe. This is Samantha. Yeh, Dad is acting distant, strange. Of course, maybe I can arrange a meeting. Maybe we should surprise him. The Comic House up here is bitchin'. I'm sure he misses you too." She hung up. Her mind flitted from one thought to another, a slam-dunk, the mousetrap was set, the flypaper was out, a home run.

Brian admonished, "I hope you're happy. This one's on you."

Samantha took a deep breath. "This has been agonizing, terrifying. I never took a risk...on my own...before now. Brian don't desert me, please, it'll screw up my courage." They looked at each other like faltering little children.

Brian reminded her, "It's like when we sawed the legs off the dining room table."

"Yah! It was all over. We were like all the 'Kings horses and all the Queen's men'." Gulping air she wheezed, "We couldn't glue the mess back together again."

Brian pontificated, "You got that right. Now it's time that you face this wild Bambe scheme, a possible disaster, on your own. Think of it like a solo flight. You might crash. So you skin one knee. You've got another one. You'll survive."

Apprehensive, she twisted her hair, "What are you hinting at Brian?"

"You're scared you made a mistake? The only way up from a fall is to get up, dust off and keep going, charging to the finish line."

"That's what you do when you're tackled, huh?"

"Dah! No, I just lie there and let another two tons pummel me." Hanging his tongue out of his mouth, Brian feigned punch-drunk.

Gazing at her giant-toad brother towering above un-nerved her with his moral strength. Strike that illusion, it was his physical strength that zapped her confidence to the bone! Uncertain like a bug underfoot, she whimpered, "Okay, so I have to deal with this mess all alone."

Taken by her helpless quirkiness, Brian free-styled a lyric. "You're a big girl. In life's jagged cruel city. All alone, wandering. Looking for pity, Ms. Pretty."

All she heard was the word 'pretty'. Flickering like a candle, she asked, "Pretty, ya' think?"

"I think my hands are clean on this one." He said with conviction.

Wanting to believe him she playfully bowed and curtsied. "Yes, my master mind-manipulating bro'." Twisting her hair tight to the scalp with a finger, her merry heart quickly shifted to doubt. "How about your heart, Brian. Is it bleeding red or black?"

Sometimes it's difficult to forgive and forget, especially in matters of the heart. Tanya felt used and abused by Brian. The quandary sent her lurching like a piranha to the Campus Crisis Center. Lori, a dressed-down plain-Jane senior counselor performing community service, listened intently to Tanya's peeves.

"Brian bull-shitted love baits on me, 'You're so fine, Tanya, a guy can't help raining love all over you.' Believing that bull kicked me into heartbreak. My triumph – he didn't score. His triumph – he probably has another fish wiggling, trapped in his net."

Lori set the ground rules. "Please no names, this is confidential, not tabloid stuff."

Chastened, Tanya explained, "Sorry. I just wanted love. To have fun, hang with someone special. He was the one. Self-centered, cocky, sure of himself like an 'arrested-development' kind of guy."

Lori congealed, "Exactly what every healthy liberated woman wants – a 'yes' man."

Tanya burst forth, almost frothing at the mouth, "Look, I'm no women's-libber out marching for rights."

"You mean you won't stick your neck out for anyone?"

"I do okay," her vulnerability surfaced, scraping under authority's radar."

Lori offered her chocolate from a box. "The dark creamy ones are to live for."

Tanya shook her head 'no'. "You mean to <u>die</u> for."

Lori stuffed one in her mouth. "So, what is going on with you?"

"How about being raised by my sixty-five-year-old grandma. Always hung-up, saying, 'Got to fight for it, there's no equality being a woman.' She was a poor depression baby, a saving everything penny-pincher. My first bra was a cinching nipple flattener. A 'hand-me-down' – Granny's first bra – yellowed after thirty smelly years rotting in a hope chest."

"How awful." Silencing herself Lori slid her fingers across her mouth. She wanted to avoid fueling Tanya's pent-up emotions.

"She hoarded rice, box's of bulky two-inch Kotex. My tenth disaster birthday gift was her black little typewriter with terminal ribbon jams instead of a computer. I cried and cried, 'I'm the only kid without Spell check'. No wonder I'm illiterate. 'Make do' was her favorite saying. When she died, she donated the old Victorian house as a museum."

"Sounds like a conservationist, a real survivor."

"Oh yeah! Our age-warp gave me a flaming survival thing. To use my sexy-self to my advantage."

"Aren't you right on time? A Millennial! Sexy, savvy, a 'Gen 'Y' chick."

Squinting, Tanya was confused." Doing what on time?"

"Giving no respect for male dominance, or hierarchy's. We women control the work force, even as executive assistants. Once denounced as secretaries, the underrated power job, a 'do-goody' assistant can send up a corporate red flag. She simply deletes a vital email. Result? A mean-spirited boss is justifiably whipped to demolition, eliminated, fired."

"Whew! I don't have a boss and I'm not planning to be one," Tanya confided, relieved.

"Unfortunately, here at Stanford, we're a 'three girls to one guy' ratio." Responding to Tanya's blank look Lori clarified. "Meaning, this is truly a no-man-zone. Available guys are hard to find."

Tanya agreed. "It's the pits. Tell me what I don't know!"

Trying to lighten the mood, Lori bombs with, "Take a number. Line up, you lonely-hearts waiting for love."

Ready to explode a fountain of repressed pain and anger, Tanya gripped Lori's hand. "Don't call me that! Is it wrong to want a real family with brothers and sisters? I'd sign up for triplets if it meant having Brian and Samantha in my life forever." She started to sob.

Handing her a Kleenex, Lori observed, "Seems like you hit breakpoint. Are you tired of doing life alone?"

Wiping tears and sniffling, Tanya warbled, "Who am I kidding? That would lead to incest – the very thing that's freaking me out. The father-son thing is way too raunchy to even mention." Tanya got up to leave. "Thanks for the ear."

Lori pointed a finger at her, warning, "If I were you, I'd think 'secretary-kill'. Send up a smoke signal and red-flag the jerk."

Seething and lost in retaliatory thoughts Tanya replied, "I'm going back...to dump it on the dykes."

Astounded by this absurd person, Lori mustered a mealy wave, "Bye-bye." Taking a breather, she imbibed a quote on her desk that read, "Dealing with difficult people? Shoot 'em in the ass."

Heartsick, Tanya's quandary lingered. With her guard up and ready, she stepped into the Campus Security Office. Helga's intimidating presence, a bulldozer with breasts, didn't make the pursuit easier. Convinced that justice must be served, Tanya fielded a question of inquiry with conviction. Staring Helga directly in the eyes she said, "This is the third time I've been here. Please, where is Ms. Hallbally?"

Helga answered flatly. "On an indefinite leave of absence. What's so hellacious?"

Tanya blurted, "Lecherous old men on campus are posing as students."

Helga bristled. "Lurking vermin-sloats." Pulling a form from a stack of papers on her desk, she handed it to Tanya. "Make a complaint. We'll take 'em down before they kidnap or..." for a scare tactic effect she pounded a fist on the desk, "...mutilate some unsuspecting soul."

Tanya gasped, "I never thought of that. I was thinking more like hanging him on a clothesline to dry so everyone could see he was dirty laundry."

"Hmmm...that veers on homicidal ideation. How often do you have bizarre notions?"

"I felt that one really strong for maybe a minute, then medium strong for like a few seconds...um, that's about it." Tanya glanced at the form doubting her ability to fill it out correctly. "I really need to talk to Hallbally."

"Actually she is an apt choice. Thrives on smutty details." Realizing she revealed too much, Helga coughed loudly, as a diversion.

Tanya was persistent. "Please put Hallbally on it."

Helga studied the teen's shard-like face, crushing with insecurity. Going soft, she admired and sympathized with Tanya's ardent pursuit. It reminded her of when she was young and had no one to turn to, or to listen to her complaints, imagined or real. Picking at her tooth with her fingernail, she opted to offer Tanya a sense of support.

"I'll see what I can do. You show courage. Being a snitch isn't for the weak-hearted."

Tanya grasped Helga's free hand and earnestly shook it up-and-down. "Thank you, thank you, somebody finally listened to me."

Helga just nodded. She knew listening was the first part of a trust equation; understanding was the second. "I understand" she assured.

"So radical. You got where I was coming from." Tanya received more support than expected. No black eyes, sexual harassment, or loitering tickets. Floating on a cloud, she left the Campus Security Office super-charged.

Sequestered at Brian's apartment for days, tending to Billy Goat bedded in the laundry room, Richie confided, "I love seclusion," when the kids suggested a movie. Without Brian's help, suggestions, or game planning, Samantha choreographed a rendezvous for Richie with Bambe. It was Saturday night at the most touted place in town, the Comic House.

Swabbing grease gunk, crumbs, and natty droppings from the kitchen floor, Richie's shirt was crumpled, frayed, and grubby. "Disgusting," Samantha whispered, exercising control not to criticize his every move, or stalk him from room to room yelling, "Stop this crazy B.S. Come back, Dad, please!" She moved closer, ripping the dishrag from his hand. His knuckles were a raw bright red, discolored, and chaffed. "Let me do this. You go get ready. It's our big night out," Samantha said in a cheery voice.

He shoved a dirty rag in the garbage can. "Changed my mind, can't abandon the fort."

"Dad, this is 'Father and Daughter' night at the Comic House. I can't go alone."

"Right! Of course! Can't let my daughter down, now can I?"

She muttered to herself. "He looks the same, the same nose, eyes, and that's his dimple. But, this isn't Dad. Who is this madman? Maybe Brian is right, he is pod-bound."

Richie showered and dressed with the same precision and intensity he seemed to give to all his routine tasks. He sported a navy jacket, grey shirt and matching Armani trousers. He looked in the mirror. "Left over right," he recited as he adjusted the Gucci tie.

While he was dressing Samantha hovered about filling Parrot's water and feed bin, a foul-mouthed multi-colored parrot abandoned by Brian's ex-roommate. "Rake your snake." Parrot screeched. Startled, Samantha darted back a couple of steps. Looking spiffy Richie surprised her with, "Well, how does your old man look?"

She gazed into his young spirited eyes, thinking, "What a handsome man." This was the example her future guy would have to live up to. She smiled, "You look stylish, Dad. Maybe twenty years younger."

He beamed at her. "That's my girl."

Samantha had done her best. She'd been patient and calculating, waiting for her plan to take hold. However, doubts intruded, sweltering hot beads of perspiration on her hands, swallowing her confidence. "What if this encounter is a mistake? What if Brian was right and the setup was a betrayal?" 'What ifs' wreaked havoc in her mind.

Richie was quiet and self-absorbed as Samantha drove them to the Comic House. Covering anxiety, she small-talked. "So, Dad, how's the new cat food?"

"Not bad. I taste every morsel before any pet gets a sniff. It's a little grainy when you first chew it, but saliva seems to melt it and it blossoms into a yummy purée."

"I thought you like crisp and crunchy, opposed to drippy and chewy."

"Only for Billy Goat's oats."

"I see," Samantha said with a slight tinge of disbelief that they were having such a bizarre conversation. The interchange waned when she stopped prying. Strange how he showed little volition to inquire, to prod or have interest in her personal thoughts or life. She couldn't decide if she felt free or abandoned. Flashing neon letters, 'Comic House' caught her attention. "We're here." Samantha whipped the SUV over to the curb in front of the building. "This is the spot, Dad."

A line of college kids and locals formed down the block. He remarked, "Popular place. Looks like half of the town showed up."

Handing Richie the tickets with the guile of a turncoat, she smiled curtly, "Special seating. You don't have to wait in line."

"Me? What about you?" he voiced with concern.

"I'll catch you inside. Get a good seat." A car horn blasted behind her. "Gotta move." Richie got out of the car. Waving good-bye Samantha peeled off, leaving him to fend for himself. He lingered outside on the sidewalk for a few minutes, and then walked over to the entrance. A middle-aged hefty man with a younger taut woman stepped up beside him. Richie smiled, "Good idea, 'Father and Daughter' night?"

Gruff and blunt the man answered, "Not funny, creepo."

Richie was puzzled. "No humor, no joke?" Sneering at him, the couple entered the club. Richie followed, careful not to walk too close behind them.

Inside the Comic House Richie scrutinized the eclectic crowd that ranged from young teens to the elderly. Everyone was talking and drinking in an animated way. An air of excitement and anticipation permeated the room. Mingling through the crowd, Richie settled at a table near the stage.

Out of sight, hidden up in the rafters, Gritty focused a camera on the crowd. Panning and scanning the room, he located Richie. Zooming in on a close-up, he snapped several shots. Continuing to scan through the lens he zeroed in on Bambe milling through the crowd, searching. Spotting Richie, she sneaked behind him, covered his eyes, and nibbled his ear. "Guess who, lover boy?"

The hair on the back of his neck nearly stood straight up in fright. "Please God, don't let it be Tanya."

She grimaced, "Who the hell is Tanya?"

Turning around, instantly apoplectic at the sight of her, he blurted, "Bambe! What are you doing here?" Trying to scoot away from her, she pinned her body against his, snuggling close. "I vant you Richie. Tonight! Forever!"

Backstage Jenny struggled, handcuffed to a chair. Aggie warned her. "Bolt now, you'll be ranked a felon. Judge Hickey will hijack your freedom key for a permanent jail cell."

Jenny wriggled in the chair, peeking out at the audience. Up front Bambe fondled Richie. Enraged, Jenny thumped the chair up-and-down. "Aggie, please. Take the cuffs off. Raspberry butt-ass is here."

"You'll try anything won't you, girl?" Aggie finagled the mummy headdress on Jenny. Emerald green eyes loomed out from the opening, glowering frostbite cold, desperately seeking revenge.

Onstage Grunge appeared before the crowd. "Hi, everyone! Are you having a good time?"

Voices shouted, "You bet!" "Yee-Haw!" "Let's get on with the show!"

Grunge laughed. "It's going to be a great night! Thank you all from coming! And now...it's 'Showtime'. Here's 'Funny Mummy'."

Backstage Jenny continued pleading with Aggie. "Forget 'Showtime'. This is a meltdown."

"Go get 'em before they eat you alive." Aggie rubbed her shoulders, preparing her like a fighter going into the ring, removing her handcuffs.

Breathing hard, Jenny worked herself up for the kill. "This is no mess-around warpath time. The enemy has treaded my turf." Aggie released her and pushed Jenny's tush through the drapes.

On stage 'Funny Mummy' strutted her stuff. Pointing to a burly guy at a front table, she challenged, "Hey, stud-horse, having trouble relating to a mummy-face? Well, if you think you have a problem, imagine me trying to get around town. I get on a bus – everyone gets off, including the driver." A few laughs bellowed in the crowd. She dug in her heels, undulated her tummy, and did a couple of hip rolling belly dance moves. A few wolf-whistle's echoed from the audience.

"Or how about when I checked in at the airport. They checked me with the other bags. Rode with some scraggy dogs. We barked and howled all the way home." Throwing her head back, 'Funny Mummy' howled, "Woof-Woof."

Richie admired her tone. "Mmmm. What a set of lungs."

Bambe answered. "You mean chops, Richie."

'Funny Mummy' sauntered offstage circulating through the audience. "Now folks, let's get real. Can we talk? Anybody out there who's bored?"

Shouts rang out, "Yeah!" "Right on!"

She turned her back doing a 'fanny jiggle'. Lifting one cheek, then the other. Gritty sneaked to the foot of the stage and with a camcorder, began taping her performance.

Still mingling with the audience, she riled, "Anybody pissed off?"

The crowd jeered, "Damn right!" "No work!" "Finals, babe."

Sashaying up to a biker chick in black leather, body-pierced from head to toe, 'Funny Mummy' leaned into her and saucily asked, "Brave little 'Biker-Mama', what got you off your Harley?"

The biker chick boldly bragged, "To get laid."

"Crude and lewd," 'Funny Mummy' said dismissively. She shimmied her shoulders. Looking around the room, she moved toward the bar. "Any other horny-takers in need of some lovin'?"

Voices hollered. "Give it to me, 'Mummy'." "Lay it on."

Strutting back toward the stage, her eyes grew into tiny, beaded slits. "Your 'Funny Mummy' getting down. Any cheater's here? Home wreckers?" She strolled closer to Richie and Bambe, stopping in front of their table. "What about this happy little couple?" She plopped on Richie's lap, facing him, straddled her legs tightly around his, gyrating over his crotch. "Getting turned on, hot boy? The 'Mummy' here could be a real home wrecker." Richie began to sweat. Casting a glaring stare at his befuddled, flushed face, Jenny held herself back from strangling him. Standing up, she pressed her hip against Bambe. "And how about you, Bambe-bimbo, isn't that what you do? Grab the leftovers, devour the family?"

Bewildered, Bambe stood up and backed away. "How did you know my name?"

Jenny pointed to Bambe's panty hose, ridiculously slipping to her knees. "Looking to hang yourself?" At the silly sight the crowd let out cackles and a few roars.

"See, you're a known joke, everywhere. A punch line, punch board, girlfriend."

"How dare you call me a 'punch board'?" Bambe huffed.

"Excuse me. Is 'slut-able douche bag twit-banger' a better fit?" Jenny leaned in closer to Bambi's face.

Bambe fumed adrenaline, attacking 'Funny Mummy' like a cat, claws out. Instead of taking Bambe out with a karate chop, 'Funny Mummy' taunted with swift offensive moves. Bambe air-punched, tripped over a chair, flipping backwards. The panty hose twisted on the back of the chair, holding her captive. Ripping at the mangled stockings, tearing them in shreds, she eventually tore herself loose.

Funny Mummy

The audience loved the mayhem, whopping, "Go, 'Funny Mummy'." "Get her!" "Blotto!"

Bambe struggled to her feet. In a futile attempt she pummel-attacked, hitting Jenny open-handed like a child and not landing one hit. Jenny egged her on, avoiding contact. "Come to 'Mummy', girly-girl." Finally, Bambe let out a wrenching gaggle and collapsed.

'Funny Mummy' singled out Richie. "Everyone, I'd like you to meet Mr. Richie Forrest, AKA dick-head." Strolling around him, running her fingers through his hair, she grabbed a strand and yanked. "Why don't you just wear a trench coat? Dead-beat wanker! Cradle-robbing Daddy-O." Without mercy she aimed a straight-legged karate kick at his thigh. Richie quickly moved aside. The blow swiped the biker chick. Taking it to the gut, she doubled over. The leather-clad toughie recouped with a high-kick through the air at Jenny. "You're toast, 'Dummy Mummy'!"

The crowd rumbled in a 'free-for-all'. Total mayhem ensued. Patrons were either fighting or fleeing. Waving a DVD Gritty chickened-out of the chaos, racing for the front door, screaming into a cell phone, "Evidence secured!"

A muscle-bound-freako held Richie over his shoulders, spinning around and around. "Strap this one on, scrounger." Tossing him like a football, Richie flew into the air, crash-landing on a table. The room appeared to spin.

Blurry-eyed Richie watched 'Funny Mummy' and the biker chick wrestling on the floor. "Take this you ugly pie-hole, "Biker Chick yelled. Richie witnessed the biker brute lift the 'Funny Mummy' headdress. In that split second Jenny's face was revealed. Richie mumbled. "Jenny? ' Funny Mum'...uh...'Jenny Mummy'?" And then he passed out. Blood immediately drained from his face, crumbling to the floor, like a raggety-man-doll.

'Funny Mummy' cuckolded the biker chick. "Your last ride tonight, sweetie." Staring at the fallen opponent Jenny rubbed her hands together, signaling she was done -- the battle was over.

Disheveled onlookers waited for 'Funny Mummy' to say something special to them. She searched within. Thoughts bounced like balls between her ears. "Should I run or step up for my true self?" In a moment of decision, she faced the crowd. "Well, folks. May the truth set you free." Breaking into the song "Bobby McGee" she began to sing, "Freedom's just another word for nothing left to lose. Nothing, nothing if you are free."

Onlookers applauded, basically going wild. "Bravo!" 'Funny Mummy' brought down the house captivating newfound fans.

The crowd cleared. The house lights dimmed. A clean-up crew carried out a ton of trash. Backstage Jenny wallowed in the notorious letdown – the aftermath of a performer's adrenaline rush. However, her real remorse came from a more sacred place.

"I'm a loser! I used humor to hurt." On the verge of tears, her voice quivered as she admitted, "I lived for retaliation. I rehearsed it over and over. 'Get Richie! Get Richie!' " She wailed, "I misused the funnies. I gutted, de-balled, de-frocked."

Grunge interrupted. "And you triumphed as 'Funny Mummy'."

The bright yellow hospital room trimmed with smiling giraffes, elephants, and chimps surely belonged in pediatrics. Confined to bed Richie groaned, laid-up in traction with a bandaged leg. Brian performed one-arm push-ups in front of the TV.

Samantha fed Richie through a straw. Trying to rationalize his rambling she said, "Dad, you think you see Mom everywhere."

Richie mumbled, "This was the physical, tangible, three-dimensional human. Ask anyone who was there. She called out my name and Bambe's."

Brian tried reasoning with him. "You had a reservation, didn't you? They had your name, right? It was just theatrics. A set-up."

"Bambe didn't have a reservation."

"Yes she did. Samantha made it." Brian shot an 'oops I slipped' look at Samantha.

She snapped back, "Thanks, traitor, black evil one."

Richie tried to get up, falling back down in pain. "How could you? You betrayed your mother. Poor thing! No wonder she showed up."

Trying to salvage the moment Samantha replied soothingly. "This should be quiet time. We can bond, family-like and build treasured loving memories."

"When you've been married twenty years, you'll get a clue what real love is." Richie's face glowed, reflecting sweet memories.

Collapsing in a chair she relinquished her will to his whimsical state of mind, "Okay. What is it Dad?"

With a tad of interest Brian twiddled a finger on the bed, and then slyly asked, "Spill it, what is true love?"

Richie patted his stomach. "Beer bellies, stretch marks, arguments, 'I'm sorry', kiss's and make-up sex." Exhausted, he closed his eyes.

Samantha felt both flustered and amazed. "Right out of Cosmopolitan. You think he reads that stuff?" she asked, looking over the bed to Brian on the other side.

Brian added, "It's a real simple take on life, especially for him."

Samantha walked to the doorway. "I need a junk food fix. Wanna come with me?" Brian nodded. They walked down the corridor to a vending machine. Sticking a five-dollar bill into the slot, she hit ten buttons. Gobs of candy, cookies, and a box of Cracker Jacks fell out. "Doesn't this remind you when we were kids and we stuck our hands in the nutty peanut butter jar and pretended it was brains and livers?"

Brian grimaced. "Kind of. Whatever's happening sure doesn't feel real."

She tossed the Cracker Jacks to him. "It's my fault," she said. "Dad wouldn't be lying there crabbed-out, sulky and maimed. He was a happy cleanaholic, safe at home feeding frogs and parrots and God-knows-what. Why did I have to call Bambe?"

"You were trying to help."

Melted chocolate smeared, dripping from her lips, "Now I need to fix a wrong. I'm calling her back."

"Logic, Sam. How do two wrongs make a right?" Brian asked as he opened a box of Cracker Jacks.

"I'll take my chances." She pulled her cell phone out of her bag and punched Bambe's number, turning on the speakerphone. Brian listened.

Black-eyed, Bambe held a frozen pea bag to her face. Her arm floated in a sling. "Hello." She answered meekly.

Skipping the niceties Samantha got to the point. "Bambe dear, this is Samantha. Did you happen to see that 'Funny Mummy' person's face?"

"Face? Vhat face? If I deed, I'd have the sleet-eye arrested." Bambe ranted, "She almost keeled me."

Samantha was adamant, "But, Dad says he saw her."

"He's delirious. Rants on about zee walking dead, voices in his head. He hugs trees for zee 'oneness' vibe. You must know all that?"

Samantha played dumber than dumb, "Not really!"

Suddenly Brian's interest peaked, popping into the conversation. "Hey Bambe, it's Brian here. Anything else he said, like cosmic or weird?"

Bambe fiddled with the frozen pea pack on her eye. "Where should I start? Raindrops send messages like Morse codes. And he's cracking zee secrets of zee universe."

Crunching her knuckles Samantha became defensive. "Maybe he is. What would a bimbo like you know about genius?"

"Zhat you are not one, dunce." Intentionally Bambe threw the mean-spirited remark.

A body kick to her vulnerable spot, Samantha squirmed, hurt and insulted. "Who told you that?"

Going for the juggler Bambe attacked, "Your father...ees impossible to reason with, just like all of you."

Samantha lashed back, stuttering, "A dark.. twisted frightmare...like you...could never get his alcohol-fermented brain."

"He's a cracked nut, if zhat's what you mean, a fruitcake loop, however you say it in English." Bambe banged the receiver in Samantha's ear. The frozen peas dropped on her foot, ice to bone. Screeching in pain, Bambe hopped on one foot, shouting, "Curse zee Forrest clan!"

In frustration, Brian added to the flame, "Great job Samantha. Now you've alienated our one resource."

"Dad is definitely cracking, isn't he?" Samantha fear flashed in her eyes.

Brain paused, "Or maybe he is on to something. In quantum physic's it's proposed that vibrations emanate from light-years away, affecting our emotions, thoughts, and the collective core of humanity. We are actually in touch with realities that hold the memory of the universe."

Samantha remained clueless. "Good try. That's school theory, Brian. We're talking planet Earth, here."

It was a 'Grand Central' bedlam in the Grunge Group Rehab office. Phone calls, emails, groupie lines around the block, all signals that 'Funny Mummy' had become a hit. Jenny read a slew of emails. "I have over a hundred and fifty new phone messages," she said in amazement to anyone within earshot. "Listen to this one. 'Ms. Funny

Mummy, I'm desperate. I have three teens and a six-month-old baby. Either I commit hari-kari or get some funny survival tips from you'."

The phone continued to ring and the announcement clicked on, "Comic House. Leave your reservation at the giggle." A cacophony of giggles overlapped.

Grunge returned to the office from a break, quickly checking the answering machine.

"Please reserve fifteen VIP seats for Lorsch on Friday." "Six tickets for the Fox's for Saturday." Ecstatic, he bragged, "Phenomenal, 'Funny Mummy' struck a primal chord. The rage is just beginning. SNL here we come!"

Aggie chimed, "It's like Seinfeld on campus."

"There's a mega distinction. No one ever wanted to be Seinfeld. They just wanted to watch him."

Jenny answered, "That's what TV is for...to watch."

In a convincing tone Grunge summed it up. "Your fans want to be funny and dump their pent-up anger. They're sick of their drab, drone-ish lives. They want to be 'Funny Mummy' types."

Jenny was baffled. "That's ludicrous and unreal. Who is 'Funny Mummy', anyway? Neurotic little Jenny disguised as Hallbally."

Aggie applauded, "So you're finally coming out. We saw your sad-sack husband searching for his Jenny on TV." Laughing at the thought, she added "You've been hiding-out with a hag-mask over your face."

Clearly a covert sleuth like Grunge traced and knew her identity all along. He stayed on task and expulsed philosophical rhetoric to Jenny, "Don't worry, fans love neurotic, dysfunctional multi-dimensional's. You know their pain, the agony, the rage of your followers."

"Followers? If I'm the leader, they are majorly doomed," Saddened by the thought, Jenny shook her head.

Grunge encouraged, "You're their inspiration. A Muse."

Aggie supported him, "A blooming boomer-babe holding the funny bone key."

Grunge added, "A hip, uncensored nut-case."

Scowling at him, Jenny snipped, "I knew it. I'm just a case study to you, a horny lowly specimen."

"More like low on self-esteem, a little uptight, needing to unplug. It's time to unplug, 'Funny Mummy'." He held her arm, she pulled away, growling "Up yours."

"Don't tempt me," he teased. Then Grunge shot Jenny a hypnotic look that jolted through her. Gently wrapping his arm around her waist he guided her into the studio. "Relax. Breathe. Sit." His voice was commanding, and so she obeyed.

In a semi-trance, Jenny sat cross-legged in the center of a circle. The Grunge Group drummed hypnotically. In tribal-style they moved rhythmically around her while Grunge performed a shaman ritual. "Debrief. Reprogram. Own it. Claim it." Tickling her with a feather, "Can't you see you are every woman, every man?"

She jiggled and squirmed. "Every child."

"It's the sign of a leader, a chosen one with a higher mission."

"You're the leader, Grunge." She shouted with joy.

"Try to tell that to your fans." Grunge opened a window, revealing a sundry group of misfits, college kids, and locals who were all waiting for a glimpse of her.

No longer enraptured by Grange's hocus-pocus Jenny poked her head out of the window. Cameras flashed. Fans chanted, "We want 'Funny Mummy'!"

Jenny spilled-out mixed emotions as groupie fanatics swarmed like killer bees wanting to devour, to taste a snippet, of the host. Opting to make a humble plea, she called-out to the crowd, "Go home, you stalker-ratzie's. You've been duped. Mummy's just a Grunge stunt."

The crowd answered with a chant. "We love 'Funny Mummy'."

She fired bits of her perceived truth, "Grunge is a Svengali-trickster warped with a master plan to make you..." Spellbound, they hung onto her every breath, waiting for wisdom, direction, prophecy, or the shoe to drop. Jenny was searching for the right words. "He wants to make you into...'Funny Mummy' clones."

The crowd happily chanted, " 'Funny Mummy' clones." A break-dancer spun around on his head, and lifted his body off the ground with one arm. Grunge nodded with a twisted smile at the vulture-brewing crowd, wrangling Jenny from the window.

Inside the studio the Grunge Group participants drummed and chanted. " 'Funny Mummy' equals money." Jenny covered her ears and shouted over the chant. "Gobbleegook money-mongers."

They stopped chanting. "Gobblee what?"

"Gook, kooks. You'd throw better odds spitting wooden nickels, or playing a slot machine than banking on me."

Willy contorted his face, "Tell that to Goldie, Bette or Lucy. Funny is money."

Jenny raised her arms, "Back off for a sec, would you please?" Jenny began to cry. "It's all happening too fast."

Grunge came to her rescue. "Come on guys, let her rest and get a grip."

"And get a new ID fast," Jenny whispered under her breath.

Grunge held her close, appealing to her in a comforting tone, "What do you want, Lucy?"

"Don't call me that, anymore. Role-playing is wearing tread-marks on my psyche." She scrunched her face like a two-year-old on a potty-train. "I want to be left alone. I was sentenced to this funny farm to stay out of jail. Not to exploit fortune, hype and fame."

Grunge appealed logically, "Be honest with yourself, which one sounds better? Jail time or a star on the Hollywood Walk Of Fame?"

A bright big grin crossed her face. Grunge sighed, believing he had finally reached her. Then she asked. "Depends. How long is the sentence?"

Grunge baited her, "How about high-kick stakes, big bucks and notoriety?"

Jenny frowned, not going for it." No doubt a felon's dream come true."

Not letting up, Grunge was intent on convincing her to commit. "Well, let me sway you with an air of truth. How often do you think talent gets star-crossed with good management and lucky timing?"

"How often?"

"Never, to once-in-a-lifetime. Those are your odds Jenny, you're beating the game."

"Beating the opponents?" Jenny's interest peaked.

He nodded. "Most certainly."

Jenny feet positively challenged. "Now you're on to something, Grunge. I hate losing, you know. Did I ever tell you I was a star soccer player in grade school? The fastest runner on the team! The hardest kicker with my head, foot and knee."

Remembering his gonads, Grunge replied, "Don't remind me, you definitely have some mean knee-caps."

Ready to put her desire on the table, she wanted clarity, "Now you're talking a 'win-win', aren't you?" Grunge nodded with his disarming grin, thrust his hand out for a handshake. Jenny smiled and welcomed it.

Minutes later, Grunge and Jenny returned to the office where Aggie was fielding one call after the other. " 'Funny Mummy'. One moment please." She picked up the next call, "Hold your britches, okay!" One caller caught her full attention, "Hello. My name is Mac and I'm from the Celebrity Channel." Aggie flicked on the speaker, "Is 'Funny Mummy' available for interviews?"

Aggie jubilantly quipped, "You bet your sweet Mummy ass."

Grunge snatched the phone from her hand. "Excuse the profanity, vulgarity and insanity. This is Grunge, Ms. Mummy's manager, at your service."

"We'd like to schedule her on 'Dandy Man's Inferno' – live."

"She is totally, radically, irresponsibly at your disposal." Grunge promised.

Jenny watched the commotion, listening to the raves and the affirmations. A bug of satisfaction eagerly crept into her like the measles lying dormant before the blister's fester.

The hospital stay grew thin on Richie's nerves. Hobbling on crutches, he felt cranky and grouchy. Samantha assisted him into the bathroom. "I'm not an invalid! I can do it," he snapped.

On the hospital room TV, photos of 'Funny Mummy' were streaking across the screen. A reporter announced, "Good afternoon, everyone. Welcome to 'Dandy Man's Inferno' on the Celebrity Channel. Today, we have a very special live, exclusive 'Funny Mummy' exposé." A fan waved a sign, 'We Love De Mummy'. Dandy Man approached the crowd and asked a young man, "What makes you fans frolic in 'Mummy' chaos?"

The teen quickly answered, "To get free, man. We're trashing the stash." Escorted by Grunge, 'Funny Mummy' stepped up to the camera, stiff-backed and clearly disoriented. Dandy Man announced. "Here she is, folks. The degrading, elating 'Funny Mummy'. Welcome, Ms. Mummy."

Playfully Jenny said, "Greetings unfair and unbalanced, Dandy Man schmucko." The onlookers cheered. She rattled on, sound-bite driven, "Listen up, Trendoids, life is short, rottenly sweet. It dumps daily bird-do on your headache."

Grunge whispered to her, clutching her arm. "Do the 'Hah-Hah' promo. Now!" As if on cue she recited, "Feeling down and out? Wash away dumpy blues. Pop your 'Funny Mummy' happy pill. It's only a laugh away. Hah-Hah!" Dandy Man and the fans cheered and laughed at the strange cackling tone of her laugh.

♥♥♥

Back in the hospital the family leered at 'Funny Mummy' on TV. Open-mouthed and startled, Samantha turned up the sound, listening intently. Suddenly, she railed, "It's that annoying cackle!"

In elation Richie thumped his crutch. "It's our hanky-panky-mama!"

Brian shot into the air. "Holy shit! It can't be!"

Samantha leaned on the bed for moral support, "Dad's right.' Funny Mummy' is <u>Mom</u>!"

Richie held his gut, groaning in pain, blasting a bizarre belly laugh. "Haddy-Ho-Hah!" Within moments, a seemingly divine intervention took place: the room shook and the TV faded to black. Richie, Brian, and Samantha clutched each other as the bed, nightstand, and vital-sign monitors skidded across the room. "It's the wrath of Satan!" Richie shrieked, scaring the life out of the twins.

Back at the ground-shaking interview, Dandy Man screamed into the camera, "We're in an earthquake!!" People scattered around him, running out of their shoes, scampering away from falling debris. 'Funny Mummy' posted signs flew like torpedoes past the camera. Dandy Man ducked out of view.

Grunge and Jenny escaped into the alcove of the Comic House. "Oh, the power you have, Lucy." He drew her near, pushing his thighs against hers. His heart thrummed loudly, her heart registered dead calm. Pushing him away, she snarled, "A smooth cad aren't you...an uncouth delusional womanizing fool."

"You are adorable, delectable and womanly...even when you're testy."

Rolling her eyes, "Save your humdrum renegade repartee for when it really counts." She was exhausted she collapsed onto a couch. Knowing not to push her, Grunge slipped out the door and into his office to handle pressing business for his newfound star.

PART FOUR

CLIMAX – TWISTED FATE

An 'eye for an eye' is one option for betrayal, abuses and lies. Or 'turn your cheek', 'there goes I', 'stepping-out in another's shoes'. Incensed beyond reproach, the Forrest twins chose unadulterated retribution for their mother's unforgivable sham. Adding to the fire, Samantha overheard a security babe claiming

Hallbally was Funny Mummy. The revelation of their mother's triplicity - ignited the twin's revenge torch. Brian was the designated driver on the stalwart mission. They bantered, ruminating about Jenny's shortcomings. Samantha chided, "How dare Mom hide, lie, and humiliate herself!"

Brian admonished, "How dare Mom put Dad in harm's way?"

Samantha scathed, "Or decimate the family by sneaking and peeping."

Brian exuded disappointment, "Or spout ugly profanities against the human race!"

They reached their destination: Samantha's dorm. Brian leaped three to four steps at a time. Samantha held onto the railing as she ran up the steps at a high-speed pace. Once inside the building, the siblings dashed up another flight of stairs to the fourth floor and down the hall to Jenny's room. Measuring a minimal window of opportunity they had to work fast. Brian slid a credit card in the doorjamb to gain entry. "It's payback time."

Samantha declared, "She's no relation to me, the lying smothering old lady."

Honoring the intent to do havoc, Samantha scribbled graffiti on the wall. "XXX Super-Mom. Go

Home!" Brian emptied Jenny's closet, chest of drawers, and medicine cabinet. He tossed everything out the window. T-shirts, security uniforms, army boots, shampoo, and cosmetics, sailed down onto the street.

"Take that, you faking phony!" Brian yelled.

On the street below Tanya walked toward the building. A slinky dress dropped from the sky, covering her head. She pulled it off. "What the hell was that?" she wondered, startled by the blow. She looked up to see where it came from. Peering out from a fourth-story window was Brian.

He called out. "Tanya! Wait! I miss you!" Rapidly tying a sheet on the window latch, he slid down like Prince Galahad to meet her.

On the street passers-by snatched scattered clothes, loading cars with whatever they found. A barefoot homeless woman tried on a left-foot combat boot, and then march-limped in search of the mate. A funky punk kid had found the right-foot boot, put it on, and march-limped beside the old woman. In formation, one boot kicked forward, then the other. Another woman grabbed a security jacket, buttoned it, and saluted Tanya. "It's Christmas. I'll be a 'Witch's tit'."

Brian caught up to Tanya and swooped her off her feet. Holding her in his arms, he twirled around in a dizzying circle, grinning. "Can you forgive me?"

Coquettish, she teased, "Remind me for what?"

He gently set her back on her feet. Relieved she didn't demand a lengthy apology or explanation, Brian happily proclaimed. "Not! Let's just forget the past. Start now, have some fun."

She brushed strands of raven hair from her eyes, "You just want to get it on." Going for the jugular, she sighed, "Tanya wants more, maybe a happy future, huh?"

Lovingly cupping her chin in his hand, he went for the truth, "I've got big plans in the next five minutes. How about joining me?"

Overpowered by his charm, unable to resist him, without hesitation she smiled, "I'd love to."

"You're on!" Off they went on Brian's private mission. He tried to explain. "Let's just call it the demise of 'Funny Mummy'." They scoured the campus parking lot in search of Jenny's Caddy.

He spotted it. "Come on, it's over here." He jimmied the lock, put the gear in neutral, and rolled down the driver's window to steer. With his arm on the wheel, he pushed from the side. "Go in back and give it all you've got." Tanya pushed from behind, as Brain guided it into a tow zone. "So freaky. Hallbally is your mom's...what did you say?"

"Alter-ego. No, make that more like an inbred-clone. And, my Dad's reformed. A covert-convert! A 'at one' with everything, boner."

"The boner part...sounds way right," Samantha mused. And, whatever slam your mom gets wouldn't be enough – for betraying everyone.

Jenny searched the parking lot for the Caddy. Furious, she kicked a lamppost with her foot. "Ouch!" Limping, she paced through the parking lanes. There was no pink Cadillac in sight. Flipping-out, she rattled, "It can't be. No. No. No! My future is in that trunk!"

She jogged across the campus, through the greenery, climbing a fence for a shortcut to the tow area. Aggie was on duty in a kiosk. Breathless, Jenny implored, "You towed my car...I hope."

"Not me. Why on earth would I tow your car?"

"Maybe someone else did?" Aggie checked the records.

"Yep, parked in a tow zone. Try stall thirteen."

"That's good luck."

Jenny dashed to stall 13. Shiny pink glistened: there was her beloved Caddy. Anticipating the worst she pleaded, "Please be in there." Swiftly opening the trunk she tossed everything out, flailing items onto the ground. Staring in disbelief. "It's empty. My satchel...with fifty-thousand dollars...gone." Sinking to the ground, she put her head between her legs. "I've been cursed."

Working up to hysterics she crawled into the trunk, "Got to make sure." BAM. The trunk door slammed shut. Trapped inside the darkness Jenny panicked. "I'm going to die...all because of greed, stupidity, and moronic behavior." Just as she worked-up a death sweat she heard someone tampering, turning the key. It was Aggie.

In a desperate frenzy Jenny cried. "My satchel! It's not in here! What did you do with it?"

"Nobody had the keys to your trunk."

"You criminal-thieving frauds don't need keys."

"Watch that mouth, Hallbally. Or whoever you are. You left them hanging in the trunk-lock, bozo."

Jenny was beside herself. "I'm a faceless nobody. A washed-up disgrace without means."

Aggie just shook her head, "Helpless. Hopeless. Haggard, is more like it."

"Ah, shucks. Screw that 'que sera sera' attitude," Jenny jabbed, caustic and rude.

Aggie had heard enough insults. She closed the trunk with Jenny in it. "Ah shucks, the trunk shut."

Jenny pounded, "S'cuse me, open the damn trunk!" Aggie went back to the kiosk. Her tactic was to wait until Jenny calmed down – a security balance procedure when someone showed signs of having a meltdown.

When Agnes let Jenny out, she was zombie-like. "Where's my key?" she softly mumbled. Sensing it might not be safe for Jenny to drive, Aggie weighed the options and covered with, "They're in the main office, I'll get them later." Jenny ignored her and climbed in the caddy and just sat there. Finally she got out and headed back to the dorm without uttering a word. "I'm here if you need me," Aggie called to her. Jenny kept on walking without looking back.

Descending the tiers of an identity crisis, Jenny plunged into an inferno. She paced back and forth, trotting over smashed items in her trashed room. Stripped of her valuables, launched in a sea of guilt, she uttered, "I'm a shameless freak vampire. I preyed on the hopes, schemes and dreams of the trusting and the innocent, even my own children's."

Next to Samantha's graffiti putdown Jenny scribbled, "Demise of X Super-Mom".

Simultaneously, letters were being sprayed in bold red on the Comic House wall: "DUMMY MUMMY – GO HOME."

Samantha, Brian, and Tanya, the spray-paint culprits, high-fived each other. Performing a series of hostile, seething payback attacks, they ripped down 'Funny Mummy' posters, tossed them in the trash, and flung lit matches in the bins, setting the posters on fire.

Helga spotted them, giving chase. "You're fried buns. Toast." She saw Brian swiftly push Tanya's butt over a fence, climbed up after her, and disappeared on the other side. Samantha headed for the fence,

Helga fiercely pursued her. Samantha couldn't get over fast enough. Trapped, she backed into a tree, and with all her might shimmied up to a low shaking branch. Helga pulled at her legs. "Arson-girl? Caught you in the act."

On a break from his watch, Gritty sat on tree branch above, munching on a sandwich. Struggling to hold on, Samantha grabbed his pant leg. Helga pulled harder. "Got ya'." Samantha fell, clutching fast to Gritty's pant leg. He toppled off the tree with her, landing on the ground with a thump on top of Samantha, face-to-face, actually lip-to-lip – an instant lusty attraction.

Samantha whispered, "Don't I know you from somewhere, maybe like...in a dream?"

"I wish," he said. An uncontrollable mutual desire, craving and yearning mounted. Lips touched: brushing, lingering. They kissed.

Helga screeched, "Finster, is that you?"

Grinning, he quipped, "Gritty here, tree-trimmer."

Grinning back, "Right! So, the folks let gorilla boy out of the cellar."

Caught, confused, and embarrassed, Samantha seized the opportunity to run away. She dashed off. Gritty trailed like a bloodhound. Catching up with maximum precision, he tackled her, tumbling and rolling in the wet, soft grass. Pinning her down, they dizzily and dreamily gazed into each other's eyes. In an instant Helga handcuffed Samantha - squirming and thrashing she wailed, "That sucks!"

Gritty accused her. "You kiss and run?" He winked at Helga, who nodded in recognition.

Helga chastised Samantha. "I don't think you're right...hurting Hallbally."

"You mean the great impostor," Samantha hissed.

Helga admitted, "I'm not the judge. You can work that out with Judge Hickey."

One phone call and they escorted her directly into the judge's private chambers. Samantha stood zoned-out at first, and then escalated to a rebellious brat in front of Judge Hickey. Helga and Gritty were flanked beside her. "You have one second to pull it together. No one contaminates my chambers with toxic attitude."

Samantha tried to hold it down, "My Mom's a phony mummy. A fraud."

"You Forrest women are a rowdy bunch." Judge Hickey read a document. "Predisposed multi-dimensional's. Gene-pool, DNA delusional."

Samantha defended her position. "Told you! She's not worthy of my wrath or revenge." Suddenly, Samantha's mind began to whirl. Looking at Helga, then back to Judge Hickey, she asked. "How do you know who my mother is? That's she's a 'Forrest' and not a 'Hallbally'?"

Judge Hickey glared at Samantha. "I ask the questions here, not you! Now, let's get back to your predisposition for violence...such as the current issue for why you are here."

Samantha protected herself. "Revolting was a clean body scrub. Like an exfoliation of my wounded spirit."

"So you'd prefer to break the law, young lady? I suggest you choose to break your inbred genetic chains. Stop the madness. End this absurd pattern of self-destruction. Are you following me, Ms. Forrest?"

"Are you talking about being sane or rebelling against it?"

"Do not insult this court, young lady."

Samantha cowered, "Nobody understands me."

"To support the choice of being sane you are hereby sentenced to Grunge Group Rehab behavioral therapy and community service."

Cringing, Samantha reported, "I don't do groups. People don't like me."

"Just like yourself. Get with the program, or you'll get a one-way ticket to a lock-down cell. Got that?"

The Judge's tough love was disarming. Samantha's bottom lip curled. Her body stiffened. Trying not to break, tiny tears trickled down her chin. Gritty pulled on his tie, gently wiping a tear from her cheek. "Don't worry. It'll be okay." Then he escorted her out of the chambers. A heckler outside screeched, "Cry-baby."

Judge Hickey addressed Helga with disdain. "Brouhaha on your watch again?" Leaning close to Helga, she said, "Keep Gritty's penis-puppet away from baby-girl Forrest."

On the court steps Samantha and Gritty locked in a quick embrace, lingering in a moment of ecstasy. Helga reached from behind, lifting him up by a nappy collar. "Get a grip, lover boy. Lucky for you I can't find my baseball bat." Tugging Samantha in tow, Helga barked, "Come on Forrest, your sentence starts now!"

Nighttime often brings out the madness even in those who appear subdued by day. Jenny had been alone in her room fretting, fussing, and vexing for too long. Her coping level decomposed to 'mad as a hatter'. Popping out like animated characters, Jenny morphed into Hallbally and 'Funny Mummy'. Caught-up in multiple personalities, the personas vied for dominance, colliding like dodge-cars, grumbling prickly putdowns and debates.

Jenny demanded, "What are you doing in my room?"

'Funny Mummy' answered, "I wouldn't trust a tightwad like you to iron my pillow cases."

Hallbally reamed 'Funny Mummy'. "Oh yeah! Why don't you put on your clown-suit and fly out of here."

Jenny's head swirled in confusion. "Will you please shut up! I can't concentrate. I have an important paper to write." Hallbally declared. "You know the penalty for plagiarizing mama's around here, don't you?"

"'Funny Mummy' cackled, "Turn you into a sass-hole 'Funny Mummy'."

Jenny bemoaned, "You're a hierarchy of replicant sadists."

Hallbally heard a key turn in the door. "Shush! Someone's coming."

Aggie entered. "Hope you've calmed down. Now your daughter is in a tizzy."

Jenny affected her Mrs. Forrest persona, "Who the heck are you?"

"Drop the act, Hallbally."

"How dare you swear at me! You will be de-striped for rude insults."

Scanning the trashed room and the scathing graffiti, Aggie knew something serious was afoot. "Look, I'm with Campus Security. Doing my job. What did you say your name was?"

"I didn't. But, for your edification, I am the <u>real</u> Mrs. Forrest."

Jenny sat up with a dignified air. Aggie's calamity training kicked in; she implemented crisis management 101 – lie through her teeth. "Mrs. 'Real' Forrest...uhh, there's an emergency...a bomb scare. I need you to come with me. Pronto." She bellowed, "<u>Evacuate</u>!"

Jenny froze, dumbfounded. Aggie took advantage of the moment and lobbed her over her shoulder. Jenny shuddered, "I should have known this rattrap wasn't safe."

Aggie ignored the schizoid-behavior of her load and headed to the parking lot, secretly enjoying the potential chaos that she knew would happen when they reached the Grunge Group Rehab studio. What else could she do? It was time for Hallbally, or Mrs. Forrest, or even 'Funny Mummy', to face the music.

Convinced Grunge was a perverted, quasi-nemesis, Samantha remained tight-lipped and grim in the Grunge Group Rehab studio. With folded arms, reluctant and non-compliant, she spoke in a haughty tone, "Being in captivity feels like an assault on my dignity."

In her mind the only point of personal control was refusing to participate.

Making a concerted effort to win her over Grunge encouraged. "Trust yourself. It's your teen scene. Take it from the top."

"How about 'take your top off, little girl'. Aren't you a pervie? Oh no, I forgot, you're a 'one on one' kind of guy...am I right, Grunge sucker? Yeah, I remember you from the parking lot...peeking into my car."

The group squealed, "Nihilistic!"

Rank Rhonda blurted, "Doomer-Gloomer."

Willy the Worm nonchalantly stated, "Not good. Not bad."

Amazingly assertive, Samantha resisted the group pressure. "I'm no guinea pig and neither is my mother."

Howdy challenged, "Does Ms. Piggy say she hears 'Squeaky Oink-Oink' voices in her head or thinks other little piggy's are chasing after her?"

"Very funny." Insulted, Samantha turned her back on him.

Grunge intervened, "This is no joke, is it Samantha? How about a humongous 'teen-scream'? Let out your anger, the hurts that block you from you."

"I'd rather rot in solitary."

To amplify the already chaotic vibe, Aggie entered the room with Jenny muddled in the midst of an identity crisis.

Aggie jumbled what had happened to Jenny. "She's trapped, hiding from a messy, gloomy reality. It's whacking her silly."

Howdy defended Jenny, "You're a troublemaker, Aggie."

Jenny slap-happily babbled Hallbally and 'Funny Mummy' personas. Rapidly cursing and conversing.

Jenny cried out. "Sleep! I need sleep!"

Hallbally shouted. "I have to keep the peace! Where's my piece?"

'Funny Mummy' jived, "Horny Hallbally wants a piece, carries a piece. Sleep on that one, Jenny Jen-Jen." Then 'Mummy' ripped a contagion of outrageous laughter. "Hah. Ha. Ha!" The group laughed like hyenas magnifying a cartoon-wackiness.

Samantha covered her ears, screaming, "MOTHER, STOP CACKLING!" Samantha's voice reverberated. The furniture in the room shook. A crystal vase shattered.

Grunge and the group screamed approval, "What a smokin' teen-scream." "Bravo!" "Rad!"

Jenny beamed at Samantha. "You called me 'Mother'? Quit bad-rapping, blaming, trying to please. Do it for yourself. Grow up, whiney-piney."

'Funny Mummy' applauded. "Mummy-Yummy's roastin' yo' teen-queen."

Hallbally asked, "Who's a Mutha?"

Samantha broke down. "It's too late. She cracked, split."

Grunge interjected, "Multi-dimensional episode."

Samantha felt scared, vulnerable and on the edge, "Am I too? What say you?"

Grunge answered. "Gene-pool misfits. This episode is just a misfire, a synapse glitch. No fear! Got that one covered! Just acknowledge her spirit – the soul will reveal her real self." He reached for Jenny and began rocking her in his arms, soothing her. "You're a sweetheart, aren't you?"

Jenny sighed. "I am loved. I am the <u>real</u> Mrs. Forrest."

Grunge waved a pendulum, penetrating deep into her eyes. His voice deepened into a hypnotic drone. "Yes to all of the above. To all of the below."

Grunge spouted what seemed to be dialogue from a 17th century melodrama. "Prince Grunge salivates the mystical, a necromancer's dream. Integrate the ladies three. Grant their wishes, invoked by me."

The pendulum shined a bright blue. "It's time for Jenny-Jen to come through. What is your life's fancy?"

"Life? Do I have a life?" Jenny meekly asked.

"Your intention is your salvation. Name it. What's your 'Lotto-win', Jen? The biggie!"

"To have my family back."

Samantha kneeled by her side. "Even dad?"

'Funny Mummy' replied, "He is she, honey-dummy."

Incredulous, Samantha glared in disbelief. "You knew. He knew. He was you?"

Grunge prodded deeper, " 'Mummy', 'tis you speaking, me thinks. Pray tell your bidding?"

"I want to kill 'em with the giggles. Laugh 'til I die."

Hallbally revealed another agenda. "Suspecting. Suspects. 'Who done it'?"

Grunge asked, "Hallbally! What's your poison, babe?"

"Fifty-grand singing in a Caddy's trunk."

Grunge waved the wand, throwing a pinkish hue. His voice deepened, otherworldly. "Fulfill their wishes three. Demented merge, into oneness – be."

Captured under his spell Jenny gyrated, arms flapped, toes wiggled, and then she was motionless. He leaned over to kiss her.

Samantha tugged his arm. "Don't even. No one takes advantage of my mother."

"It's the vital kiss. The NLP programmed cue. The hypno-breaker."

"I'll give you a friggin' hypno-breaker." She reached for Aggie's handcuffs. Aggie, quick on her feet, readied to subdue Samantha. In a surprising turn, she flipped Grunge onto a chair and cuffed him instead.

Aggie accused, "Stop the insanity! You mutant-felon!"

Samantha ranted into her cell phone. "Where's dad? It's an emergency.

A menagerie of stray dogs, cats, and a raccoon took over Brian's apartment as they caroused every room and corner. Samantha paced past Billy Goat who was happily crunching grains. The parrot named "Parrot," shrieked in a cage. "Screw the babysitter. Suck my beak."

Brian picked hairballs off his shirt. "Raccoon fuzz. Dad trashed my clothes, washed, rinsed, and fluff-dried my Cub Scout raccoon hat."

Samantha, insistent, was demanding, "For the fifth time, cut the nonsense. Where is dad?"

"Saving furry critters for the Forrest Family Petting Zoo." Brian bragged, feeling proud of Richie.

"Dad, into humane causes? Give me a break. You've got to be smoking something. Where is he?"

"Don't you see, it's our duty, our destiny, to save the helpless, nearly extinc,t creatures? Noah was the man, a rad pioneer. The ark was the ticket, "he grinned enjoying his analogy.

Twisting her hair, she mumbled, "Dementia. Definite signs."

Parrot squawked, "Shake a tail-feather. Burble-Gerbil."

Losing patience, Samantha screeched in Brian's ear. "OKAY! Brian, for mankind or whatever's sake, where the hell is our father?"

Brian shrugged. "I don't know. Haven't seen him all day."

A hedonist who once lived by the aggressive man's golden rule, "Do unto others as they'd do unto to you – only do it first," Richie was mending his screwed-up ways, transforming his motto to "Care, share, be aware of other's needs." He used to detest those very words, labeling people who said them as 'Bleeding heart liberals' who are the source of society's ills."

Richie now romped in his controlled little world, laden with concocted humane rules and obscure selfless tasks. Honoring a choice priority, he chased Mutt, a newly named stray dog across a park lawn. "Come here, Mutt boy," Richie wiggled a bone. Mutt edged over, tongue hanging, panting. "Come on, good boy." Richie lured him near a metal cage. Mutt played along, grabbing the bone, running in circles. Richie spun after him. Mutt ran faster, getting away.

Richie called-out, "Cheater! Bring back the bone!" Breathless, Richie fell onto the grass. "I called him a cheater," he realized.

Pausing, he scratched his head. "That's interesting. We say to others what we need to hear ourselves. What's the message, the deeper meaning? The 'cheater' – was me." Still mumbling, he touched a tree trunk. "Bring back the bone. Back where?" He caressed the tree, humped up against it. "I feel the vitality, the power." He pressed his ear to the bark, listening. "You say it's obvious, douche-ably transparent? Ah ha! Got it." Smiling in delight, "Bring the boner home."

Lying on the deep-piled lawn Richie gazed at the clovers in the grass. With a savant perception, he saw the clovers lined-up in a swirl. Instantly, he counted them. "Six hundred-and-fifty clovers." Zeroing in on the lone four-leaf clover, a sense of discovery and synergy enveloped his spirit. "Aha! A lucky four-leaf clover." Richie tilted his head and leaned into it. "Tell me, what am I to do about Jenny?"

The clover seemed to answer in a sexy-raspy voice (at least in Richie's needy ear), "Courage, big boy. Don't walk to her. Run, in your mama's shoes."

Grateful, he kissed the clover. "I won't pick you and destroy your life. You entered my lucky heart." As he lifted his head, Mutt's rear end smutted him in the face. Its rear legs flew backward, digging a hole. Dirt whisked in Richie's face while Mutt buried the bone.

Standing up and dusting off his jeans, Richie's eyes glowed with joy and determination. "Mama…here Daddy comes." Richie dashed off like a marathon runner. Mutt followed.

The whine of a lawn mower could be heard in the distance. Coming closer, it unmercifully mowed the four-leaf clover down. An ironic completion; as if its sole purpose was to connect with Richie's soul.

As he ran, Richie imagined a new reality. Feeling connected to all sentient beings, animal, vegetable and mineral. Scattering joy and counting blessings took a front row seat. A well deserved respite, a sabbatical for his over-worked analytical mind, he kept on running for posterity, for joy, for life.

During Richie's afternoon outing, Samantha and Brian continued to engage in the push-and-pull lack of

communication with each other. Deliberately teasing, Brian strummed a guitar, exaggerating long-fretted twangs. "Neeee...Yo-Maa."

Samantha was nearing her wit's end, "Why don't you listen to me? This is a life-threatening crisis."

Improvising, he sang, "Dad's on afternoons, gets food, and strays! I serve on nights, instead of days."

Losing her patience she shook Brian's shoulder, "Cut it, Brian! Can't you hear me? Mom is a hostage of comic freako's."

Hitting an extended high-pitched riff, he was dismissive. "Sam, your nerves are electrified, on the verge of short-circuiting."

Shaking like a leaf, teeth chattering, she stuttered, "Dad has...to...to kiss her, to bring her back...to reality...to normal...no, she was never normal."

Tanya slinked out of the bedroom flaunting a black silk teddy and eating a bag of Goober's. "Hi guys, it's sugar rush time."

Brian blew her an air kiss. "Yeah, a kiss could work." He smiled at Samantha. "Tanya and I kissed and made up."

Samantha froze, glaring at Tanya she said,. "Don't tell me you made Kappa Kappa."

Rubbing it in Tanya bragged, "Actually I made Brian. Your surefire, devilish twin."

"Oh really? Then, what's his most distinct trait?"

Nibbling on his neck, Tanya gushed, "He's adorable, smart, funny."

Samantha taunted, "Nah-ha. You didn't do it. No Kappa Kappa."

"Oh, you mean his ass-tribute. The cherry-busting raspberry?"

Samantha cowered. "Save it. You beat me. I'm screwed. The last living virgin on campus."

Tanya brushed her fingers through Brian's hair. "Not screwed. No Kappa Kappa."

Attempting to diffuse the sparks and mediate, Brian stood between them. "Cut the cat-nipping, babe. Both of you try chilling. Get a life, Sam."

Incensed, Samantha went on the offense. "Me? What about your 'kiss and tell' life? Keeping a chick scoreboard, bragging 'Girls all love me.' Or your ballet lessons and wearing my tou-tou?"

Brian the master of comebacks replied in a condescending tone, "Sam, we were in pre-school. Catch up, will you?"

Samantha threw her arms in the air, "I'm done. Stick a fork in me." In a dramatic gesture, she poked herself in the chest. Sibling rivalry usually has no bounds. Nevertheless, this was the cut-off for Samantha, "Sexual humiliation, and my best friend dumping a bout of shame; my brother, a conspirator in my demise? I'm out of here." She flung her purse over her shoulder and headed to the door

Gritty had been lingering outside, eavesdropping. As Samantha opened the door, he fell forward, catching her in an embrace. Smitten like a schoolboy he flashed a document, informing her in a seductive way, "There's a problem at this place. It's called, 'Pet overload', a major infraction that requires the removal of the violator's possessions."

Taken aback she asked, "What are you talking about?"

Pushing past them and making entry like a zany circus troop was Moe, a beefy no-neck, and Curly, a four-foot dwarf. Both wore gloves, dark shades, and black zoot suits. Moe lifted two sound speakers and carried them out. "Check out those woofers, "he beamed at the value of the take.

Curly expertly examined a watch. "Dispossessed and stylish."

Brian grabbed it, snapped it on his wrist. "What's up, dude? Hands-off."

"Shove it, punk face." Curly threatened.

"'My father's a criminal lawyer, so lay off."

"Who cares yo' daddy's a scummy hellbender. Protest or mutiny?" he challenged. The culprits continued ransacking and pillaging like thieving pros.

"Get bent," Parrot shouted, as he pecked furiously at the latch-closure on his cage, managing to open it. Sneaking a glance at Curly, Parrot lifted into the air like a mini-jet and landed on Curly's head. Jabbing and biting Curly's ear, Parrot screeched, "You big turd! Take a leak."

Curly fumed. "Lip-wrestle someone your own size." He grabbed a chopstick from a moldy take-out carton and whacked at Parrot. "Take that, you twerping-twerp."

The bird hopped quickly, dodging the blows. Parrot hooked its claws, mounting the chopstick. Curly twirled and whirled the stick around and around. Hanging on, Parrot spun about in a blur.

Brian tapped Billy Goat on the rear, edging him toward Curly. "Go, Billy boy." Billy Goat nudged Curly, and then butted him. The chopstick with Parrot clinging for life flew out of his hand. Parrot sailed airborne, banging against a wall. Screeching "Bottoms up!" he bounced, and then rolled across the floor.

Oblivious to the ruckus Gritty and Samantha, with closed-eyes, gently touched each other's face. Gritty writhed in anticipation, "I'd know that face anywhere."

She gurgled, "Me too." They stepped outside, hugged each other with tight squeezes then finally swallowed each other in a kiss.

Inside, Billy Goat butted Curly full-force. Curly propelled through an open window, past the lovers and crash-landed onto a flatbed truck.

"Cat", a nomad feral taking refuge behind a cabinet, spotted Parrot knocked-out on the carpet. Cat raised its back, fur standing on end. "HISSS." He pounced. Parrot flew into the air screeching, "You dirty cat!" Feathers scattered. Parrot winged back into the cage. Barely escaping, he managed to close the door just as a cat claw tried to push through.

Richie arrived after the ordeal wound down. Brian and Samantha were both eagerly waiting for him. They blurted out at the same time. Samantha wailed about her Mother being captive. "Grunge has Mom under a hypnotic spell, he's controlling her. You have to save her, Dad. Brian wailed about the thieving crooks, "A dwarf took the woofers, you should send him away for life."

"Screw the woofers, you nincompoop," Richie yelled at Brain. Cornering Samantha, Richie was crazed, "Grunge who? Did what!! I'll kill him with my bare hands."

Samantha expounded, "No Dad, you just have to kiss Mom...to break the hypnotic spell."

"Where the hell is she?" Richie asked in a frenzy.

"The Comic House, next to Grunge's rehab den. Please hurry Dad, we could lose her to that"...searching for the right word, she mistakenly picked "pedophile."

'Pedophile, a real scum roach." Richie raced into the bedroom and put on his cowboy regalia. Within minutes trouncing toward the front door, he paused and tipped his Stetson, affecting a slow drawl, "Grunge ain't seen real balls until he's seen mine." Brain and Samantha were frozen in place watching their father, whipping out of the door like he was on his way to the OK Corral. Mutt followed in happy pursuit.

Richie parked his car and stepped out onto the pavement. His boot-spurs clanged macho-masculinity as he swaggered up the street. Mutt nipped at his heels as they approached the Comic House. Richie caught his reflection in a window. "Looking good, compadre." Wincing beady-eyed like 'Billy the Kid', he adjusted the well-worn Stetson hat, pulled the leather cords, tightening a turquoise Hopi bolo neckpiece. He stuffed a wad of chewing tobacco in his mouth. Two chomps and the wicked sour-burn snuff lodged in the back of his throat. Gagging, he spit out black gunk, sputtering, "Damn redneck nicotine." Wiping his lip, he went inside.

The Comic House office area was dark and empty. A foghorn 'hum' reverberated from another room. Richie and Mutt followed the sound. Sensing danger Richie edged his back against the wall, creeping along like a bandit in the night.

In the cavernous darkness, Aggie, Grunge, and Jenny exhausted from the hullabaloo that had been going on at the Grunge Group Rehab office and studio, had left the building and slipped into the Comic House next door to take a nap. In unison they resonated a symphony of snores, snorts and retching sounds. Jenny quietly remained a 'Sleeping Beauty' of sorts. Onstage a key light focused on Grunge. Aggie had dragged him away from his studio, still tied-up and gagged. Waking-up, he struggled, handcuffed to a chair. At the sight of Richie, he could only manage a series of gurgling sounds. "Osh...eee...glurpie...de."

Richie climbed onstage. Unsuspectingly he removed the gag. "What the hell? Where's Jenny?"

"Did the 'Rocking-Chair Bandits' send you?" Grunge asked in a completely disoriented state of mind.

"Do I look like a rock bandit in some punk group?" Richie smirked, at the absurdity.

"No psychic spies are claiming the Grunge turf. I am the King!"

"Oh, yeah? Well, for your information, the boner's back home," Richie snarled.

Mutt, rustling around Richie's legs, looked up at Grunge, raised his head and howled as though he were a coyote sending a warning of danger to the moon. Grunge, sensing his ego was in jeopardy, retorted, "Dream on, 'Mr. Indulgent'. Grunge rules."

Lowering his Stetson over his eye, Richie commanded, "Take the challenge, victim-slayer. A show-down of wit and brawn."

Grunge laughed at Richie. "And who might be a worthy opponent?" Mutt snarled, showing snagged teeth. Grunge deepened his voice. "No contest, lapdog." Mutt cowered, lowering his tail between his legs.

Grunge bemoaned. "I sacrificed my own persona rescuing marginal societal dregs. Cracking the veils of delusion. Piercing the mask of the isolated. Healing the hearts of the lonely."

Richie grinded at him, "Words are birds, Mr. psycho-babble. You are a cock-twisted manipulator. A destroyer of free thought. A mind-zapper of boggled-brained slaves!"

"You are a parasitic rodent of a husband. An embalmed dead-beat dad! A hard-hearted declining alcoholic toad."

"Oh really?" Richie snarled in sarcasm. "The booze gave me up: <u>Richie's</u> heart rules." A lightning bolt shot from Richie eyes, striking Grunge. Gyrating, Grunge flipped backward, his legs and arms flailed like a porpoise out of water. A phantasmal fear-factor ensued: A duel of minds, spirit, and hearts. Bluish lightening bolts shot back and forth between the rivals. Caught in a time warp of supernatural phenomenon, the scenery instantly changed. Walking a tight rope

Richie fell, rolling down a ravine. Mutt crept down the hill, licked his face, reviving him.

Proving their manhood the challenges and feats escalated. With visions of jungles, they traversed across surreal worlds. Grunge dove into a pool of water. An alligator surfaced. Richie mounted its back, "Yippeeeee!" he exclaimed, riding it like a water snake, pursuing Grunge. The alligator's mouth opened wide like Jonah's whale lapping at its prey. Jangled teeth clacked and snapped mere inches from Grunge's flapping feet. In a hair-raising swim for his life, Grunge made it to shore and then ran for his life. Mutt chased after him, nipping madly at his heels.

High up in the Comic House rafters Detective Gritty focused a video cam on the continuous perilous action. The surreal moments didn't photograph - they were in the eyes of the participants. The competitors wore metal helmets, slashing at each other with gleaming swords. Charging, they banged heads. CLUNK! Lying side-by-side, flat on their backs, knocked-out, the duel ended in a standoff.

Groggy and suspicious, Richie opened his right eye. Grunge opened his left eye, leering. Jenny seemingly floated in the middle of the room, three feet in the air, fast asleep. Simultaneously they called out, "Jenny?"

Racing toward her, Grunge tripped Richie. Grunge arrived first to rescue the damsel-in-waiting. He leaned over her. "Jenny, your wake-up kiss. Be mine." Grunge kissed her with the intent of Prince Charming. Nothing happened. She remained still.

Richie pushed him away, kneeling down. "I'm yours, my Jenny. Be mine." Richie kissed her. Nothing happened. He tried again. Nothing.

Aggie pushed Richie away. Aggie kissed Jenny.

Time altered to a slow-motioned pace. The room blurred into a scintillating white light. Jenny's apparition oozed out of the sleeping Jenny. The apparition leaned over her sleeping self. SMACK! Planting a sizzling hot-kiss on herself.

Aggie waited expectantly. Jenny stirred. Flabbergasted, Aggie cried, "It's me! I'm the one."

Grunge feebly remarked, "Whatever."

Richie screeched, "Over my dead body!"

Jenny opened her eyes. The anxious threesome – Aggie, Richie, and Grunge – hovered over her.

Jenny mumbled, "Love yourself. To yourself be true."

Richie declared, "I love...the three...all of you."

Breaking the moment, Hallbally's persona took over, threatening, "Back off, creep. I barely know you."

Richie played along. "Maybe we could go on a date...sometime."

Mischievously grinning, Hallbally broke rank, and hammer-locked Aggie. "Where's my loot, you thieving con?"

Squirming like a guppy, Aggie garbled. "One day at a time: 'No muss. No fuss. No cuss'."

Hallbally registered the familiar saying. Releasing Aggie, she hissed, "Those snaky Barton's set me up didn't they?"

Aggie backed away, "They're <u>nobody</u> to mess with."

Jenny's face tightened in a stern expression. Staring icily at Aggie, she stated, "Rather than pull every strand of your hair out, I'm regrouping and making a decision."

Fearing the worst, Aggie appealed to her sensibilities. "Don't be rash. These are desperate times."

Hallbally declared a quiet revenge, "...to take desperate measures."

Aggie soared beyond worried. "Be rash. Don't do anything weird or terminally screwed-up."

Hallbally gathered Aggie's combat gear - handcuffs and full combat wear. "Well, I'll be vendetta-bound."

Aggie shot Richie a desperate look and hissed, "Do something, you idiot."

Richie piped-in. "Going on a payback mission alone could be fanatically dangerous."

"I have a score to settle. And, I won't function as a human being until I do." She bolted out of the Comic House building. Richie trailed after her, spouting. "I'll back you up through thick-and-thin, which is an unprecedented sacrifice in this cold and lonely world."

Bowled over, she turned to him, "You'd be my backup?"

He nodded. "Until the bitter-end." Whispering under his breath, "Oyii vey, what the hell am I saying?" Mutt, who had never left his side, answered with a "Woof, woof."

Richie assumed a subservient stance. "A chauffeur at your disposal, Hallbally."

"At my command! You're disposable, Forrest. It's 'Sergeant Hallbally' to you."

In the perfect role reversal he stood at attention and saluted her, "Yes sir, ah, ma'am. Right this way." They headed for the yellow pickup truck. Hallbally admired it. "Retro, huh? Just my style."

Richie seized the welcomed communiqué he'd been praying for, "Yep. One-of-a-kind retro. Totally

refurbished with new chrome and rolled leather seats."

The yellow pickup barreled along the highway rolling over familiar territory. Richie and Hallbally, quite the odd couple, sat side-by-side. He queried under the guise of small talk. "A gal like you must have a lot of suitors?"

"Trying to get personal on duty? A no-no. Infraction! Invasion!" She slipped on Aggie's combat jacket.

Reversing his approach, "No. No. I'm copping to...I'm fundamentally unlovable, not typical soul-mate material, that's all."

She scoffed, " A reject! Guys like you butchered, hammered, and decimated my faith in romance."

Eyes glowing, a teasing delight filled his heart. "Then maybe a guy like me could restore that cold front?"

On guard, denying the tingles on the back of her neck, Jenny snapped," Button your lusty-crude lip."

Swallowing his libido, he read the sign, "Medville. That's our place." Jenny reached over and put the storm helmet on him. "You're on formal duty, Forrest."

In the distance, on a tactical watch, a man with binoculars spotted the retro truck coming up the road. "They're in view," he spoke into his Bluetooth informing his co-conspirator. Clearly waiting to ambush them, he dumped a bag of nails in the road. Shouting into the Bluetooth, "Clear the coast. Mayday. Get ready."

The pickup approached the ambush, bouncing over the nails. Bang. Bash. Thump. The tires blew and the car fishtailed across the pavement, avoiding an oncoming car. Jolting onto the soft shoulder and changing directions, Richie whipped the truck back on the road. "We're down to hubcaps."

Hallbally belted, "Keep on going." Metal wheel frames knocked and smoldered, sparks spewed, banging down the road.

On the edge of the Barton's driveway the pickup metal-ground to a halt. Inside the house Festus peered through the peephole. "Sounds like a Sherman tank." A fish-eyed view distorted Hallbally and Richie's images into stocky action-figures. "It's like the dag-gone militia."

Clad in a mish-mash of storm-trooper gear, armed with walkie-talkies, quietly sneaking toward the house, Jenny led the way.

Festus 'Yahooed' his excitement. "No foolin'. Lookie who's a visiting."

Elma peeked out, "None too early. Down the hatch." Festus and Elma hurried through the wooden trap under the hallway linoleum.

Jenny and Richie scooted on their bellies, creeping toward the house. She whispered, "Cover the back. And watch my rear."

Eyeing her tight-rear bumping by his face, he happily remarked, "My pleasure." His pants slipped down exposing his butt-crack. She eyed the tip of the red raspberry birthmark with a lusty smile, "Fair game." They split up. Hallbally squiggled down to one side of the house, Richie wiggled down to the other.

Excruciating loud animal sounds pierced the rural silence. As if greeting a long-lost friend, Sam, the crow whizzed, around Richie's head. Little chicks squabbled and pecked at his ears, a sheep nuzzled next to him. Big Bull reared his legs, chanting a guttural "MOO!" The racket was a dead give-away; their attempt to sneak-up in silence was potentially blown.

Hallbally stayed on mission. Focusing on picking the side door lock, she huffed gruffly into a walkie-talkie, "What the heck is all that noise? It'll bust our cover."

As a sheep licked his face Richie clumsily negotiated his walkie-talkie. Squirming and chuckling he answered, "No problem. Just the family."

"What! The Barton's know we're here?"

"Baa-Baa." "Caw-Caw," blasted her eardrum.

Thinking it was Richie she scowled, "Darn static! These talkie-walkies aren't worth a damn." Jangling the lock-pick, the door opened and she stepped inside. A rope swung across the room, hitched her by the waist, lifting her up in mid-air. "Holy Toledo!" she blustered.

Richie entered the back door, cautiously stepping inside. A full water barrel dumped on Richie like a Tsunami, drenching him. Stumbling about, eyes doused like a blind man, arms stretched straight out to feel his way in the hallway, he thumped and bumped into walls like Frankenstein. Within seconds he fell through the trap door and landed in the cellar, flat on his back. Festus and Elma, sitting on matching overstuffed leather recliners, rested in wait. Festus startled Richie. "What took you so long, cow-daddy?"

Meanwhile, Hallbally dangled, swinging like a chimp, twisting in the air, trying to untie the rope. "Forrest, you baboon! Where are you?" she said under breath.

Back in the cellar Richie glowered in amazement at a fully equipped high-tech broadcasting studio. In a corner a few telemarketers manned phones, answering, "ID-4-Identity, at your service."

Richie accessed the equipment. "State of the art. Festus, my savior, has a high-tech war room. Impressive! Satellite broadcasting, digitized editing bays, the works. This is amazing!"

Festus rallied, "No shit-a-la."

Hallbally finally freed herself, and slipped down the wooden hatch that led to the cellar. Her attention fixed on "Active ID" photos stick-pinned to a corkboard on the wall. Helga, Aggie, Grunge, Dean Chase, Judge Hickey, and even Hallbally, were among them.

Creeping into the high tech room she took the old couple by surprise. Taking a shooter stance, gun-drawn, she aimed at the Barton's. "Jig's up, you slacky-jawed yokels. You're busted! Going up the river."

In a firm voice, Festus replied, "If it isn't that heartbroken, jinxed, side-spitting wretch."

"Cut the small talk Caddy raiders. Where's my fifty-G's?"

Richie interjected, "<u>Our</u> fifty-G's."

Elma motioned to the elaborate studio equipped in surround-sound. "You're looking at it, folks. Fifty grand invested in a broadcast studio."

Richie was aghast. "That's stealing. Embezzlement! Bunko-fraud!"

Elma's lips curved into a sly smile. "Unless you jingle-jangle the law to the 'nth degree. We hold the Caddy's title. Untouchable and bulletproof!"

In a rapid-fire negotiation Festus threatened, "An ethical hijack. The said cash is circumcise-ally ours."

Richie cowered, protecting his crotch. Backing off, he knew the old codger meant business. Stammering, Richie said, "No problem...uh, 'you haven't seen nothing until you seen one hung low'."

Festus clapped his hands three times in Riches face, commanding, "Buck up." Richie's head bobbled as he stuttered, "Sending me to a lawyer's twelve-step program?" He decided to play the game. "Well, the deal sounds airtight. Any profits?"

Everyone's attention turned to a large TV monitor where a video began to play. The title was "The Birth of Funny Mummy." Highlighting uproarious footage of Jenny's transformation to 'Funny Mummy', there were shots of her onstage, and a series of the machinations that surrounded her journey.

Watching the footage, Hallbally's' 'rough and ready, down and dirty' persona dropped. Jenny's scrutinizing sophisticated persona emerged. "Me! It's really me!" she exclaimed.

Elma clapped her hands three times in front of Jenny's eyes. "Drop the act. You got the part, girlfriend."

Jenny piped, "Don't you think I'm sick of one-liners? No meaningful communication! No human connection! Except head-trips, sound-bites from Grunge-droned warlocks."

Gritty, Samantha, and Helga entered the house. One by one they slipped down the wooden hatch. Gritty was all smiles, "This is the moment I've been waiting for." Samantha echoed, "Me too." The threesome joined the group. They snickered at the footage. Samantha hugged Gritty, "Awesome! Aren't you the next Spike Lee!"

Richie convulsed at the sight of Gritty touching his sweet young daughter. "Samantha! What is going on?"

Festus stood proud. "Greet our daughter, Helga. And this here is our grandson, Finster. He's your new partner in crime."

Richie balked, "I don't do crime or time."

Making amends Gritty offered an outstretched hand for a handshake. Reluctant, Richie caught an evil twitch in Elma's eye. His arm shot out and he honored the gesture with a clenched grasp.

Gritty rubbed his hand. "You've got quite a grip. Well, we meet again, Mr. Forrest. Hope you enjoyed 'The Birth of Funny Mummy'. It's <u>our</u> Webcast hit."

"<u>Our</u>!" Richie had a fit. He stomped, trampled, clogged in place. "A lame con! A setup with my innocent, naïve, virgin daughter!"

Samantha lovingly stroked Gritty's hair, "No virgin setup, Dad." She gushed and blushed. "Twisted fate, we found each other, didn't we, Finster?"

Elma beamed with pride, "Keeping the high-kick stakes all in the family."

Festus added. "Lean and clean legal tools. No FBI minefields in our backyard."

Richie paced with intent, his lawyer's mind calculating. "So this is a well-crafted conspiracy. And you are...'The Rocking-Chair Bandits' Grunge was so afraid of?"

All eyes magnified and were glued on Elma. She remained stone-faced. Close to peeing in their pants, the group waited with great anticipation. Elma spewed, "The first rule of good managing is: Never tell anyone more than they need to know. Only confuses them."

Festus stepped-up to Richie and Jenny, " Ready for your 'Funny Money' bonus?" He motioned to Gritty, who presented a giant-sized check to Richie. Jenny and Richie gazed at it, jumping up-and-down like Lotto winners. "Two-hundred-and-twenty G's!?" Gritty snapped photos of the momentous occasion.

Jenny touched the check with reverence. "Made out to...'Richard B. Forrest and Jennifer Forrest.' "

Elma challenged Richie, "Community property, no doubt."

In a moment of poignant sharing the couple gazed deep into each other's eyes and souls, morphing into their wedding day. Jenny packed a huge baby bump protruding from a full length, Belgium lace, and four-foot satin-train wedding gown. Lovingly Richie rubbed her belly, gently placing an ear on it, listening. "Oops, they're thumping. I marry you, Jenny...and the baby bumpkins."

She beamed, "Me, too," slipping a platinum band on his finger. He tried to slip and twist a matching one on her triple-sized bloated finger. It wouldn't fit, finally squeezing it on her pinky. They kissed in heated passion, sliding to the floor, still locked in a fervent embrace.

Back in the reality of the present time, Richie and Jenny rolled on the floor enmeshed in each other's arms, tender kisses, lovingly squeezing, and devouring. Everyone stared in disbelief and relief. Coming up for air Richie asked tenderly, "So, what do you say, Miss Hallbally?"

"You mean...<u>Ms</u>. Jenny Forrest?"

`Richie affirmed, "The one and only, Ms. Jenny Forrest."

Filled with anticipation she tickled his fancy, "You may come a-courting."

Steeped in a marinade of desire Richie responded, "That seals the deal."

Festus whispered to Elma, "Told you he'd get her back."

She answered proud and sassy, "Our hocus-pocus never failed, yet."

Elated with the outcome, Gritty kissed Samantha. Elma laid a French kiss on Festus. Overcome with desire, he conked-out.

The fortuitous makeup, the soul-cleaning between Richie and Jenny, couldn't happen in a split second. Much discussion, boundaries, and rules were established; dreams revisited a new plan for the future. They pursued the heart-mending tête-à-tête by enjoying a romantic rendezvous in a candle-lit cabana overlooking the ocean.

Jenny pondered, "So, is 'love never having to say you're sorry'...or is it love makes you sorry that you loved?"

Wanting to gain her confidence, Richie assured her, "I'm on the wagon, clean as a whistle, Jenny, and you're garbling like I used to."

"I need an answer now. I need to know are you sorry...or just happily in love to see me?"

Jenny telegraphed mixed-up girly messages. Push-pull, commit forever, or we can make love, anyway. This was a 'now or never' moment for Richie. Could he, a male, penetrate the female psyche, obliterate the boundary of the sexes once-and-for-all and find true intimacy and reach her soul?

He held her hand and locked into her glowing emerald eyes. "I'm sorry if I hurt you, disappointed you. I'm sorry I was a dummy, a louse, made stupid choices...and that I let you down." Choking on words, hoping not to push too far, Richie added, "I'm not only happy to see you...I want you back in my life, forever."

Jenny absorbed his words with childlike innocence, wanting to believe. "You were my everything, my lover, my friend, and like my dad, I did it all to please you. Tried to be what you wanted, but you judged me. Burned food, my clothes were too tight, too short, too long. I was never what you wanted." She stopped herself from continuing, then closed her eyes for a moment and centered herself. Taking a deep breath, she opened her eyes and told Richie, "I don't want you to feel guilty, and I don't want to be laying blame on you."

Richie knew he was straddling the razor's edge with the woman he loved. His mind raced. "Don't defend. Don't attack. Don't go there. "Without attitude he reminded, "You judged me, harping, 'Richie, you don't listen, don't hear me or care what I think. "To Jenny's surprise he said the magic words, "You were right."

It was as though a plethora of cobwebs instantly cleared from her heart and mind. "I was right? You just said I was right?" A stunned expression radiated over Jenny's face.

Richie had settled the issue. Brilliantly, he had declared the revenge-buster: there could be no comebacks to that admission.

"We can't go back and pretend can we?" he said softly.

Her lip curled, confessing, "I've been pretending my whole life...except for one thing."

"Yeah, what's that?"

"A hard man is good to find." She giggled, twirled in a skimpy tank top, showing lots of skin, "How's this look?"

"Like you'd need a fake ID to go out clubbing," he laughed.

They giggled and hugged. Jenny smiled. "Clubbing and dancing on our second honeymoon? I've let my hair down, and if you shave to bald, we're GQ and Cosmo."

"Anything but bald!" Richie rubbed his bald spot.

"Anything?" Jenny put her hand on his and slid it around her.

One kiss led to another. Bursting with desire, gently moving his fingers down the curve in her back, his tongue gently caressed her neck. Breathless, she whispered, "Just make sure you keep those cowboy boots under my bed." She melded into his solid-rock arms...knowing this was the man she loved.

In the moonlight their silhouette's writhed visibly through the cabana' nylon-mesh. Surfer-bums that were slumbering on the beach witnessed the display, humming, "Whole lotta love..." A gentle breeze fluttered in the cabana window, tingling flesh-to-flesh, then blowing-out the candle. The lovers disappeared from the voyeur's view. Left alone to enjoy their well-deserved, private love-nest, Yin and Yang merged; their bodies surrendered to the electrical energy of lovemaking, combining into one vibrating pulse, a melodic rhythm. Spiritually elevated through sexual freedom, Richie and Jenny were lovingly entwined in warm bubbling ecstasy.

The auspicious day arrived. Kappa Kappa pledges lined-up in front of the sorority house. A sorority sister, Big Sue, crowned 'Queen Frump', presented Samantha a Kappa Kappa sweater. "Samantha Forrest – our hippest-hotty. I ordain you a bona fide Kappa Kappa 'Ho'."

"Thanks," Samantha beamed. "It's been a long time coming."

A few Kappa Kappa members snickered at the innuendo. Tanya and Brian watched from afar. Samantha waved.

Big Sue snidely asked, "What's with Tanya – still has her cherry?"

"Way gone. Doesn't do groups, hangs with my brother, not with wallflowers."

Insulted, Big Sue glared, "What does that mean?"

Standing tall, Samantha owned her ground and switched gears. "Summing it up...I'm proud of being who I am! Who've I've been! And who I will be."

Giving her a "thumb's-up", Big Sue beamed, "That's way cool, for a frosh."

Samantha slipped on the coveted Kappa Kappa sweater. "Being ordinary, nobody-ness, doesn't scare me anymore. Being grateful for just how it is right now, this moment is the ticket."

Big Sue was dazzled by Samantha's lightness of being. "Sounds like you're ready to handle whatever comes – good, bad, indifferent, or maybe something unexpectedly extraordinary." Grinning, she pushed her finger between Samantha's eyebrows.

Feeling a jolt through her body, Samantha was filled with energy, "Whoa, what was that?"

Big Sue informed, "Third-eye opener. Centers where we see it all, know it all. You're on an evolve roll!"

Rolling her eyes Samantha admitted, "Spooky, but I like it...and I want to know more."

Big Sue smiled knowingly, grasped Samantha's left hand and led her into the Kappa Kappa house. Lining the murky flocked walls were photos of women, some pictures were in black and white, others in sepia-tone, faded through time, and newer ones were in color. Big Sue bragged, "There are Kappa's in high-ranked positions splattered all over the globe."

Under most faces were names, graduation dates, and the college they went to. Universities, vocational and traditional schools from every continent were represented. The women were in every known profession from dignitaries to school chancellors. Pointing to a life-size portrait, Big Sue announced, "Look at our svelte Oprah, graduate of the 'school of life', a one-woman thunderbolt zapping and illuminating decency into our vapid culture."

"I love Oprah. Isn't she the bomb!" Samantha brushed her finger across a framed Mother Jones magazine cover. "I'm no history wiz, but this Mother Jones never went to college. How's she a Kappa Kappa?"

"Ever hear about the 'school of life'? She took on the militia, held her hand over a musket, and led a children's crusade against slave labor. Kids never saw the light of day. They went to work at dawn and came out at night. Someone asked Mother Jones where she lived and she told them, 'Wherever there's a fight. I'm no humanitarian. I'm a hell-raiser'." Big Sue bowed her head to the magazine photo. "Mother Jones, my dear Samantha is a revered sister."

"Jeez," Samantha bowed her head. "I wish I could be like her."

Big Sue penetrated Samantha's aura, sizing her up. "You could be. Kappa's plugged-in, major connected. You need, we provide. Forever, until you're buried and, some say, beyond the grave. You're in a secret society, a world opinion-shaper, media trendsetter, and money machine. For life, we are with you, and you are with us."

"I never knew about all this." Samantha lowered her eyes, "Look, I don't want to disappoint you. I'm not the smartest star in the sky, you know."

"You found us, you passed initiation, and you hung in there. That's better than book-smart. We support blue-collar, lunch-bucket Sally's to Condi's as Secretary of State. You know the corporate glass ceiling? We built it, sweetheart. Keeps those male-mongers inside where we can control them. The 'good-old-boy's' club for your info' is run by the 'good-old-girls' pulling their chains and ding-dong's."

"So that's why...lose the cherry bit?"

"Not totally. We need your special caring, your humbleness."

Rubbing her Kappa Kappa sweater, Samantha smirked, "Stop the shine-on. What do you really want?"

"To have a 'Teen Scream' sit-in. We heard you let out the biggest primal release ever seen in Stanford Territory. It can be your gig. "

Samantha registered stunned, "Come on, that was just a reaction to my Mom and that madman Grunge."

"It's a winner idea, very promote-able. We'll make one of ours – YOU – a brighter rising star."

"Don't joke me." Samantha blushed-pink, excited to be included. "Jeez, I can't believe you asked me... I mean all you had to do...was ask."

Big Sue patted Sam's back. "Seriously, how cool a rush is that?"

"So the plugged-in, big connection rap is a bunch of bull?"

"Dah! You still don't get it. We deliver. Take us to test."

Skeptical, Samantha rolled her eyes, naive and girlish, "You sure can dish it, wheeler and dealer."

"You don't know who you're dealing with." Pointing to herself, "Big Sue...is 'Queen Frump'."

Astounded that anyone would boast about the demeaning title, Samantha bumbled, "Guess you're proud...being the most frumpy...leader of the pack."

"You don't have a moldy clue. What an honor it is, or what 'frump' means. It's an acronym. Stands for

F = female. R = recruiter. U = under-wraps. M = managing. P = pledges."

"Oh, my...head's exploding!" Samantha dizzied with mind-blowing images. Female hard-hats constructing skyscrapers, women with briefcases marching down Wall Street, dominating New York stock exchange bids and global markets. Local tribes-women being trained to administer medical aid in an African village. Women controlling Congress and M&M's candy production lines. "Kappa's are the CEO's of international corporations, at the helm of MTV and battleships, saving dolphins," she visualized. Ideas swirled at a fast pace as if the Hoover Dam just overflowed.

Samantha jumped in the air shouting, "The 'light bulb' just went off... I mean on. My brain's clicked-in. I'm inspired, whacked-out of the box. I just envisioned my future, being part of leading women on the path to greatness."

Big Sue whispered in her ear, "That's Kappa Kappa's legend. You just tapped-in to Ing Ma...traces back to the Chinese dynasty, ancient Egypt, and it spread like wildfire. Women wrote and spoke Ing Ma, a secret language. Disguised as poems and letters they protected each other from male barbs, abusive husbands, passing down the wisdom of the ages."

"I got it!" 'Teen Scream' is the ticket! Pulling together, men and women, a union of spirit, venting their problems and finding solutions for the higher good." Samantha was ecstatic, riding on a vision-roll.

Big Sue nodded in agreement," What's to lose? How many folks do you need to show up?"

"Make it... a hundred..." still wanting to impress Big Sue, Samantha blurted, "or how about thousands. Teen Scream' deserves to serve."

Big Sue rattled on. "Do I have a news release for you!"

Within hours Kappa Kappa's echelon dominated the Internet, spitting out umpteen emails. People hung posters, phone-trees jammed circuits. Kappa Kappa volunteers networked in full-force, touting and spouting, "Come hang with us...at 'Teen Scream'. "

Jenny reveled in celebration. She was coming into her own, integrating her personality dimensions. Hard lessons learned were shared with her family. Her hilarity of wisdom spiraled into a "Funny Mummy Boot Camp." A sign read, "Hoot 'n Truth Life-Change", on the Security Boot Camp property.

Jenny walloped her improvisation antics at the women boot-campers. "Jenny is my core, heart and soul. Hallbally is the doer, gets the job done no matter what. 'Funny Mummy' is my wisdom, my funnies, my love of life."

A 'BoHo-Mom' with curls tied under a kerchief nursed infant twins. One on each breast, heads covered with burp-throws. "I'm not so complicated. I'm just ME," she said matter-of-factly.

Jenny laughed, "Which me? The feeling or thinking me? The happy me, the sad, confused me, the smart, the angry me? Or the REAL me...the great one, the ME beyond it all, with no earthly limits?"

Heads nodded. Voices rang out, "I want the <u>real</u> me" "I'm the <u>stuck</u> me." "<u>All of me,</u> please!"

Jenny roared a guffaw. "Laugh. Breathe! Giggle. Breathe." The group swooned, laughing and breathing.

Jenny smiled, "I'm getting stronger in my personal convictions. I don't give a twat about whoever says whatever about me, good or bad. I'm getting past praise or blame. So now there's a chance to see me, feel me, know the real me."

A tight-wired suburbanite slouched in her seat. "How the heck do you do that?"

"By the end of 'Funny Mummy' bloopers, you'll be telling me how to find peace of mind. You'll be laughing your fanny off every day in spite of it all." Jenny inhaled, holding her breath for a moment. "So we're going to let it all go and flow." Only able to share experiences up until now, she faced the camper's eyes. "She smiled, holding on to her truth. "It's a NOW happening. It's only yours when you can give it away."

From Jenny's "Funny Mummy Boot camp" the Forrest family had turned their lives around. They were kinder, more loving, humane and compassionate with each other. Together, supporting each other they blazed a positive force in the community. Richie learned what counted most: Love, family, being of service. His client base included foundations that were fighting for equal rights for the disenfranchised, low-income and middle-class people. Lobbying on the Senate floor he cried, "There is no crime greater than passing a beggar on the street and pretending he's not there. Or dropping a coin in a tin. We need to find out how he got there, and help him get back on his feet." The room rang with applause. Jenny summoned a standing ovation, "Yahoo, Richie!"

Reuniting with Richie held the wild card of betrayal, forgiveness...and never forgetting where you came from. That kept Richie jumping through flaming hoops. "Something every good husband should do, anyway," Jenny often said and thought. Her new philosophy became, "No more waiting. Be waited upon."

Luckily, Richie had become a seasoned gourmet chef and often served Jenny with pride. "Darling, do you want escargot with the clam sauce or would you prefer a hot-fudge sundae?"

After many heart-to-heart talks, they solidified a 'Mr. & Mrs.' agreement, "For better or the worse, re-heating the marriage flame." A fresh agenda emerged on how the Forrest household was to be run. "Smart wives don't bitch, they itch for intimacy. Give it – to get It. Smart men don't say 'why'? They ask 'when and where'?"

Dealing with their newfound Internet Webcast fame took a front row seat. They moved their digs out of the Burbs. The fortune they continued to receive from the 'Funny Mummy' franchise purchased acres of high-desert land. It made sense to them to convert the property into a retreat site for "Funny Mummy & Boner Adventures", a retreat for both men and women to self-actualize, have fun, and find their life purpose. Their new home was located two miles due west from the Barton Farm, as the crow flies.

Twisted-Fates intertwined. The unfolding of the Forrest family's destiny had not yet played out.

One evening, the family gathered for dinner. Richie and Jenny held hands. Brain and Tanya dazzled as a couple with their adopted Parrot in tow. Samantha and Gritty played chess. Everyone's focus was on the upcoming 'Funny Mummy' Webcast: how, when, what, and where.

Each took turns playing leader. They laughed, played, and brainstormed. There was no competing or cheating. No one-upmanship's or putdowns. Such camaraderie was a first for the

Forrest clan, until Parrot busted their chops. "Ah, shucks. You phooey-phony's, get bent."

Grunge, producer of the Webcast production, arrived for dessert. Nibbling on Jenny's prize Apple Betty, he pumped the cast and crew. "It takes a dream team to get a job well done." That was the launching point for Grunge and Richie to make amends. Through macho-minded jabs, they bantered back and forth. "Power respects power," Grunge had conceded. "And, the best man gets the girl," Richie had retorted.

On a TV sound stage, at the Forrest Retreat site, Grunge masterfully helmed the video crew. Gritty rolled the video cam, taping the "Funny Mummy" Webcast.

Featured as a rising star Samantha rallied a 'Teen Scream' group. She commanded, "Jump, leap, fly, fall down, get up, dust off. Do it again." On pogo sticks the participants, Big Sue, Grace, Tanya, Brian, and Jax, among others, hopped like rabbits, some falling, others leaping for joy. "Yippee!" Brian knocked Jax off balance, "Rip. Fly. Conquer", Brian roared. Tanya hung in, getting Big Sue, "Aye! Gotsya'!" she barked in a devilish Irish accent.

Samantha, motivated with bravado, shouted, "Take the plunge to wholeness. We need our spaced-out freedom to screw it all up. Now let's hear the fear, let out the pain, claim your name. Blast it! This is our 'Teen Scream'!"

Primal-yelps reverberated, pent-up angst, memories from eons past. Mouth's opened wide with reddened tonsils bursting, vocal cords waggling, spilling inner wrath. Some fainted, others pounded, seats rattled. The audience shook like jackhammers digging up the nasties, releasing ingrained traumas, finally pulsing with laughter and joy. Mesmerized teen faces glowed in recognition and admiration of their triumph.

Sitting on top of a crane, Grunge directed the continuing action. Gritty juggled a bouncing video cam, panning smoothly to another set. On stage Jenny and Richie co-hosted another segment of the 'Funny Mummy' Webcast special. Overhead lights flashed a strobe effect. The couple's image eerily faded in and out. Jenny joyously pontificated. " 'Funny Mummy' zaps you right out of the nest. Hang in with us for your journey into you, at your best." Richie pitched his heart out. "Jumpstart your 'Id-4 Identity'. Get a new lease on living! It's guaranteed to bring the boner home!"

The scene flashed to a small oasis in desert wasteland, the converted "Funny Mummy & Boner Adventures" retreat site. Gritty zoomed in, focusing on the rock, which was inscribed, "Frog hair cut in four directions. Sit in East, follow sun."

In all his glory, Richie guided a 'Vision Quest', a replica of his own experience. Sitting in a circle surrounded by stones were several men, closed-eyed and cross-legged. A shocking surprise to the Webcast viewers, Shaq, Tommy Lee, Bill Maher and non-celebrities were among the group. All faced east following the sun. Flies buzzed like fighter jets around their noses. "Join the brotherhood of the bees. Hear the buzz, what is it saying, be one with it." Richie instructed.

Bill Maher whimpered like a coward, "No sting, please. Don't bite me." In total panic, he ran away like a madman as bees encircled him, chasing and stinging.

Tommy Lee swayed, singing a haunting lyric, "Mend the split in your soul. Ravaged, torn apart. Commune in the innocence of a child. Hear bees and trees 'buzz zing' oneness in your heart, no longer torn apart."

In a close shot, Richie and Jenny yodeled a duet with Tommy Lee as the sound overlapped to the next scene.

The video crew caught the action that was going on at a Stanford campus street corner. It was "Community Service Day." Cats, dogs, and even Billy Goat, yelped, jamming in a rhythmic harmony. Tanya and a few football jocks held up signs. "Animals are People are Animals".

A staunch 'street' Samaritan, Brian strummed his guitar, singing with Parrot on his shoulder, "Turn evil darkness, waste, and greed into sustainable humanity. Adopt a pet. Adopt yourself, for all eternity."

Parrot joined in with a cackling, "Tweak my beak. Hee-Hah." The sound overlapped into the 'Funny Mummy' theme song.

Continuing the show, a crane operator zoomed in on a choreographed chorus line 'high-kicking'. The dancers were incognito, bright-eyes shining through 'Funny Mummy' headdresses. One by one removing the masks, they revealed the 'Funny Mummy' all-star cast: Jenny, Richie, Samantha, Gritty/Finster, Brian, Tanya, Helga and Aggie. Bambe with M. Barrett, Festus and Elma, Judge Hickey and Grunge, high-kicked, triple-spinned, rocking out, ending the show.

Reuter's wire coverage raved, " 'Funny Mummy'—A hilarious life-transforming, trend-setting phenomenon!" TV blurbs gave two-thumbs-up. A contagion socked it to the nation, 'Funny Mummy' clubs, workshops, and online courses were affecting pop culture, cutting reality's edge with wacky, zany togetherness.

♥♥♥

Jenny typed joyously at her computer, writing an overdue FUNNY MUMMY BLOG:

Friends, you probably wonder what happened to me, or maybe not. **I am no longer the lily-white control-monger princess. I have tasted the seedier, shadowy side of myself. Well, with that said, I'd like to share with you my thirty-day life-change recipe. I morphed from negative thinking, a crummy life filled with self-deceit, lies, and chaos, into a positive, hopeful, self-actuating fun-filled existence.**

If you want the full low-down how you can do it for yourself I've prepared a giveback, an offering − **the 'Funny Mummy Workbook'. It's full of recipes for creating authentic joyous life adventures. Find the way out of nightmarish heart-quakes and mind-bakes, 'singing the blues' or grinding your teeth. Create giggles and fun, love and laughter, daily in your life's party. I'm not saying it'll work for you.**

Nevertheless, I will admit, 'Freedom is just another word for nothing left to lose…' It's your choice! Your life. You choose how you live it. I hope that this isn't your last

day on Mother Earth. However, I choose to live every day as my last. Milking the goodies for all it's worth.

Have patience, 'Funny Mummy' BLOG readers. Slow but sure I'm answering your questions and reader comments. Loved whoever called my journey into oblivion as 'Funny Mummy' a 'joy ride'. Their life must be hankered in a hellhole. In the meantime I would like to give you a heads-up on my reality filter.

Hurray for Samantha! She's getting engaged. Brian opted-out of his football scholarship to work on the 'Forrest Petting Zoo'. Richie's consumed with our 'Funny Mummy Boner Adventures' retreat. Proves that there is a universal collective intelligence operating out there or maybe he is a drone clone walk-in.

And Bambe? I've lightened up. She's the best assistant Richie ever had. Who else could stand his meticulous, ridiculous ways? And since she's dating billionaire heir M. Barrett, her life is so extravagant. In fact, she's an honoree at the 'Pink Ladies Brunch' coming up. She'll be a smash of trash.

With the kids off to college and living life, I have so much extra time to obsess. Well folks, you are it. I vow to devote my 24/7 to you lonely hearts out in cyberspace. Yes. Yes. Yes! I'll be able to dote on every little aspect of your life and growth. My ticket to self-evolve—it's a vicarious experience. You don't have to go to hell to know what it's like. You can do it for me. I'll benefit. Sound selfish? Me first, with compassion. Try it. Then you get the benefit of the evolved one, instead of the blamer, controller, and complainer!

OKAY – there is a required payback. Or as I prefer, 'to pay it with a smile & hug.' Here's an offering, a 'Funny Mummy' teaser I'll share with you right now. A simple truth recipe for 'Living a happy life" is to <u>**GET OFF OF 'WHAT IF' THAT HAPPENS.**</u>

I spent my lifetime negatively dwelling on 'what if'? What if that happens? In addition, if it does, then this could happen. And if that did…then DOOM. Holy Moly! If If If. That's how I arrived as your 'Funny Mummy' – imagining the 'what ifs'. And praise the lord, the wacky saga's not been fatally devastating or crippling as imagined. IF it… Oops, that was close. It's so easy to slip. Remember the obsessing 'what if' is not akin to brilliant brainstorming, finding usable, doable possibilities. So what happens when a 'what if ' becomes 'What is-Is?' That leads to our second simple truth:

<u>*DON'T LIKE IT – CHANGE IT*.</u>

Take responsibly inside and out – no blaming it. (On someone else or laying guilt.) Be mindful. Alert, aware, awake. So life's not an accident, but lived with purpose. The third simple truth: Prefacing, life seems to come in threes. For instance, taking off on a relay race, we count: 'On your mark. Get Set. Go.' (That's three.) Or a musician counts down, 'A one, ana' two, ana' three' before starting a tune. So now your curiosity may be up wondering, "What's behind the number three door?"

BE GRATEFUL FOR WHAT YOU HAVE.

Celebrate the journey. You are entitled to imagine it could be worse or better but only for 3 seconds, and then flip back to grateful. Live in 'grateful' for what is. Then imagine improvement, dreams coming true. OK, so much for the little teasers! Much more is in store, in-house, online for you. Until next time, imagine there are no limits. Life's all a 'wonder' of extraordinary possibility. Here's a 'Funny Mummy Workbook' title quote, "BOUNCING OFF THE WALLS? LAND ON YOUR FEET." BLOGGED IN AND OUT.

♥♥♥

Hi Guys & Gals. This is Richie. The rodent you've heard so much about. I won't defend, pretend, or make any amends to you. I do have one confession. I've been a BLOG reader since day one. Under the code name: DeathSport.

Call me a coward if you like, but it was easier for me to be a stand up guy, anonymously in print than to show up like a mensch in real life. I wanted to be there for my Jenny, and until I mended my ways, her Blog was a safe place to connect with her. You lazy bums have ignored so many gem opportunities that I had to step in and regurgitate and pontificate. Leaving less room for future disappointments, I'm working on giving up expectations about how other's react or act. Therefore, I don't 'expect' you to believe I've given up BS-ing in exchange for "If I say it, I mean it. If I talk it, I walk it." Here's a skinny-dip fact 4 U. We'll be doing 'Funny Mummy' workshops and retreats. Just ask and you will find. I'm still growing, slowing down to enjoy, laughing lots, and showing-up. MY LOVE TO MY JENNY!

♥♥♥

Hey Dudes. Brian here! I'm stepping-up and tripping-out. Yes, I know I was born with a silver lining – fitting-in came easy. Philosophy changed me. Had great dialogue with Dr. Ron comparing Cant to Descartes. I meditated, studied Buddha, the TAO, and realized, "Ideas don't matter. It's the sense behind it." Therefore, I was whipped and humbled like a toad. Everyone I meet is my teacher. What a lesson for a bully, who got off watching flies drop in my brew. Still hanging with Tanya, lucky me, love opened my heart! Don't believe the rap I quit football. It's rough playing with the big guys, so I'm keeping my Mom safe from herself. Nobody wants to see her son under three tons of tackling flab. Heading for the majors. Wish me luck! FOREVER TRUNCATED.

Guess what? This is Samantha. I started a Twins Club. Isn't it lucky to have another half that can take the best and leave the rest? That's what I'm doing. I quit college and I'm running the biz with

Finster. I'm pregnant. Due date – twins on my birthday. Exactly the same age as Mom when she had me, rather, us.

NOT! JUST KIDDING! I've learned to face-off with a sense of humor. My major life study includes pranks, put-ons, jokes, laughing, no comparisons, like no one is more or less unique than me. Giggles and love-me-first-fest's reign. My Motto, 'Don't take reality too seriously. It cremates you into a dread-head.' I put on a happy face for me and the world to see. And it smiles back. I'm running 'Teen Scream' and I'm the most downloaded web-chick <u>I know.</u>
THAT'S ALL (that counts) FOLKS!

It's Jenny. Just taking a moment to share- 'Never Say Never!' Hard lesson learned from foibles and folly. We're here in the produce department of our favorite suburbanite grocery store. No crow eating for changing my mind. I grew into a new perspective. Yes, I came full circle. While guests are tutti-frutti tasting, I'm in the midst of my book-launch. This is where it all started. Where I cracked-up, had a heart-quake and bake, tuned inside to live and face it all. So isn't it perfect sharing a 'Funny Mummy' workshop with needy produce patrons? Fruitcakes just like us. Feigning normal? Afraid not! Gobbling life's peaches, sour grapes, or lemon tarts. Smiling, lusting, and chanting. No Muss!as No Fuss! No Cuss!

BLOGGING ONWARD AND UPWARD

BOOKS BY MERRIE LYNN ROSS

Bounce Off The Walls- Land On Your Feet

The Bully Solution – Peace Smarts

Life As An Improv' - HAHA Healers Series

Happy Heart Journal

Adventures of Funny Mummy - Kindle

Peace Smarts Curriculum

Morph America Curriculum

Nartikki – Soul Dancer

Courses/Workshops/DVD's

The Bully Solution- Peace Smarts - DVD, course materials.

Peace Smarts Within E-Course with MP3's /mini book

HAHA Healers Teleseminar, E-Course, Live Workshops

Life As An Improv'-E-course, MP3's + Bonus Teleseminar.

Merrie Lynn is available for media interviews, live events, lecture and motivational speaker engagements, Tele-seminars, and workshops.

ABOUT THE AUTHOR

Merrie Lynn Ross – multi award winning filmmaker/author/actor has starred in 35+ TV/films. Best known as daytime's first comedienne, she giggled into millions of viewer's hearts on 'General Hospital'. Internationally acclaimed as a child advocate, honored by President Clinton and President George W. Bush she created "Morph America" and "Peace Smarts" curriculums: helping over two million families to create a culture of peace.

After suffering a personal tragedy, and rediscovering a way back to living in purpose, Merrie Lynn was guided to share her healing and life altering recipes. With a contagious joyous energy she proves to be a beacon of light for everyone she meets.

She currently stars on 'MerrieWay Day' TV - filled with uplifting news, red-carpet folly, and fun global treks. Dedicated to empower youth, she's producing, "Bully Proof Vest! " a short film, written by Byron Fox, to be used in tandem with "Peace Smarts".

A hill-dweller in Southern California, Merrie Lynn lives with her shelties, and enjoys a 'green healthy' life with her circle of colleagues and loving friends.

Enjoy this FREE Gift!

BYRON'S SERIES
BE REAL, LAUGH & LOVE

BE Real, Laugh & Love's Inspirational content
will be sent to you with instructions. An amazing way into
your heart's desire and how to actualize your truth.

Go to ~ www.bereallaughlove.com

MediaMorphUs - publisher
www.merrieway.com

Merrie Lynn Ross

www.ingramcontent.com/pod-product-compliance
Lightning Source LLC
Chambersburg PA
CBHW032058090426
42743CB00007B/166